THE NEXT WAR

BEYOND BOUNDARIES: CANADIAN DEFENCE AND STRATEGIC STUDIES SERIES

Rob Huebert, Series Editor
ISSN 1716-2645 (Print) ISSN 1925-2919 (Online)

Canada's role in international military and strategic studies ranges from peacebuilding and Arctic sovereignty to unconventional warfare and domestic security. This series provides narratives and analyses of the Canadian military from both an historical and a contemporary perspective.

No. 1 · *The Generals: The Canadian Army's Senior Commanders in the Second World War*
J. L. Granatstein

No. 2 · *Art and Memorial: The Forgotten History of Canada's War Art*
Laura Brandon

No. 3 · *In the National Interest: Canadian Foreign Policy and the Department of Foreign Affairs and International Trade, 1909–2009*
Greg Donaghy and Michael K. Carroll

No. 4 · *Long Night of the Tankers: Hitler's War Against Caribbean Oil*
David J. Bercuson and Holger H. Herwig

No. 5 · *Fishing for a Solution: Canada's Fisheries Relations with the European Union, 1977–2013*
Donald Barry, Bob Applebaum, and Earl Wiseman

No. 6 · *From Kinshasa to Kandahar: Canada and Fragile States in Historical Perspective*
Michael K. Carroll and Greg Donaghy

No. 7 · *The Frontier of Patriotism: Alberta and the First World War*
Adriana A. Davies and Jeff Keshen

No. 8 · *China's Arctic Ambitions and What They Mean for Canada*
P. Whitney Lackenbauer, Adam Lajeunesse, James Manicom, and Frédéric Lasserre

No. 9 · *Scattering Chaff: Canadian Air Power and Censorship during the Kosovo War*
Bob Bergen

No. 10 · *A Samaritan State Revisited: Historical Perspectives on Canadian Foreign Aid*
Greg Donaghy and David Webster

No. 11 · *Working for Canada: A Pilgrimage in Foreign Affairs from the New World Order to the Rise of Populism*
Geoff White

No. 12 · *Polar Cousins: Comparing Antarctic and Arctic Geostrategic Futures*
Edited by Christian Leuprecht with Douglas Causey

No. 13 · *Deterrence in the 21st Century: Statecraft in the Information Age*
Edited by Eric Ouellet, Madeleine D'Agata, and Keith Stewart

No. 14 · *The Next War: Indications Intelligence in the Early Cold War*
Timothy Andrews Sayle

Indications Intelligence in the Early Cold War

Beyond Boundaries:
Canadian Defence and
Strategic Studies Series

ISSN 1716-2645 (Print)
ISSN 1925-2919 (Online)

TIMOTHY
ANDREWS
SAYLE

© 2025 Timothy A. Sayle

University of Calgary Press
2500 University Drive NW
Calgary, Alberta
Canada T2N 1N4
press.ucalgary.ca

All rights reserved.

This book is available in an Open Access digital format published under a CC-BY-NCND 4.0 Creative Commons license. The publisher should be contacted for any commercial use which falls outside the terms of that license.

LIBRARY AND ARCHIVES CANADA CATALOGUING IN PUBLICATION

Title: The next war : indications intelligence in the early Cold War / Timothy Andrews Sayle.
Names: Sayle, Timothy A., author
Series: Beyond boundaries series ; no. 14.
Description: Series statement: Canadian defence and strategic studies series, 1716-2645 ; no. 14 | Includes bibliographical references and index.
Identifiers: Canadiana (print) 20250142325 | Canadiana (ebook) 20250142384 | ISBN 9781773856230 (softcover) | ISBN 9781773856223 (hardcover) | ISBN 9781773856247 (PDF) | ISBN 9781773856254 (EPUB) | ISBN 9781773856261 (Open Access PDF)
Subjects: LCSH: Intelligence service—Canada. | LCSH: Intelligence service—United States. | LCSH: Intelligence service—Great Britain. | LCSH: Cold War.
Classification: LCC JF1525.I6 S29 2025 | DDC 327.1209/045—dc23

The University of Calgary Press acknowledges the support of the Government of Alberta through the Alberta Media Fund for our publications. We acknowledge the financial support of the Government of Canada. We acknowledge the financial support of the Canada Council for the Arts for our publishing program.

  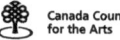

The manufacturer's authorized representative in the EU for product safety is Mare Nostrum Group B.V., Mauritskade 21D, 1091 GC Amsterdam, The Netherlands. Email: gpsr@mare-nostrum.co.uk

Copy editing by Kelly Laycock
Cover image: "1928 Russian Map of Soviet Caucasus," from *Atlas of the Union of Soviet Socialist Republics*, ed. Central Executive Committee of the USSR, 1928, Wikimedia, https://commons.wikimedia.org/wiki/File:1928_Russian_map_of_Soviet_Caucasus.jpg.
Cover design, page design, and typesetting by Melina Cusano

Contents

Acronyms	VII
Acknowledgements	IX
Introduction: The War of 196?	1
PART 1: IMMINENCE OF WAR, 1944–1954	15
1 A Third World War in the Making?	17
2 Agreed Intelligence	47
3 The Most Important Question	77
PART 2: INDICATIONS OF WAR, 1954–1966	105
4 The Origins of Indications Intelligence	107
5 The Tripartite Intelligence Alerts Agreement	121
6 The Alerts Agreement in Action	149
Conclusion: A Semi-Dormant but Continuing Agreement	177
Notes	181
Bibliography	223
Index	233

Acronyms

ABAI	American-British Agreed Intelligence
ABCI	American-British-Canadian Intelligence
ACAI	American-Canadian Agreed Intelligence
ADC	Air Defence Command
ALE	Alert
BJSM	British Joint Staff Mission
BSP	Basic Security Plan
CAS	Chief of the Air Staff
CBNRC	Communications Branch, National Research Council
CCOS	Chair, Chiefs of Staff
CDC	Cabinet Defence Committee
CGS	Chief of the General Staff
CIA	Central Intelligence Agency
CIG	Central Intelligence Group
CIIB	Current Intelligence Indications and Briefing Section
CJS	Canadian Joint Staff
CJS(L)	Canadian Joint Staff (London)
CJS(W)	Canadian Joint Staff (Washington)
COMINT	Communications Intelligence
CSC	Chiefs of Staff Committee
CWC	Cabinet War Committee
DAI	Director of Air Intelligence
DEA	Department of External Affairs
DL(1)	Defence Liaison (1) Division
DL(2)	Defence Liaison (2) Division
DMI	Director of Military Intelligence
DND	Department of National Defence
DNI	Director of Naval Intelligence
DSI	Director of Scientific Intelligence
G-2	United States Army military intelligence
FBIS	Foreign Broadcast Information Service
GCHQ	Government Communications Headquarters
IAC	Intelligence Advisory Committee (Canada and the US each had IACs)
ICBM	Intercontinental Ballistic Missile
JCS	Joint Chiefs of Staff
JIB	Joint Intelligence Bureau

JIC	Joint Intelligence Committee (Canada, the US, and the UK each had JICs at one time or another)
JIC (London)	Informal name for the United Kingdom's Joint Intelligence Committee
JIC (Ottawa)	Informal name for Canada's Joint Intelligence Committee
JICLO(L)	Joint Intelligence Committee Liaison Officer (London)
JICLO(W)	Joint Intelligence Committee Liaison Officer (Washington)
JIG	Joint Intelligence Group
JIR	Joint Indications Room (Canada and the UK each had JIRs)
JIS	Joint Intelligence Staff
JISC	Joint Intelligence Sub-Committee
JPC	Joint Planning Committee
MCC	Military Cooperation Committee
MOD	Ministry of Defence (UK)
NIE	National Intelligence Estimate
NATO	North Atlantic Treaty Organization
NIC	National Indications Center
NORAD	North American Air Defence Command
NSA	National Security Agency
NSC	National Security Council
ORE	Office of Reports and Estimates
PCO	Privy Council Office
PHP	Post-Hostilities Planning Committee
PJBD	Permanent Joint Board of Defence (Canada and the US)
RAF	Royal Air Force
RCAF	Royal Canadian Air Force
SAC	Strategic Air Command
SACEUR	Supreme Allied Commander, Europe
SG	Standing Group
SIS	Secret Intelligence Service (UK, sometimes known as MI6)
SIGINT	Signals Intelligence
SLS	Service Liaison Staff (UK)
SNIE	Special National Intelligence Estimate
SSEA	Secretary of State for External Affairs
TIAA	Tripartite Intelligence Alerts Agreement
UN	United Nations
UNEF	United Nations Emergency Force
USAF	United States Air Force
USIB	United States Intelligence Board
USSEA	Under-Secretary of State for External Affairs

Acknowledgements

It is common for authors to write that their book would not have been possible without certain other people and their contributions. This is definitively true in my case. Almost every archival record cited in this book was security-classified and closed to researchers until very recently. Without Alan Barnes' efforts to seek access to the archival record of Canadian intelligence history, and his sharing of those records with the Canadian Foreign Intelligence History Project, I would not have been able to conduct research (or even read) the records cited here. Alan's work has fundamentally changed what is possible for students and scholars of Canadian intelligence history.

Processing *Access to Information Act* requests, in turn, is an unnecessarily difficult task in Canada. I am grateful to the staff of the Access to Information and Privacy, or ATIP, section at Library and Archives Canada, as well as the investigators and others of the Office of the Information Commissioner of Canada who helped ensure these documents were made available for research. Some other government departments remain confused about what information about Canada's past is now publicly available, what can be released, and the benefits of releasing more information. I hope my book can contribute to their education and the further release of more historical records.

It has been my great privilege to hire a number of excellent students to work with me on this project, as research assistants for the Canada Declassified website. Elisabetta Kerr helped me make sense of many documents from the "Imminence" era. Lindsay Grant helped make sense of the documents, too, and then made her own original research contributions on the Hydra communications facility that I am pleased to cite. Angus Lee and Kenneth Wong did a wonderful job preparing Canada Declassified briefing books that will make the primary sources I used in this book easily accessible to other students and scholars. Grace van Vliet helped me pull key elements of this book together for publication. Sam Eberlee read more drafts than he probably cares to count, and I am grateful to him for his interventions. My friends Susie

Colbourn and Asa McKercher read my introduction in draft stage and provided encouragement at the right time.

Support for research assistance and my larger project to make the primary source collections available on Canada Declassified was provided by the Social Sciences and Humanities Research Council (SSHRC) and a University of Toronto Connaught New Researcher Award. I had early opportunities to share my ideas at the International Studies Association, King's College London, the Society for Historians of American Foreign Relations, the Canadian Historical Association, and a Canadian Foreign Intelligence History Project workshop. I also wrote about some aspects of the diplomacy I cover in Chapters 5 and 6 of this book for an article that appeared in *Intelligence & National Security* 38, no. 3 (2023): 427–46. I am grateful for these grants and opportunities.

At the University of Calgary Press, I have had the benefit of working with Brian Scrivener, Helen Hajnoczky, and Rob Huebert. I am also grateful to the two anonymous referees, who provided helpful comments that improved the manuscript. I owe special thanks to Kelly Laycock for her excellent editorial suggestions. JoAnne Burek prepared an excellent index that will be a great help to researchers.

As you will see from the above list, I have relied on assistance from many quarters to write this book. Still, and as always, any errors or omissions are mine alone.

There is a certain tension in writing about one's family in a book about intelligence warning of nuclear war. Does anyone want a book on the subject dedicated to them? Probably not. And so while I will not dedicate this book to my family (or anyone else), I still owe great thanks and all my love to Nicole and our boys Henry and Charlie; to Eric and Cathy, my mom and dad; to Brian and Jo; and to Hilary and Miles and Hudson and Russell.

INTRODUCTION

The War of 196?

No one sought a nuclear holocaust, but it came anyway.[1] The origins of the Third World War lay in Finland, on the Soviet Union's border. In a parliamentary election at the end of July 196?, the Finnish Communist Party won the most seats of any party. But a coalition of non-Communist parties insisted that they had enough members to form a non-Communist government. The dispute escalated, leading to a scramble for power in Finland. The Finnish military splintered into factions. Commanders threw their weight behind competing camps. Rioting and street-fighting escalated into civil war.

As the conflict escalated, the Soviet Union supported the Communist factions with arms, advisers, and technicians. A small group of Soviet troops, searching for quicker routes by which they could send arms to their Finnish allies, lost their way and mistakenly entered Norway. Small skirmishes broke out between Soviet and Norwegian units. The Norwegians, who had been so instrumental in the creation of the North Atlantic Treaty Organization (NATO) two decades earlier, called on the alliance for help. The NATO allies issued Moscow an ultimatum, insisting Soviet troops leave Norway without delay. The USSR did not comply.

The president of the United States appeared on national television. He told his fellow Americans and the world that the American nuclear sword — the missiles and bombers of Strategic Air Command (SAC) — was on alert and that the United States was ready for "instant retaliation" in the face of aggression. From Ottawa, the prime minister told Canadians that Canadian troops were also on alert, "ready for whatever might befall."

As in the Second World War, US servicemen streamed into Canada, this time bringing with them fighter squadrons and air defence missiles to better defend North American aerospace. During the build-up, Canada's minister of

National Defence misspoke badly. When he stated that Canadians were ready for war, trying to give the nation a boost, it sounded too much like a warning that bombs would soon strike Canada. The statement unleashed panic. Wealthier families from Toronto who owned cottages on Lake Muskoka or on Lake of Bays stockpiled food in their summer cabins, leaving the grocery store shelves of Ontario's cottage country empty.

The actual exchange of nuclear weapons seems to have begun by accident. But it remains little more than speculation. So few records survived the war that it is difficult, if not impossible, to know for certain. Two United States Air Force enlisted men — the only two survivors of one SAC base destroyed in the war — were interviewed after the war and recalled communicating with a bomber on the night of September 3. The bomber had radioed back to base, warning of a failure of its navigation equipment. It seems likely that the bomber strayed off course and unwittingly entered Polish airspace. Neither the bomber nor its wreckage was ever found. Soviet leaders seem to have believed the bomber was the vanguard of a pre-emptive strike. They decided to retaliate.

The first three hydrogen bombs fell in the dawn of September 4, near Washington, DC. One crashed into Arlington, Virginia, and failed to detonate. One burst in the air over Georgetown, destroying most buildings in the capital's core. A third missed its target by a large margin, falling just off the Atlantic coast. Its detonator malfunctioned and it exploded in the water. Wind carried radioactive fallout across Washington, Baltimore, and beyond. Over half a million people were killed in the burst over Washington, and the severe radiation prevented efforts to rescue those who had survived the first blast.

The attack on Washington was followed in quick succession by attacks on twenty more United States cities and several SAC bases. The initial blasts, combined with the subsequent effects of radiation and starvation, reduced the United States population by ninety million souls. A simultaneous attack on the United Kingdom destroyed London, Manchester, and Liverpool in a split second. Western Europe was showered with weapons.

Canada was targeted with five missiles, but more than twenty missiles aimed at the United States malfunctioned en route to America and landed throughout the country. None of the malfunctioning missiles hit Canadian cities. But of the targeted strikes, the first direct hit destroyed Montreal. Two missiles fired at Toronto landed near the city's edge, severely damaging the city. The single missile sent to destroy Ottawa exploded in southern Quebec, and senior officials and the senior defence leadership were evacuated successfully from the capital. The next morning, however, a Soviet bomber pilot searching for targets of opportunity dropped a high-yield weapon on Ottawa. The city was levelled.

The bombings unleashed chaos. In Washington, the United States government collapsed, and the United Kingdom was nearly obliterated in the war. But the nuclear capabilities of both states, honed for quick action and delivery, still dealt equal devastation on the Soviet Union. Ballistic missiles rained down on Soviet cities, and while early bomber sorties were met effectively by Soviet interceptors, Soviet air defences were quickly rendered ineffective by missile attacks. Later sorties by American bombers continued until their bases ran out of bombs and fuel. Crushed under this devastating bombardment, early Soviet offensives into Europe collapsed without support, and ultimately Moscow's forces were recalled home to assist in survival operations.

In the days after the bombing, the Government of Canada worked to restore authority and assert control over the country. Early efforts were successful because Ottawa had been evacuated and most Canadian cities were spared incineration.

The real challenge came after the war. An exodus of American refugees, somewhere on the order of twelve to fifteen million people, flooded north across the 49th parallel. Bands of armed Americans and Canadians roamed the provinces. Murder and brigandage became the new way of life. Swarms of refugees descended on the Muskoka region, plundering the supplies hoarded before the war by cottage owners.

Slowly, very slowly, Canadian and American military units were reassembled and reorganized to execute rudimentary policing duties. They established a semblance of order. With the world's missiles expended, North America was once again protected by the vast Atlantic, Pacific, and Arctic Oceans. Insulated from predatory powers in this way, the two North American neighbours co-operated to send relief workers to Europe. They pooled their resources and efforts with recovering states in South America and Europe to establish a new political entity: the Atlantic Federation.

The Soviet Union, however, had no great moat behind which it could shelter as it repaired and rebuilt. Only one year after the end of the Third World War, Chinese forces poured north and west, seizing control of an enormous swath of territory: China dominated from the Pacific Ocean in the east to the Ural Mountains in the west, and north from the Arctic Ocean and the

Himalayan Mountains south down to and including Taiwan and Singapore. China's preponderant position raised the spectre of a future conflict.

Newspapers in the Atlantic Federation started reporting on the new "bamboo curtain" that had descended across the world. "The framework of World War IV is becoming increasingly clearer." General war would continue to beget general war.

The war of 196? did not happen. This scenario was written by a member of Canada's Joint Intelligence Staff (JIS). While this war was not "real," it was conceivable. It was, in fact, the war that Canadian intelligence officials worried might be imminent in the first decades after the Second World War.

Indications of the Third World War

This is a book about intelligence and general war. The war in question — what would have been the third world war in the twentieth century — did not come to pass. Or, to put it more starkly, such a war did not occur in the decades in which it was first expected. It has not come yet.

That general war did not break out for a third time in the twentieth century has been interpreted by some as evidence that the fear of war between the nuclear-armed superpowers was misplaced, or that the possibility of such a war was overestimated. One element of the Cold War era, the unceasing preparation and rehearsal for nuclear war, is easily regarded as a mistake, or a cruel joke.

Newly declassified intelligence records make clear that such simplistic judgments misinterpret the views held by government officials and policymakers during the years of highest Cold War tension. Making extensive use of these documents — which showcase some of the most deeply held secrets of Canada and its allies — what follows is an examination of how Canadians tried to understand the likelihood of war in the first two decades of the postwar world and, if the Cold War was to turn hot, whether they could recognize such a change in time to act. It is a history of Canada's Cold War thermometer.

In retrospect, Canadian conclusions about the imminence of war were judicious. Canadian officials understood that general war was a real possibility, that it might be brought on by a host of different conditions, from superpower miscalculation to the escalation of a regional conflict into full-blown war. But they concluded in their final estimation that general war remained unlikely. The records from the 1940s through the 1960s reveal an impressively clear-headed appreciation in an era when mistaken judgments might have had enormous financial, political, societal, and even existential costs.

This book draws on recently declassified records from Canada's Joint Intelligence Committee (JIC), the body that wrote Canada's intelligence estimates and liaised with Canada's intelligence partners in the early Cold War. The early Cold War period saw Canada develop an extensive intelligence-sharing network, principally via its Anglo-American allies, and, to a lesser extent, with Australia and New Zealand. This network was developed during an era in which Canada expanded its involvement in world affairs, especially through its peacetime alliances with the United States and NATO. What political scientist James Eayrs wrote about Canadian foreign and defence policy, that Canada "grew up allied," is entirely applicable to Canadian intelligence history, too.[2]

The historical record reveals that officials in Ottawa made their judgments about the prospect of war both in co-operation and, occasionally, in disagreement with their key allies in Washington and London. Recently declassified records in the United States and United Kingdom National Archives help provide a more complete picture of both the co-operative and competing efforts to assess whether war was imminent, and how the three closely allied capitals would warn each other if they detected indications that this move to belligerence was the case.

A study of Canadian intelligence records from the first two postwar decades reveals much about this era. It helps explain what leaders in Ottawa feared, and what they judged to be the mistaken fears of others. It was not, as is often caricaturized, a period in which mandarins expected that Moscow was dead set on conquering the world with the bayonets of the Red Army. Rather, Canadian views showed a nuanced appreciation of the international situation — and of the threat emanating from the Soviet Union.

And yet the Canadians still feared a return to general war. They understood that such a conflict might come as a result of decisions and mistakes made by both foes and friends alike. By examining the first decades of the Cold War from this perspective, we can dispense with the pernicious cartoons of Canada's Cold War strategic policy as the fever dreams of rabid anti-Communists; erase the idea that allied strategic thinking was the work of a deranged Dr. Strangelove; and do away with the notion that Ottawa was little more than Washington's powder monkey.[3]

The Canadians agreed with their American and British counterparts on many things and got much of their intelligence information from these two other states. But the Canadians, at times, disagreed with the conclusions reached by even their closest allies. They sought to air their differences, and to change the thinking in other allied capitals. They did so by representing their own views in secret conferences. They encouraged and helped build a trilateral intelligence communications network that would insert Canadian and British views into any American decisions to use nuclear weapons. This system would allow Ottawa, London, and Washington's top intelligence bodies to send specially coded messages to each other with the highest precedence.

What follows is not a history of the entire Canadian postwar intelligence structure, although questions in Ottawa about the prospect of general war did contribute to the evolution of the intelligence bureaucracy in Ottawa.[4] Nor is this a history of Canadian strategic thinking or defence planning, although these issues are closely related to the question of whether and how war might return to the world, and how Canada should be armed. It is, instead, a history of Canadian efforts to grapple with the most important, even existential question of the postwar era: is war imminent?

The six chapters below describe how Canadian officials assessed the prospects of war in the aftermath of the Second World War. In the first section of the book, "Imminence of War, 1944–1954," Canadian officials, spurred to the question by joint conferences with their American partners, and to a lesser degree, British colleagues, sought to assess the imminence of war.

The road to posing this clear question — is war imminent? — was anything but straight. As explained in the first chapter, Canadian and American planners began making defensive plans for war long before they asked whether this war was likely, let alone imminent. The implications of these joint defensive plans for Canadian finances and sovereignty led to calls in Ottawa to rethink the assumptions underlying the plans. And when it became obvious that American war planners were thinking of offence as the best defence (which, in the age of atomic strategy might mean pre-emptive war), the Canadians became even more concerned with the question of whether the Soviet Union was seeking a conflict that the United States might try to pre-empt. This change in thinking, and the inclusion of Canada in both bilateral and trilateral intelligence conferences with the United States and the United Kingdom is the subject of Chapter 2.

In 1950 the imminence question was complicated by the outbreak of war on the Korean peninsula. Did the North Korean invasion of South Korea in 1950 suggest that general war was imminent? Chapter 3 traces the arc of concern during the conflict, and the Canadian preoccupation with how the war itself, rather than the goals of either Moscow or Washington, could bring war to the world. By the end of the war, however, the Canadians had answered the question: war was not imminent, nor was it likely.

What came next, the subject of Section 2, "Indications of War, 1954–1966," is one of the cruel ironies of history. Despite the assessment in 1953–54 that general war was not likely, the potential implications of a such a conflict had changed dramatically. The introduction of the hydrogen bomb into the arsenals of both the United States and then the Soviet Union, along with the coming massive deployment of nuclear weapons to NATO formations in Europe, seemed to finally confirm that any third world war would look nothing like the sprawling Second World War. Rather, it would be a short and utterly destructive nuclear holocaust not unlike that sketched out in the draft history of the War of 196?.

With this change came the paradox: just as the weapons of war had convinced leaders that no one could benefit from a third world war, the risks and consequences of such a war had metastasized. The only sure way to deter such a general war, according to the American, British, and Canadian planners who crafted NATO's strategy in the 1950s, was to be prepared to launch a massive nuclear response to any major Soviet challenge to the status quo in Europe.

This strategy lay with delicate balance upon a knife's edge: the United States, whose president controlled the decision to wage nuclear war, believed it had to convince the Soviet leadership that it would use these weapons if necessary. The corollary was the need, in Ottawa and London, to be assured that the president would only use these weapons if absolutely necessary.

The trigger for the use of nuclear weapons was an indication that the Soviet Union was preparing to wage general war. Intelligence assessment came to focus on identifying and evaluating these "indicators." It is a quirk of history that after years spent studying the "imminence of war," and the repeated conclusion that war was not imminent, the allies began searching for "indications of war."

Chapter 4 traces the origins of postwar "indications intelligence," meant to provide rapid definitive proof of an imminent attack. A special point of emphasis here is on how American and British thinking about such indications led the Canadians to consider developing a national system for managing this intelligence. It quickly became clear, however, that any Canadian system had to be integrated into American and British evaluations of indications intelligence. For their own reasons, the British came to agree with the Canadians that it was crucial to try and insert themselves into the American intelligence apparatus for evaluating indications. This move was just as much about influencing American decisions as it was accessing American intelligence information, but both were important to London and Ottawa. Ultimately, the Americans agreed to their allies' plans.

Chapter 5 examines the creation of the Tripartite Intelligence Alerts Agreement (TIAA) and explains why the allies believed such an agreement was necessary. The chapter investigates the Canadian role in reaching a trilateral agreement among Ottawa, London, and Washington. Once an agreement had been reached in 1957, however, the three states had to decide how such an alerts network would work—and when it would be put into action. Chapter 6 traces the early operation of the system that resulted from the tripartite agreement, the development of procedures and the communications network that supported the Agreement, and finally the fall of the system into a semi-dormant state in the 1960s. The Tripartite Intelligence Alerts Agreement itself, however, outlived the Cold War.

A history of how Canadians judged the imminence of war, and how they engaged in these judgments with their allies, helps reconfigure the history of the Anglo-American "Special Relationship." That relationship was not bilateral with an occasional Canadian addition, but in many ways it was fully triangular. In the case of the TIAA in particular, Ottawa was the bridge between London and Washington; it really was how the North Atlantic Triangle was joined.

The point of this history is not to cheer on Canadians of the past from the present, or to insist that the world needs more Canada. It is instead to convince the reader that the organization of postwar intelligence sharing and diplomacy, even between the United State and the United Kingdom, cannot be understood without the Canadian dimension. The conclusions, estimates, and appreciations reached by these three states, independently and jointly, when placed alongside the diplomatic and bureaucratic wrangling that allowed for co-operation in intelligence analysis and warning intelligence, explain the origins of the intelligence relationship among these powers.

More fundamentally, the history of tripartite intelligence co-operation reveals the three respective governments' views of the nature of the international system and the risk of war, and the unending challenge of assessing such a risk. The habits, practices, and systems built to assess whether or not the Cold War would turn hot forced officials to consider the possible sources of such an escalation. And as a result, it provides one of the explanations for why the twentieth century contained two — and not three — world wars.

The Last War

There is one important piece of pre-history that readers should understand before reading this history of early Cold War Canadian intelligence. Readers should keep in mind that the Canadian officials who assessed the likelihood of a third world war did so with constant reference to their experience during the Second World War. As they prepared Canadian intelligence appreciations, negotiated and debated joint assessments with their American and British allies, and built an intelligence alert network, they were on guard against certain tendencies their allies had exhibited in the fight against Germany and Japan.

There was one important difference, however, in thinking about the last war and preparing for the next. When Canadian officials harkened back to the Second World War, they were thinking about what it was like to fight alongside allies in a war that had already begun. The war started for the allies at different times — the United States, of course did not join until 1941 — and so there had been no "allied" intelligence appreciations of how and when the Second World War might start.

Instead, the experiences of the Second World War that would inform Canada's postwar intelligence diplomacy were not strictly related to intelligence. They were issues of command, of planning, of sovereignty — of the fundamental relationship between states or what officials in the Department of External Affairs (DEA) at the time called "Canada's national development."[5] This is relatively easy to reconcile when one recalls the belief of officials at the time that the national and joint intelligence appreciations and apparatus of the early Cold War era would, and did, shape Canada's place among its allies in peacetime, and would dictate Canada's place in a war if war came.

The Second World War marked a transition from close, if guarded, co-operation between Ottawa and London to deep co-operation between Ottawa and Washington on defence issues. This occurred while Anglo-American co-operation, with the Canadians largely excluded, set the direction of war.

In the earliest days of the war, when Canada fought alongside Britain but the United States remained neutral, Canadian diplomats complained that, in regard to the broader direction of the war set by the British, Canada had "practically no influence on decisions and little prior information concerning them." Lester Pearson, who wrote these words from the High Commission in London, noted that "we do not seem to have been concerned at our exclusion from the Councils of our Allies in a war in which our whole future is at stake."[6] Canadian troops were one of the means of British strategy, but Canadians had little role in deciding its ends. "I dislike," wrote Pearson, "this role of unpaid Hessians." Canada, he thought, should have a seat at the table — to attend the crucial meetings and have staff participate in committees. The machinery by which governments stayed in contact in times of peace were "dangerously inadequate in wartime," and Pearson called for their re-examination once war was joined.[7]

It was during Pearson's tenure as secretary of state for External Affairs, a decade and a half later, that Canada would make major contributions to the development of one of the most important pieces of intergovernmental machinery — the Tripartite Intelligence Alerts Agreement — that would allow for communication among London, Ottawa, and Washington in the murky moments between peace and nuclear war.[8]

In North America, during the war, the sheer number of interactions between Canadians and US civilians and military and naval officers ballooned. These interactions left the Canadians confused and exasperated. Dealing with the US military services revealed an American "obliviousness to the prides and prejudices of others." This was not a Canadian appreciation of the good qualities of individual Americans. Canadians noted that American officers showed a remarkable generosity of spirit: Canadian officers "hardly ever make an appeal for help to Senior American Army and Navy Commanders without the latter leaning over backwards to meet them."[9] The source of the exasperation, ultimately, was the friction inherent in a great power, on the cusp of becoming a superpower, dealing with a significantly less powerful neighbour.

In 1940, Prime Minister Mackenzie King and President Franklin D. Roosevelt agreed to create the PJBD (Permanent Joint Board of Defence, or for the Americans, "Defense"). The board, co-chaired by an American and a Canadian, seated high-ranking civilian and military officials from both countries and allowed for consultation on defence matters. In the spring of 1941, the PJBD set to work drafting plans for the defence of North America in the event the United States joined the war on Germany. The discussions ultimately produced a "Joint Canadian-United States Basic Defence Plan," ABC-22. But there were bruising battles along the way, especially over matters of command and "strategical direction."[10]

ABC-22 was developed in relation to ABC-1, a plan developed by American and British officers earlier in 1941. (The purpose of ABC-1 was to create a plan for co-operation between the United Kingdom and United States if and when the latter joined the war.) The Canadians were not invited.[11] This irritated the Canadians deeply.

Chief of the General Staff Harry Crerar warned of "an increasing danger that the U.S.A. and U.K. will decide 'grand strategy and major tactics' between them" — and this before the United States had even entered the war.[12] The minister of National Defence was advised by the Chiefs of Staff Committee that the Anglo-British bilateral talks were facing Canada with "various defence arrangements importantly affecting her own and contiguous territory concerning which she has not been consulted."[13] Pearson, who at the beginning of the war in London had written about Canada's exclusion from supreme bodies there, had returned to Ottawa and worried that Canadians could only observe Anglo-American planning.[14]

In the negotiations over ABC-22 in the PJBD, the American chair, Fiorella La Guardia, implored the Canadians to accept the plans and arrangements the Americans saw fit. He told his Canadian counterparts that it "is far better to trust to the honor of the United States than the mercy of the enemy." La Guardia said there was "no protocol" for how to operate, and so the plans should be "guided by the law of necessity."[15] This high-handed approach sat uneasily with the Canadians. It echoed previous struggles with the imperial centre in London. The Canadians listening to La Guardia's request heard him seemingly suggest "that Canada should surrender to the United States what she has consistently asserted vis-à-vis Great Britain."[16]

The Canadian-American plan, ABC-22, was ultimately agreed. The Canadians had held their ground and gained the concession that the plan would be coordinated by "mutual co-operation" rather than exclusive American direction.[17] But the process left its mark on the Canadian officials.

Allied — that is, Anglo-American — grand strategy for the war against the Axis powers was set by the Combined Chiefs of Staff (a combination of American and British Chiefs of Staff). Canadian officials learned about the establishment of this staff from newspaper reports, despite the British and

American expectation that the staff would have, at its disposal, Canadian troops.[18] Major-General Maurice Pope was sent to Washington to try and liaise with the Combined Chiefs, and he would ultimately lead the Canadian Joint Staff (CJS) in Washington whose officers did their best to keep in touch with various subsidiary bodies of the CCS.[19] As C. P. Stacey, the historian of Canada's war effort, put it, "the Canadian government had no effective share in the higher direction of the war."[20]

Following the Japanese attack on Pearl Harbor, ABC-22 was put into effect.[21] But the organs that had been established to manage US-Canadian defence relations, such as the PJBD, were initially forgotten or bypassed by the Americans. The US minister in Ottawa made a direct request for permission to install airplane detector equipment in British Columbia on the Pacific Coast. The request frustrated the Canadians, who saw such a direct and ad hoc request from the US legation to the Government of Canada as avoiding the whole system of co-operative discussion and planning that the PJBD was meant to provide.[22]

American entry into the war had paradoxical effects: Canada would, for the most part and as expected, be left out of the broader direction of the war. But Canadian territory would become extremely important to the United States. There was a frantic effort by Americans to ensure that Canadian territory could be used to support and defend Alaska from the Japanese. Yet, at the same time, there was no effort to include Canada in the broader direction of the war, and the Canadians noticed a tendency for the Americans to continue their 1941-style brusqueness and domineering attitude toward Canada as a lesser power.

The effort to defend Alaska led to the development of airfields and other logistical bases in Canada. One was the building of the Alaska Highway: a route that would allow reinforcements from the continental United States to travel by land to Alaska, via British Columbia. Another was the development of a series of airfields, the "Northwest Staging Route" that allowed for the rapid movement of aircraft to Alaska. The Americans later expanded the air routes to allow for the delivery of bombers to the United Kingdom and to the Soviet Union. Another was the development of Canol (from "Canada Oil"), a pipeline that transported crude oil from Canada's Northwest Territories to a refinery in the Yukon, from which the refined product could be transported to Alaska.

In 1942, there were 15,000 Americans in Canada building logistical facilities. Six months later, by June 1943, the number had risen to 33,000.[23] Legends arose that US Army telephone operators working in Canada were answering their telephones with the greeting: "United States Army of Occupation."[24]

The massive projects on Canadian territory, and the tens of thousands of Americans defending North America from Canadian soil, caused Canadian officials to fear that Canada might find itself "committed to the consequences of future United States policy."[25]

Canadian officials, despite their frustrations, had a clear-eyed sense of how power dictated roles in wartime. It is critical to keep in one's mind the role of this history and memory to understand the wariness with which Canadians approached the matter of assessments of the imminence of war and indications intelligence during the last war as they considered the next war.

PART 1

Imminence of War, 1944-1954

1

A Third World War in the Making?

Partner or Prophylactic?

In late May 1944, Canadian troops in the United Kingdom were training to storm the beaches at Normandy. D-Day, June 6, 1944, was more than a week away. France was still occupied, and Hitler's Nazis controlled Europe. But in Ottawa, a group of civilian officials and military officers was already imagining whether and how the next war would come, and what it would mean for Canada.

The Post-Hostilities Planning (PHP) Committee had been established in 1943 to advise the government on a host of issues that would face Ottawa and its allies once the Second World War had been won.[1] What place would Canada occupy in the world after the war? The one place it was certain to be, and which could not be altered by any wish or effort, was its geographic location. Stuck between the United States and the Soviet Union.

Geography put Canada smack in the middle between what, it was clear at the time, would be the two most powerful states in the postwar world. Two states, in fact, that might very well begin a new war against each other. After the defeat of the Axis, advised the PHP Committee, the only nation "physically capable of launching an attack on North America" would be the USSR. If tensions between the United States and the Soviet Union were to build, and especially if the United States itself were to begin to "make large scale preparations for hostilities" — that is, to prepare for war — then Canada's position would be "extremely difficult."[2]

This notion — that if war were to come again, it would come between the Soviet Union and the United States — was not just found in the imagination of Canadian officials. Ottawa's allies in both London and Washington also believed that the only possible enemy in the postwar world was the Soviet Union. In July 1944, Field Marshal Lord Alanbrooke, the chief of the imperial general staff, wrote in his diary that "the main threat 15 years from now" would be the Soviet Union.[3]

The British had a Post-Hostilities Planning Committee, too. It relied on an assessment by the United Kingdom's Joint Intelligence Committee, written in late 1944, to guide its thinking about Soviet strategic interests and possible postwar actions. British intelligence deemed that, after the war, Moscow would undertake a search for "security," including seeking to control buffer zones along the Soviet border. They expected the Soviet Union to "build up a system of security outside her frontiers in order to make sure, so far as is humanly possible, that she is left in peace and that her development is never again imperiled by the appalling devastation and misery of wars such as she has twice experienced within a generation." But would this aggressive search for security lead to conflict with the United States or the United Kingdom? Ultimately, the JIC concluded, the answer would depend on whether these states could "convince the other of the sincerity of its desire for collaboration" rather than conflict.[4]

In January 1945, the United States' Joint Intelligence Committee produced its own "Estimate of Soviet Postwar Intentions and Capabilities." The American JIC's conclusion was similar to the British JIC's: that the Soviet Union would not wish to embark on general war after the Nazis were defeated but would seek security by dominating states on its border.[5]

The prospect of postwar tensions between the United States and the Soviet Union was an obvious possibility, even likelihood, from Ottawa's vantage point in 1944.[6] But this is not to say that Canadian officials thought the Soviet Union wanted war. In both 1943 and 1944, the Canadian ambassador to the Soviet Union, Dana Wilgress, argued consistently that the Soviet Union would prefer peace after the devastating Nazi invasion.[7] The PHP Committee did not think that the Soviets would seek to escalate tensions, but they worried that American oversensitivity to Soviet actions could lead to conflict. Canadians, the PHP noted, would likely take "a much less serious view" of the "potential aggressiveness of the U.S.S.R."[8] than their American neighbours.

Any future war would have serious implications for Canadian sovereignty. In a wartime paper, the Post-Hostilities Planning Committee explained that in the midst of the "present war," — that is, the Second World War — the United States had constructed a number of military facilities in Canada. These facilities, especially air bases, were nominally defensive in nature. But the Canadians knew that these bases were fully capable of serving offensive purposes. And the Soviets knew it, too. If, in the postwar world, the Americans pushed Canadian leaders to develop or lend more such facilities in Canada to the United States, the Soviets might see these as threatening actions with "embarrassing results for Canada."[9] If war came, would Canada have a choice in its role? Or would the United States insist on using Canada as a launching pad, if not battleground, for the war?

Prime Minister Mackenzie King puzzled over these threats. He fretted about Canada's place "lying between the U.S.S.R. on the one side and the U.S.A. on the other." He believed that Canada's position "may have to be worked out with very special care."[10] King, who served as prime minister but also as secretary of state for External Affairs, had at least one senior adviser who thought Canada should avoid any real postwar military planning with the United States. Canada, according to Escott Reid, first secretary of the Canadian embassy in Washington, was a "buffer state between the U.S.A. and the U.S.S.R." Reid, like some on the PHP, worried that if tensions between the United States and Soviet Union pushed the two states to the brink of war, Washington would put enormous pressure on Ottawa to support the American war effort and lend it territory for bases. He hoped that if Canada remained neutral in any such conflict, "saner counsels may prevail," and Canada might find a way of preventing general war between Canada's giant neighbours. "We could," he wrote, "try and make Canada a chastity belt" between the Soviet Union and the United States.[11]

Reid, who would continue to serve in important roles in the Department of External Affairs until 1962, liked to think big, and to think creatively. The sketch he laid out, in which Canada would avoid any real participation in military planning with the United States, allowed him to imagine and urge his readers to consider a range of options for Canada in the postwar world. But Canada's options were not so broad. King had committed to deep defence relations with the United States in an agreement with President Franklin Roosevelt at Ogdensburg, New York, in 1940, which had created a PJBD with high-level civilian and military representatives from both states. He remained fully committed to the PJBD with an emphasis on "Permanent."[12] In the postwar world, Canada would find itself beside the United States, both figuratively and literally.

World War Three?

Just how likely did another major war seem as the Second World War came to a close? Given the destruction and devastation in the world of 1944, there was a general sense in Ottawa that it would be at least a decade after this war ended before another one might begin. Germany and Japan, the most recent aggressors, would be defeated. The Soviet Union, while a victor, would be ravaged by war. Nonetheless, the PHP Committee's reports suggest that some Canadian officials worried, as early as the spring of 1944, that a victorious United States might misunderstand or overestimate the actions of the Soviet Union, perceive a threat to Washington from Moscow, and plunge the world back into war.

These were not intelligence appreciations or assessments, per se. Even by early 1945, there was no formal intelligence organization for making assessments on potential Soviet actions, or the risk of war. The Canadian JIC, which had been established during the war in November 1942, coordinated intelligence for the Chiefs of Staff Committee (CSC) by streamlining the army, navy, and air force intelligence services. While the purpose of the JIC was, on paper, "to conduct intelligence studies and to prepare such special information as may be required by higher authority," it seldom carried out these duties; its actual function was to be a communicative vessel for receiving UK and US JIC intelligence assessments.[13] Not until June 1945 did the JIC expand beyond its military branches by incorporating two additional representatives from the DEA and the RCMP. These changes greatly enhanced the JIC's ability to address intelligence demands.[14]

In July 1944, the Canadian CSC directed the Canadian Joint Staff in Washington (CJSW) to query American officers on the prospects of another war. (The CSC consisted of the heads of the Canadian armed services, and the CJSW represented the Canadian military attachés in the United States.) The Canadian officers in the US were directed to ask their American colleagues whether they agreed that there was "no danger of attack on North America" in the ten years after the current war ended.[15]

The responses the Canadians received from their American colleagues were mixed. Some US officers and officials saw "no reason whatever" why the United States and the Soviet Union might go to war. But the possibility of a war between the United Kingdom and Russia, which would draw the Americans back to Europe, "lurked in their minds."

Other US officers, including the deputy chief of staff of one of the services, said the US could not agree with the Canadian assumption of no danger to North America. Not because of the Soviet Union but because of civil-military politics in Washington. The services were pushing for retaining a large navy and compulsory military service. If word "ever reached the ears of Congress" that war was unlikely, then the US service chief's hopes for continued and even bigger budgets "would be dashed against the rocks." Here was an early and important indication for the Canadians of how the US military's domestic political needs could colour their stated views about the chances of peace, and the difficulty of truly assessing the threat to North America.[16]

There was a variety of opinions in the Government of Canada, too. On one hand, Canadian diplomats in the Soviet Union, and Canadian diplomats in Washington, believed that the problems of postwar "recovery and development" in the Soviet Union were just so vast that war between the US and the USSR in the decade after 1945 was "extremely remote."[17] On the other hand, senior military officers, like Air Marshal Robert Leckie, the chief of the air staff (CAS), believed there was a "grave danger" in assuming there was no possibility of any threat of war, or assuming that there could be no future threat to North America.[18] This does not necessarily reveal disagreement, but a divide between those who thought war unlikely and those who believed it dangerous to plan as if war was unlikely. It was a distinction not easily resolved in the coming years.

What leaders in Washington or Moscow wanted, however, and what they might get, were hardly the same thing. In 1945, Wilgress reported from Moscow that the world had fallen back into that "pre-war game usually described as the 'war of nerves,'" with rumours of troop movements and possible war. He believed it was "this irresponsible readiness to play with fire that makes one uneasy about the ability to avoid conflagrations."[19]

War, it seemed, could indeed come again. But unlike the Second World War, a future general war could come to North America. Ultimately, the PHP Committee, and then the Cabinet War Committee (CWC) itself, agreed that the nature of warfare had changed so much during the Second World War that Canada could not safely assume that North America would be protected in any future conflict.

The great improvements in the range of aircraft meant that Canada would no longer be protected by oceans. And more important, perhaps, neither was the United States. Canada lay "across the shortest air routes from either Europe or Asia," and Canada was now "of more direct strategic importance to the United States." The result was that the "defence problems of Canada and the United States must now be considered as inter-dependent."[20]

This prospect of future conflict appeared vague and abstract, yet even the slight possibility of another war would affect how the United States acted. And while Canadian officials did not expect that Washington would return to the isolationism of the interwar years, they worried that those instincts may reappear in a new guise, as "a militant form of continental defence-mindedness."[21] The Americans might try to huddle down on the continent, ignore the rest of the world, and build Fortress America.

As the base-building and other co-operative efforts of the Second World War had revealed, a Fortress America would really need to be a Fortress North America, with Canada used as a staging ground for both offensive and defensive operations. It had become obvious to the CWC during the war that the existence of sprawling US air bases in Canada could "impair Canada's freedom of action."[22] In a postwar world marked with tensions between the US and the USSR, would Canada have any freedom whatsoever to make decisions of war and peace?

In the Canadian view, in early 1945, the threat to North America may have been a theoretical possibility but remained practically minimal. Ultimately, the nation's senior leaders, the Cabinet War Committee, believed that "security on the continent depends on the maintenance of peace in Europe and Asia." If there had been "any single lesson" of the current war, they agreed, it was that "no nation can ensure immunity from attack merely by erecting a defensive barrier around its frontiers." For Canada, the "first lines of defence" were not the oceans and air corridors of North America, but "far out into the Pacific in the West and to Europe in the East."[23] But did the Americans see it the same way?

Toward a Shared Appreciation

A series of meetings between Canadian and American officers in late 1945 and into 1946 revealed some of the main differences in thinking between the two nations on postwar defence issues. The root of disagreement lay in a different interpretation of the lessons of the last war.

In June 1945, the Nazis had been defeated but the war in the Pacific was not yet over. The Americans were already organizing their defences for a postwar world. At a meeting of the PJBD, US major general Guy Henry asked his Canadian counterparts a whole slew of questions about future joint defence efforts. What did Canada think of the postwar defence value of all the bases that had been built in northwestern Canada during the war? Would Canada collaborate with the Americans, as part of the US effort to organize the republics of North and South America for defence after the war? Would the Canadian public accept closer defence ties with the US? Would the United Kingdom be concerned by closer Canadian coordination with the Americans?[24]

The Canadians took time to try and develop answers to Henry's questions. While the US officers spoke about a new system of defence and closer relationships, the Canadians "had no indication" of just what the Americans were thinking. Any joint defence planning, the Canadians insisted (to themselves), "should enjoy a two-way flow of information."[25]

A few months after Henry's questions, Brigadier-General Maurice Pope offered the Canadian response in the September meeting of the PJBD. He pointed out, frankly, that Canada had no information whatsoever on just what the US Army or Navy views were on joint defence. He also recalled grievances over the installations and bases the Americans had built in Canada during the war, which the Canadians did not think to be militarily valuable at that time or since. In the future, he said, Canada needed to be "made more fully aware" of the US Joint Chiefs of Staff (JCS) "appreciation" of defence requirements. The phrase "appreciation" is key here; it was the Canadian phrase used instead of what the Americans would later call an "intelligence assessment." If indeed the US-Canadian defence effort was going to be joint and permanent, Pope was saying, the two countries needed to have a shared intelligence appreciation: Canada and the United States should "seek to agree as to the international picture of the coming post-war period in so far as this has a bearing on the question of North American defence."[26]

To achieve these goals, Pope continued, it was necessary to revise an earlier joint appreciation made in 1941, ABC-22, and "bring it into line with our new joint appreciation of our defence position." Tipping the Canadian hand somewhat, he said he doubted that "a military appreciation of our North American defence position over the next one or two decades will lead to the conclusion that the northern half of our territories is threatened with invasion."[27]

Pope, who had served on the Western Front in the First World War and in senior leadership positions in the Canadian Army during the Second World War, was worried about a third. He told his US counterparts that if a major war were to return to the world, he assumed that the "main Canadian effort will again consist of furnishing Armed Forces outside North America" while the American effort would be different.[28] His implication was that, as in the First and Second World Wars, Canada would join any conflict at its outset, while the Americans would again delay their entry into war.

The Americans bristled at Pope's comments. When they responded to Pope in November, they challenged the idea that if war came again, Canada would make "her military effort overseas on a timetable separate and far in advance of that of the United States." The Americans insisted they had learned a different point from the Second World War, and now "lean[ed] to another interpretation of history."[29] "It seems to us," said J. Graham Parsons, an American diplomat and the most senior member of the US delegation to the PJBD, that "the basic lesson of history is that in a world war the intervention of the United States is decisive."[30] And if the Americans had drawn this lesson, so too, they expected, would have potential adversaries.

"Under conditions of modern technology," Parsons continued, "we feel that a future Hitler would read the basic lesson of history correctly and regard the North American industrial base as his first target." He offered confident betting odds ("four to one") that "in any future world conflict, war would be brought to us here rather than that we would again be allowed to defend our continent in Europe or in Asia." Airplanes carrying atom bombs, he warned, would also strike Canada: "[i]f Detroit and Buffalo are attacked, Windsor and Hamilton will not be immune."[31]

This vision of future war was more significant than just an exchange across a board table. Pope had called for a revision of the 1941 appreciation. The US members of the PJBD obliged.[32] The Americans wanted the revision to take account of their expectation that North America would be a target, and an important target, for any future adversary. This was the postwar case for building a Fortress North America.[33]

These early discussions between Americans and Canadians about the future of war in the postwar world were held between military officers on the PJBD. But the strategic and political issues associated with joint defence planning were of great importance to King and the Cabinet. Because defence plans might involve questions of a US presence in Canada and raise issues of sovereignty, the government wanted to ensure that development of joint plans with the United States, and the appreciations on which they were based, not be left solely in the hands of the military.[34] Similarly, the Canadians wanted American views that were not the product only of the US military, with their internecine budget squabbles, but also the views of civilian diplomats in the State Department.[35]

In December 1945, after "considerable discussion," the Cabinet approved the creation of a new institution for joint defence planning with the United States. This new body, the Military Cooperation Committee (MCC), was to operate under the auspices of the PJBD and be responsible for developing an appreciation and then plans for the defence of North America. The Cabinet noted, however, that "any plans for joint defence had to be submitted to government," ensuring civilian oversight of the MCC's work.[36]

The Cold War Begins

The first meeting of the Military Cooperation Committee was held in May 1946. Canadian officers travelled to Washington to meet their counterparts. The two sides produced drafts of both an "Appreciation of the Requirements for Canadian-United States Security" and a "Joint Basic Security Plan" (BSP) for consideration by both governments. The BSP consisted of "essential war plans, that is, what facilities, personnel and material are considered necessary on the outbreak of war" with an unnamed enemy.[37] The plan was informed by the appreciation, which was a planning and intelligence document.

But between the creation of the MCC at the end of 1945 and before the May MCC conference, the Cold War had begun. In September 1945, Igor Gouzenko, a cipher clerk of the GRU (Soviet Main Intelligence Directorate), defected in Ottawa. The documents he smuggled out of the Soviet embassy revealed extensive espionage in Canada and the United States, including spying on the atomic bomb program. In February 1946, Joseph Stalin gave a speech interpreted by some in the West as a declaration of "World War III." In the months leading up to the May conference, there was a flurry of diplomatic reporting and intelligence analysis as American, British, and Canadian officials tried to determine whether Stalin's speech indicated a Soviet desire for hostilities.

In early 1946, the UK JIC began updating its paper on "Russia's Strategic Interests and Intentions," filling a gap in analysis left since the 1944 wartime assessments of the Soviet Union.[38] Intelligence on the Soviet Union remained sparse. As one Foreign Office official observed, the amount of information available was "insufficient for a proper intelligence appreciation," and the committee had, "as in 1944, to crystal gaze rather than to marshal facts and figures in such a way that deductions are inescapable."[39]

Lacking any secret intelligence on Soviet intentions, it was diplomats who provided the most crucial, and compelling, analysis of Soviet intentions. It was in response to Stalin's speech that George Kennan wrote his famed "Long Telegram" to the State Department from Moscow. Kennan's telegram laid out the challenges the Soviet Union would pose to the international system, but he ultimately concluded that the problems posed by Moscow were "within our power to solve — and . . . without recourse to any general military conflict."[40] In March, Frank Roberts, the British ambassador to the Soviet Union, wrote the British equivalent: a lengthy dispatch in which he predicted continuing tensions with the Soviet Union but stressed the possibility, even the need, for coexistence.

That same month, Dana Wilgress offered the Canadian version of the "Long Telegram," asking a question that would dominate Canadian intelligence assessments for the next five years: "[a]re the Soviet leaders prepared to risk another major war in the near future?"[41] Wilgress gave a negative answer. Moscow was in no position to wage war and would not risk provoking one on purpose. At the same time, however, the flux in postwar world affairs would tempt the Soviets into trying to achieve more gains: they would seek to prosecute a "war of nerves" and succeed unless their bluffs were called. The diplomatic analysis, then, pointed toward a tense and difficult future, but not one in which the Soviet Union was likely to choose war.

The draft appreciation presented to the MCC in May 1946 was a stark contrast to the dispatches from abroad. Where the diplomats thought war unlikely and unwanted, the appreciation jumped forward to what would happen in the event a war had begun. This reflects the purpose of the document itself, which was to appreciate the military resources required in case of war.

While the appreciation was presented as a joint MCC document, it was, fundamentally, an American military intelligence paper. Up to this point, almost all intelligence distributed or briefed to joint US-Canadian efforts, including at PJBD meetings, had been provided by the United States.[42] The draft appreciation followed this pattern, even down to the traditional American practice of not naming potential enemies.

Rather than assess the likelihood of war, the paper dwelled on the possible vulnerability of North America in the event of another world war. With the development of the atom bomb, but also rockets, guided missiles, submarine warfare, and biological warfare, North America was losing its "immunity" to war. While the paper admitted "major invasion" of North America was unlikely in the next several years, it assumed an enemy could develop and produce an atomic bomb in the next three to five years.[43]

War might come, the drafters explained, if a "major world power" were to start a war in Europe and overrun the continent. In that case, the United States and Canada would intervene on the side of Great Britain. And such a war would not remain limited to Europe. The US-drafted appreciation bore the imprint of the historical lessons previously described by the Americans on the PJBD: the power that conquered Europe would subject the United States and its war-making potential to attack, for "[h]ostile powers would not forget that in World War I and II this potential was the decisive factor."[44] Any state that attacked Europe would be driven to also attack North America. By 1950 or so, an atomic-armed enemy that controlled Europe would seek to use Iceland, Greenland, and even Labrador and Newfoundland as "springboards" to attack North America from the east. Alaska and northern Canada would provide launching pads from the west.[45]

On one hand, then, the appreciation was extremely specific, even to the point of certainty, in rendering a grim future in which a power managed to conquer Europe and then extend its attack against North America. On the other hand, it was purposefully vague as to what state would take this action, let alone why. When the Canadian team had wanted to discuss and assess "the intentions of potential enemies," the Americans would not agree, and so the appreciation did not include any discussion of whether the Soviet Union intended to launch a war, or whether such a war was even likely.[46] The Canadian team at the conference accepted the paper pending further consideration in Ottawa.

The appreciation, if read on paper, had obvious gaps. To try and overcome its deficiencies, Canadian intelligence officers presented the paper to the prime minister and the Cabinet Defence Committee (CDC) he chaired. The intelligence officers then orally explained what was left out of the paper: that the only real threat was the Soviet Union.[47]

Still, the briefing by Canadian officers could not alter the fact that the appreciation was the work of American intelligence officers. The formal brief to the CDC observed that the "Canadian Intelligence organization is not sufficiently developed to be able to produce very much material from its own sources, nor is it yet capable of assessing the value of Intelligence from other sources."[48] The Canadians had sought to double-check the American figures against a small amount of information they had received from the Royal Air Force (RAF). Still, the paper was ultimately based "largely on the United States assessment of the scales and probabilities of attack against this continent" and the Canadian Chiefs of Staff were "not in a position to offer useful comment on the Intelligence background on which this Appreciation is based."[49]

The intelligence available to the United States was also limited. And perhaps unbeknownst to the Canadians, there was disagreement in the US as to whether and how to understand Soviet intentions. In July 1946, the Office of Reports and Estimates (ORE), the analytical section of the Central Intelligence Group — the immediate precursor to the Central Intelligence Agency (CIA) — submitted its first report, "ORE 1: Soviet Foreign and Military Policy." The analysts concluded that the Soviets might, due to their ideology, be interested in world domination. But ORE 1 judged that a "resort to force is unlikely in view of the danger of provoking a major international conflict."[50] Like the 1944 and 1945 analyses, ORE concluded that Soviet military policy derived from "preoccupation with security which is the basis of Soviet foreign policy."[51]

At the same time, in Washington, the US JIC submitted its own estimate. Published by the Joint Chiefs of Staff, JCS 1696 was written in a more alarmist tone than the ORE paper. While it did not contradict ORE 1, it painted a grim picture of a future war with the Soviet Union in which gas and germ warfare would accompany atomic destruction.[52] The United States, then, was producing uncoordinated, if not quite conflicting estimates: one from the civilian ORE and the other by the US JIC, subordinate to the Joint Chiefs of Staff.[53]

Whether or not Canadian officials were privy to the ORE assessments, they were privy to the reporting of their own diplomat, Wilgress, and also the thinking of State Department officials like George Kennan (whose analysis matched more closely with the civilians at CIG).

The disconnect between the intelligence appreciation from the MCC and the diplomatic assessments worried Canadians in the Department of External Affairs. They did not want Canada's postwar defence policy based on the type of intelligence provided by the US military to the MCC. Further complicating matters was sensitivity in the Department of External Affairs that the MCC's appreciation had overstepped its bounds.

Hume Wrong, the associate deputy under-secretary of state for External Affairs, believed that the appreciation had strayed out of the military's lane and into the DEA's responsibilities. While Clerk of the Privy Council and Cabinet Secretary Arnold Heeney, Canada's top civil servant, accepted that it was the job of military advisers to assess military capabilities, he pointed out that it was the DEA's "to estimate the possibilities of the outbreak of such a war."[54] The MCC appreciation had seemed to estimate the possibility of war by assuming it could happen, and several senior DEA officials believed that estimate was off base.

Heeney and Wrong, along with Under-Secretary of State for External Affairs (USSEA) Norman Robertson, were wary of the appreciation. In general, they agreed with the basic thrust: North America was more vulnerable now than it had been in the past. And yet they believed that the appreciation was overly alarming, and no basis for national policy.[55]

The embarrassing situation caused by the paucity of Canadian intelligence gathering or intelligence analysis capability, combined with the Department of External Affairs' claim to responsibility, provided a catalyst for action. The result was the first attempt to draft a Canadian strategic appreciation of the Soviet threat to North America.

First Try

In early July, the Canadian Joint Intelligence Committee directed the preparation of a report titled "Strategic Appreciation of the Capabilities of the U.S.S.R. to Attack the North American Continent."[56] The paper, which was really a compilation of various shorter papers drafted by the separate intelligence branches of each service, was a failure. It was repetitive and deemed not suitable to be sent to the Chiefs of Staff Committee. Where the intent or expectation had been to determine the various "forms and scales of Soviet attack" that might be expected against Canada, the paper focused almost entirely on assessing a full-scale attack — similar to the MCC appreciation.[57]

G. G. "Bill" Crean, a member of the Department of External Affairs who would play an important role in the development of the Canadian intelligence structure, was especially critical of the paper. Crean, who had served in British intelligence in the war, thought it "seriously over-estimated"[58] Soviet capabilities. His comments on the paper mark the first example of civilian officials working to try and shape and restrain military assessments of the Soviet threat.

Where the paper had focused on what might happen if the Soviet Union launched a full-scale attack, Crean thought this was the wrong track and led to the wrong result. To him, the "chief value of a paper of this kind is not so much to show how successful the Soviet[s] would be, but really to show how difficult operations would be against the North American Continent."[59] Crean believed the idea of the Soviet Union launching a full-scale attack against North America in the near future was fantasy. He argued that it was unreasonable, at least in the next five to ten years, to expect the Soviet Union to choose war and direct all of its energies at North America. This contention would be a major sticking point in future analyses of the Soviet threat for decades to come.

By the end of the summer of 1946, the Canadians had started work on their own strategic appreciation but had not yet formally approved the joint MCC appreciation. The Cabinet remained wary of accepting any joint plans with the United States, especially ones based on a US appreciation.

US diplomats were sympathetic to the Canadian delay in approving the MCC papers. The US ambassador in Ottawa, Ray Atherton, assumed the delay was part of the postwar transition in Ottawa, as Canada looked to the US, rather than Britain, for guidance in world affairs.[60] He perhaps did not realize how much the Canadian experience with the Americans during the Second World War had made the Canadians wary.

American patience started to run out as Americans grew increasingly worried about the Soviet threat in August 1946. Soviet propaganda, according to US analysts, had reached a "fever pitch." Two US aircraft were shot at over Yugoslavia, with one forced down and the other destroyed. And the Soviets were putting enormous pressure on Turkey over the Straits of the Dardanelles, insisting that the Soviets and Turks share responsibility for the defence of the straits. This bid for influence and control over Turkey and the straits would be one of the most significant moments in the early Cold War.[61]

As a result of these events, all of which occurred in the middle two weeks of August, a US intelligence "Special Study" in late August warned that "consideration should be given to the possibility of near-term Soviet military action."[62] The study, conducted by the civilian Central Intelligence Group (the precursor to the CIA), maintained that there was no information that the Soviets were halting their postwar demobilization program (in fact they were accelerating it). Yet nor were there indications of Soviet or satellite troops concentrating, moving, or building-up supplies. The report concluded that the events of August should be "interpreted as constituting no more than an intensive war of nerves." Nonetheless, the tensions of August likely propelled the Americans to press the Canadians for an answer on the MCC appreciation.

In early September, the US representatives on the Permanent Joint Board of Defence tried to push the Canadians forward on the issues of joint planning, air defence, and the establishment of US bases in Canada. The US Army member wrote a letter to the board (the formal way in which members communicated and put key points on record) and used the appreciation as the lever. He noted that the "outstanding feature" of the joint appreciation, to which all members had agreed, was that in approximately five years "a potential enemy will be able to inflict serious damage on the vital areas of Canada and/or the United States by aerial bombardment,"[63] delivered via aircraft or guided missiles, and potentially including atomic bombs. Crucially, he observed that "military principles have in the past laid down that the best defense is the offense,"[64] but noted that strategic offensive plans were outside the scope of this defence plan. The note from the US Army member, then, contained two red flags for the Canadians. First, that a joint appreciation, agreed to by the Canadians but based on US intelligence, could be used as a lever to shape Canadian defence policy. Second, that planning purely for defence was partially artificial, as it ignored what would actually occur in war.

The Importance of Combined Intelligence

Senior Canadian military officials were aware of the political difficulty inherent in trying to gain Cabinet approval for military planning based solely on American intelligence. They needed a Canadian solution.

In October, the Joint Planning Committee (JPC), a subsidiary committee of the Chiefs of Staff Committee, and one which included a DEA member, reviewed the Canadians' almost exclusive reliance on American intelligence in joint US-Canadian efforts. The JPC suggested that future intelligence briefs or appreciations drawn up for either the MCC or the PJBD should be the work of a "*combined* Canada-United States intelligence team."[65] While acknowledging that the majority of information that made up any assessment would come from the Americans, the JPC argued it should be "interpreted and presented on a combined basis." In a nod to a growing concern in the DEA, the JPC also recommended that it would be desirable to have representatives of the DEA and the State Department take responsibility for a combined diplomatic appreciation that would form a portion of any overall assessment.

It is difficult to overstate the skepticism that Canadian and American civilians, in the Department of External Affairs and in the State Department respectively, held for the judgment of military and naval officers. Up until the autumn of 1946, the joint planning and the drawing up of the appreciation had been the preserve of the military. As Crean had noted in his comments on the first Canadian strategic appreciation, the result was to focus on worst-case scenarios and the possibility of general war.

Lester Pearson, writing from his post as ambassador in Washington, reported that his interlocutors in the State Department, men like John Hickerson who sat on the PJBD, had "a profound distrust of the military mind and all of its works — a distrust which he does not hesitate to express in no uncertain terms."[66] Pearson, from his long dealings with the Americans, knew of the sometimes impenetrable barrier between the State Department and the Pentagon. He was one of the most powerful voices pushing for civilian involvement in the development of appreciations, and the need for conversations between the DEA and State.

American planning was not put on hold just because Canadian diplomats wanted more control. While the form and process for future US-Canadian intelligence appreciations remained in limbo, the United States continued to develop military plans for the new Cold War world. In early November, Canadian officers were invited to participate in secret tripartite staff talks with the Americans and the British — plans distinct and separate from the MCC discussions about the defence of North America. Pearson was initially hesitant but came to see the value for Canada. "The more I think of it," he wrote, "the more I am convinced that a joint appreciation and forecast of the global strategic situation, developed by our two great prospective Allies in another war, would be of great value in reaching intelligent decisions on our own domestic policies, provided that is well done and carries conviction." Canada could not plan its defence policy — the example he provided was regarding air defence — "except in the light of some authoritative appreciation concurred in by both the U.S. and the U.K. of the conditions and theatres in which another war is likely to be fought and decided."[67]

Pearson was realistic enough to understand that the US and the UK would be planning for war, and that Canada's defence policy would be shaped by both the appreciations and subsequent plans made by those larger powers. At the same time, he wanted to ensure that those appreciations were the work of the civilian leaders in each country.

As Pearson came to see the advantage of Canada participating in global military planning, and not just North American defence, the broader issue of US-Canadian joint defence planning came before the prime minister and the Cabinet Defence Committee. The day before the committee met, on November 12, 1946, Pearson made a significant intervention. He wrote to King, warning that if the Soviet system did not change, "the U.S.S.R. is ultimately bound to come into open conflict with western democracy." While war was not inevitable, Pearson warned the prime minister to "not make the mistake we made with Hitler, of refusing to take seriously the words those leaders utter for home consumption."[68] A new war, however, might feature atomic bombs. Pearson offered his prime minister some hope: "All this does not mean war today or tomorrow. I cannot believe that [the Soviet Union] . . . would be ready to strike in five or ten years. But," he continued, "the way the world is now going, there can only be one ultimate result — war."[69]

King, in receipt of this gloomy warning from Pearson, chaired the CDC on November 13. Intelligence officers briefed him on the MCC appreciation and its conclusions that North America "could no longer be regarded as immune from air attack,"[70] and that a potential aggressor might hold the atomic bomb in a few years. They made clear to King and the other CDC members that the intelligence was American in origin. While the Canadian officers did not dispute the intelligence — indeed they agreed with it, and pointed out they had compared it to British assessments — they were wary of the broader plans the Americans were developing based on the appreciation. For instance, Robert Leckie, the CAS, told the committee that he did not agree with the American assumption that the Soviet Union would try to neutralize the continent through bombing. He expected attacks of a diversionary nature only. He thought the Americans plans for air defence were "extreme," and the situation did "not warrant the establishment of an elaborate defence scheme employing our resources in a static role."[71] The CAS, clearly, was wondering if the Americans were envisioning a wartime role for Canada as the gendarmerie of the North America skies, on patrols at home and with no offensive role.

The next day, the situation repeated itself in front of the full Cabinet, with the Chiefs of Staff again present and intelligence officers briefing all ministers on the MCC's draft appreciation and draft basic security plan. Major William Anderson, head of the Intelligence Branch, was the primary briefer and took two hours to offer what King thought to be an "exceptionally well performed" briefing. King wrote in his diary that he thought the rest of the Cabinet were "profoundly impressed." He even acknowledged that the information was "largely based on American sources," but seemed to take some comfort in the fact the information had been checked against the UK's. King, seemingly having taken Pearson's memorandum to heart, wrote that "the world situation is infinitely more dangerous than we have yet believed it to be. It would almost seem that we are headed into an inevitable conflict." If there were to be a war, he wrote, it "may result in a sort of Armageddon."[72] King was "coming to the belief that a third world war is in the making although it may take a decade to bring it on."[73]

The problem of joint planning, bases, and adapting Canada to "the military situation today," he wrote, "is the greatest problem which the Canadian Government has been faced since the war."[74] King, however, remained cautious. He was deeply concerned about the costs of defence, and worried that new military plans would cause the budget to explode. He worried, too, about bases and "competitive arming in the North," fearing this might begin a sort of arms race that "will not end until there has actually been war."[75] Going down this dreary road, King even began to imagine a scenario by which the Canadians and the United States built bases in the Arctic that the Soviet Union was then able to capture and use against North America.[76]

US-Canadian Differences

In November, in the days after the intelligence briefings for Cabinet, Brooke Claxton, the minister of National Health and Welfare (but soon to become minister of National Defence), wrote to King and emphasized "in the strongest terms" the "fundamental difference in the concepts of the American and Canadian staffs."[77] These differences lay in how the Canadians and the Americans interpreted the joint appreciation. The Americans, Claxton wrote, "say that they are to be the object of the main attack," while the Canadians say North America "would be the object of a diversionary attack."[78] The Americans' plans, and the level of Canadian defence expenditure and the bases the plans would require, were based on American fears that the Canadians did not share. Claxton warned that continuing to base plans on the American interpretation of the appreciation would be beyond Canada's capacity and would only achieve "a Maginot line across the north of Canada" — a reference to the enormously expensive, and ultimately ineffective, French defences against Germany built before the Second World War.[79]

Up to this point, delay had been King's preference. But, as Claxton warned, if Canada continued to wait, planning would continue, bit by bit, and "each day we allow them [the Americans] to continue along the present course" would "commit us further to acceptance of that course."[80] A high-level meeting was required, to prevent the Government from entering "upon the most important action in the peacetime history of the country on the basis of a possible misunderstanding."[81]

While scholars may, in hindsight, neatly divide foreign and domestic policy, the King Cabinet believed that its defence plans had become a "matter of major external and internal policy for Canada."[82] And the defence plans were, ultimately, derived from an intelligence appreciation made not by Canadians but by Americans.

Claxton's letter pushed discussion back into Cabinet. Ministers in Cabinet decided that before they could approve any defence plans, they would require a truly "agreed appreciation," one "prepared with the greatest care and only after full discussion between the two governments on the diplomatic level."[83] In the meantime, the Canadians would assure the Americans they would continue to participate in draft planning but would not yet concur in the draft joint appreciation.

The insistence on a joint appreciation, and one arrived at after input from diplomats from both countries' foreign service, was guaranteed to put the existing appreciation, "largely a military document," on ice. The Canadian effort then proceeded on two tracks: talks between the Department of State and the Department of External Affairs, and an effort to develop "a purely Canadian appreciation" that could be used to inform the Canadian position in discussions of a new joint appreciation with the Americans.[84]

US-Canadian Agreement

Diplomats from the Department of External Affairs were directed to examine, with their State Department colleagues, an "estimate of Soviet intentions (as distinct from Soviet military capabilities)."[85] Those tasked with the examination were permitted to assume that threat of Soviet aggression was real, but they were to consider where and when aggression any might occur.

Critically, given the Cabinet's concerns about air defence and US bases in Canada, the diplomats were to "raise the general question as to whether the principal threat of war is likely to arise in Europe or whether an 'all-out' attack on the North American continent is a probability."[86] The question of "when" an attack might be expected would affect the "tempo and scale of our defence planning."[87] The DEA already seemed convinced the existing joint draft appreciation overestimated the likelihood of an attack on North America. Furthermore, as the American PBJD representatives had said quite plainly that they viewed offence as the best defence, it seemed likely that the US and Canada would end up fighting in Europe again. For the Canadians to make the best decision about its defence policy, they needed to know about US global strategy.

In late November, officers of the Department of External Affairs drafted a "Political Appreciation" meant to assess the prospects (rather than the capability) for Soviet aggression. The document was drafted to prepare for the meeting with the Americans, but it would also serve as the text for an important component of the Canadian appreciation drawn up in 1947 (see below).[88] In December, Secretary of State for External Affairs (SSEA) Louis St. Laurent agreed to loan these documents to the Americans in December 1946, as a preview of Canadian thinking. It was, in effect, an early and informal version of sharing intelligence analysis.[89]

The process driving the drafting of the political appreciation was fundamentally different than the MCC appreciation that assessed Canada-US security needs in case of a full-scale attack on North America. The discussion and analysis now revolved around the much more difficult challenge of appreciating what might happen, and not simply planning for the worst case.

In December, Pearson and a group of Canadian officials met with the American ambassador, Atherton, and several US experts and military officers to discuss the draft joint appreciation and the basic security plan. The meeting occurred in a "most frank and cordial atmosphere."[90] This was significant for the Canadians, who recalled much more adversarial meetings with the Americans in 1941. "Happily," Pearson wrote, "it is some years since there has been any table-pounding in defence discussions between the two countries."[91]

Pearson began the meeting by laying out the Canadian analysis in the political appreciation: that "there was only slight risk of aggression on the part of any potential enemy, such as the Soviet Union, in the near future."[92] The Soviet Union would, in the meantime, strengthen its economy and build up its war potential. The United Nations, Pearson said, "would be ineffective in maintaining peace," and so it was only prudent for Canada and its allies to make preparations for security. George F. Kennan, the renowned Soviet expert, and father of the American Cold War policy of containment, had read the Canadian paper and agreed in general with its conclusions. He sketched his vision of containment: that the democratic countries could "exert some influence" on the Soviets and prevent them from "attaining by aggressive policies things it was essential to deny them."[93] The Americans said they had already set down "stop lines" to Soviet expansionist policy, a reference to Turkey and Iran.

Heeney picked up on Kennan's point regarding influence to emphasize the Canadian view that there was bound "to be some element of provocation in the overt planning of joint defence measures in the Arctic."[94] The DEA officials, from the very beginning of their consideration of Soviet intentions, understood that Western strategy, even planning and base-building, would and could influence Soviet actions. For decades to come, the Canadians would be wary that defensive moves in the West would appear as offensive measures to the Soviets, who in turn would take defensive actions that would appear offensive.

The Canadians then moved the discussion to try and learn more about American global strategy and general strategic planning beyond the defence of North America. General Henry, returning to the theme of his PJBD comments earlier in the year, said that if war were to come in five or six years, the major Canadian and US military effort should be outside North America. But over time, as enemy technology — that is Soviet bombers and possibly missiles — were developed and built, the proportion of effort spent on the defence of North America would have to increase.[95] The American strategic concept for "any future war would be to develop the maximum fire power at the greatest effective distance away from North America."[96] And while North America had to be secure, the Americans said they did not favour "the enormous diversion of resources" necessary to provide "one hundred percent protection for North America."[97] This was a far more nuanced description of American strategic thinking than presented in the MCC plan and appreciation, which had only focused on continental defence.

This meeting was of crucial importance. First, Canadian officials found themselves in close agreement with their State Department colleagues on the Soviet threat, and found "no effort on their [the American] part to over-emphasize dangers or underline necessities."[98] While the Canadian diplomats knew they could count on their colleagues at State, this also reinforced the DEA's concerns that purely military appreciations would be worst case in nature, even alarmist.

Second, the DEA was able to gain some information about how the concept of war was developing in US minds. The discussion of American thinking about general war, rather than a narrow discussion of the defence of North America, helped put continental defence in perspective. Defending North America was important to the United States, as it was to Canada. But it did not seem the Americans were expecting to build a Fortress North America, with all the cost and sovereignty implications that would entail for Canada. As Washington's plans for maximum firepower at the greatest distance from North America developed, there would be different and no less pressing implications for Ottawa.

JIC 1 (Final)

In the first months of 1947, the Joint Intelligence Committee in Ottawa began work on the purely Canadian appreciation the Cabinet Defence Committee had requested in late 1946.[99] This Canadian assessment of the Soviet Union was to be completed in time for use in discussions to develop a joint appreciation with the Americans in May. The paper, which was finalized in March 1947, was titled "JIC 1 (Final)."

The aim of JIC 1 was to "determine the capabilities of the U.S.S.R. to attack the North American continent within the next ten years," as well as "an estimate of the probable amount of warning to be expected."[100] The report was divided into seven parts, with its first two sections offering an assessment of the Soviet Union's political and economic capabilities and the potential of waging war against North America. The next four analyzed Soviet manpower, weapons, naval, military, and air force capabilities. The final section examined potential threats to Canada's internal security, either by domestic vulnerabilities and/or from the Soviets pursuing their policies through "penetrating the Canadian democratic system."[101]

DEA officials who worked on the paper believed their basic role on the Joint Intelligence Committee was "to emphasize considerations that do not occur to the military mind."[102] Ultimately, the DEA tried to achieve this by attaching the political appreciation, drawn up for discussion with the State Department in late 1946, to the JIC paper as an appendix. Its inclusion added a dimension entirely absent from the previous joint appreciation that had included only military and naval sections. But the political appreciation was tacked on to a largely military assessment. There was no effort to integrate the military and political elements of the paper.

DEA officials wondered if any such integration were possible. In a note with a cutting edge, indicative of DEA officials' views of their military counterparts, Escott Reid warned Pearson that the political appreciation might "mislead the Chiefs of Staff because it assumed a comprehension of the complexities of the problem which, because of their special training, they may not possess."[103] In the closing weeks before the paper was finalized, the DEA sought to alter the military assessment, worrying that some of the Soviet capabilities had been overestimated.[104]

In May 1947, with their Canadian-made appreciation in hand, representatives of the Canadian JIC met with the US JIC in Washington to establish a new joint appreciation. The discussions, however, contained an underlying problem. The Canadians wanted a broader discussion on the prospects for general war. The conference, however, was meant to discuss the appreciation and plan for the continental defence, and so the Americans would only discuss intelligence and planning in this narrower context. The American position was strong, for there had never been agreement that the meeting would be a full-fledged discussion of the prospects for general war. The Canadian team agreed to work within the constraints of "defence." But much to the surprise of senior officials in Ottawa, the joint US-Canadian meeting concluded that no changes of substance were required to the original draft appreciation written in 1946. The teams agreed to move forward with the original document.

Pearson was unwilling to accept this result. In the first place, the Canadians had been trying to move away from a purely military appreciation to one that included a political appreciation of both the chances of war and the type of war that might occur. Discussions with the Americans — both the State Department officials and general officers like Henry — had revealed that American strategic planning was envisioning a general war fought outside of North America. How could the original appreciation, with so much emphasis on the defence of the continent, remain relevant when the broader strategy for general war was shifting? Furthermore, as the world situation had grown more tense throughout 1946, how could the appreciation remain the same? Pearson convinced his colleagues on the Chiefs of Staff Committee that they could not accept the statement that "there had been no changes which affected the Appreciation."[105]

The experience of trying to agree a joint appreciation with the Americans had raised concern for Canadian officers, too. The chair of the Joint Planning Committee, Captain H. N. Lay of the Royal Canadian Navy, had been tasked with drawing up joint plans with his US colleagues. He complained that his team had "been handicapped by having to keep our planning within the bounds of a DEFENCE or a SECURITY plan."[106] The result was that Canadian defence planning had focused on providing "purely defensive measures on the North American continent to meet a Russian attack."[107] Lay understood the importance of maintaining defence against a possible surprise attack, and that the need for defence would increase as the Soviet ability to launch a long-range attack, possibly with atomic bombs, increased. Over time, the "period of warning" before any potential Soviet attack would only shrink as Soviet aircraft and missile technology improved, and so it was essential that Canada continually improve its "intelligence organization, methods and techniques."[108] But if war came, the Americans seemed now to agree with the Canadian view, what Pope had told the PJBD, that the fighting should occur as far away from North America as possible. And the Canadians would want a part of the offensive action. Charles Foulkes, the chief of the general staff, rejected any idea that Canada would play a "purely defensive role in any future war," leaving the offensive fights to others.[109]

Lay, and no doubt Foulkes, too, assumed that the United States had or was developing strategic plans for general war. But Canada was developing no plans beyond the joint defence plans it was negotiating bilaterally with the Americans. If the joint planning proceeded along the tracks laid down in 1946, the Canadian role would be exclusively defensive, because they were not playing a role in planning for any strategic offensive. At the same time, there was no point in Canada making "strategic war plans" on its own without working closely with the Americans and the British, who would be Canada's major allies in any general war.[110]

The problem was bigger than Canada not being able to choose a role in a future war. In 1947, the prospects of general war appeared more likely to Pearson and DEA officials than at any point since the end of the Second World War. Reid told the Chiefs of Staff Committee that "the comparative certainty of the next ten years being free from war had been reduced by events."[111] His concern was not that Moscow was seeking war, but that Washington might feel compelled to attack. The "balance of power," he told the chiefs, might alter against the United States, or the United States might presume the balance would tip and choose to act. It remained that "[i]n either event, there was a possibility that the United States might take action which could precipitate war."[112]

An American Attack?

In late August, Reid drafted a paper on the prospect of the US precipitating a war and of conflict with the Soviet Union more generally.[113] He distributed his memorandum within the Department of External Affairs in Ottawa, and to several Canadian diplomatic posts abroad. The memorandum was not an intelligence appreciation or assessment, but a thought-piece considering different aspects of the US-Soviet relationship and the implications for Canada. Reid's paper, one recipient wrote, was a "scissors and paste" exercise, cobbling together the ideas of George Kennan, several departmental memoranda, and dispatches from Canadians like Dana Wilgress writing from the Soviet Union. The responses to the paper, however, are more important than the paper itself. The paper served as something of a Rorschach test, with replies providing an insight into viewpoints and assumptions that Canadian officials held about the prospects for war between the Soviet Union and the United States.

Maurice Pope, the colourful general who had served on the PJBD and was now in Berlin, pushed back against Reid's focus on immediate Cold War crises and urged him to put the analysis in a longer-term framework. "Present Soviet foreign policy," he wrote, is "simply a continuation of Russia's age old policy of expansion." The Russian goal to create a "cordon sanitaire" on its border was, he said, "as natural and as reasonable as the United States desire for bases as far away as Greenland and Dakar."[114]

Worrying too much about Czechoslovakia's relationship with the Soviet Union, for instance, was unhelpful, as it was "really no different from Canada's position vis-a-vis the United States." Russia had existed for centuries "alongside Western Europe," even if, as he said, it was not a part of it; even if Stalin's Soviet Union fell apart, "Russia would still remain." For Pope, Soviet policy was Russian policy, and both policies were what should be expected of states concerned about their security. He even went as far as to conclude that "the United States, and to some extent British, monkeying in Polish, Bulgarian, etc., affairs has had the effect of unnecessarily goading the Russians."[115]

Marcel Cadieux, Lester Pearson's executive assistant, saw things much differently from Pope. Reid's paper had suggested an equality between Soviet and American interests, arguing that both were "[e]xpanding powers . . . scaring each other into further expansions of their defence." Cadieux disagreed with Reid, arguing that only the Soviet Union was an expanding power, and that all US efforts were warranted by the aggressive policies directed by Moscow. "To put it into a nutshell," he concluded, "the U.S.S.R. is waging war against us in all but a military means." On this basis, Cadieux called for the expansion of Canadian "intelligence facilities to learn more and more about the U.S.S.R." Only with better intelligence could Canada understand the Soviet Union, and "take advantage of its weaknesses by applying pressure at the right time and in the right manner to discourage its aggressive tactics."[116]

Wilgress was not impressed with the paper. He thought it focused too much on the chance of war. Writing from Berne, he observed that "no one thinks or talks about the possibility of war, whereas in North America this seems to be the obsession which is colouring all thinking about the Soviet Union."[117]

It was time to stop arguing about how to deal with the Soviet Union. This, he thought, had been answered by Soviet action in recent years. The United States had adopted its "policy of firmness" — those "stop lines" the Americans had mentioned to Canada in December, and what would come to be known as containment. The Soviets were not totally convinced of Washington's firmness yet, but it was the only policy that would contain the Soviet Union and prevent them from tempting steps which might escalate to war. Canada, Wilgress wrote, should "give every support to that policy of firmness upon which the United States is embarking since any wavering from that policy would be sure to be exploited by the Soviet leaders for their own purposes and hence is the most dangerous course which we could undertake."[118]

Robert Ford, the chargé d'affaires at the Canadian embassy in Moscow, offered a convincing explanation for how domestic politics in both states might lead to war: the Soviets, he worried, might risk war to divert "their people's minds from the miseries of repeated Five Year Plans." In the United States, "a strongly anti-Communist, isolationist administration" might become so frustrated with socialist governments in Western Europe that they cut off aid to their allies, creating the possibility for Soviet encroachment, and "at the same time goad the Moscow leaders into war." The Americans underestimated the strength of the Soviet Union, he thought, and the best evidence for this was the suggestion some Americans had been making "that the whole question could be settled now by dropping a few atomic bombs on Russia."[119]

R. M. Macdonnell, writing from Prague, thought such an outright American decision for war unlikely. He found it "almost impossible to conceive of a situation arising in which the Congress of the United States could be persuaded that a preventive war was necessary or desirable."[120] Charles

Ritchie, writing from Paris, agreed with Macdonnell. He thought the idea of the US preparing a preventative war "unreal" for several reasons, including the fact that "the vast and secret preparations" required for a surprise attack on the Soviet Union "seem totally incompatible with American realities as we have learned to know them in the past."[121] And yet, he noted, if the government of the United States became convinced that war was necessary for American self-defence, it "might launch the first blow in the belief that if they did not do so the Soviet Union would have the advantage of a surprise offensive."[122]

During this period in 1947, the Canadian embassy in Washington was closely tracking statements made by Americans pushing for preventive war against the Soviet Union. Joseph Alsop, a journalist for the American *Herald Tribune*, reported that a number of congressmen who had travelled to Europe had concluded "that we might as well have another war and get it over with." The Canadian diplomats in Washington had sometimes heard this sort of thinking in private conversation. The *Washington Times* provided "an almost comical example of swaggering and vicious belligerence" in response to Soviet accusations that the Americans were somehow akin to the recently defeated Nazis; the Canadians read the *Washington Times* point of view to be: "Okay; if they insist on calling us Hitlers, let's do some Hitlering."[123] Ultimately, however, Ambassador Hume Wrong wrote, while the term "preventive war" was "thrown about pretty loosely these days," the number of Americans advocating such a policy was "negligible in number."[124]

And yet they could not be ignored. As Hume Wright (then third secretary to Ambassador Hume Wrong at the Washington embassy) wrote, the postwar United States "occupies a position, in a period of nerve-cracking tensions, where her actions basically affect the day-to-day existence of whole countries." As a result, the "unstable and irresponsible side of the United States is inevitably of vital concern to the world."[125]

In a sophisticated analysis, Wright examined a number of worrying ways in which rabid anti-Communism, the nature of Congress, inexperience in international affairs, and "plain ignorance of some elementary historical facts" led to questionable American foreign policy choices. American policy, he thought, rested too heavily for its domestic support on fear of the Soviet Union and hatred for Communism. But without this motivation, the United States might slip into its "pre-war aloofness," and "the fool's paradise of the Kellogg Pact" — a former American secretary of state's treaty to renounce war. All of what Wright called the "extravagances appearing in the press and in speeches in Congress" were embarrassing, "but we must bear with them, for without them the rest of the world would be worse off."[126]

Pearson, at Reid's suggestion, sent Wright's analysis to Prime Minister King, along with a note designed to dampen King's fears the United States might launch a preventive war. This analysis from Washington was crucial in moving the Cabinet beyond any lingering notion that there was an equivalence between the Soviet Union and the United States.[127] In essence, what was happening in the United States was a process, part of it ugly and embarrassing, that nonetheless was "spreading public support for effective military preparation for war."[128]

As Wilgress and other Canadians argued, this was the policy of firmness that would, paradoxically, ensure war with the Soviet Union did not come. But it would rest on a knife's edge.

In the fall of 1947, while Canadians posted abroad were responding to Reid, the Cabinet Defence Committee received an update. Cabinet members were informed that in the coming decade, changes in the balance of power would advantage the Soviet Union, but that it was "unlikely that these alterations will make it worthwhile for Russia to precipitate a planned war, even assuming that its aim are expansionist."[129]

In fact, the Soviet Union would try to avoid "stumbling into a war." If war did come, any attack against North America would be likely to be "diversionary in character;"[130] an attempt to pin down forces in North America, rather than an all-out assault on Canada and the United States. While North America was increasingly vulnerable, and might be attacked, it would not be the primary target in a war. And yet, a war still might come if the Soviets overplayed their hand and the Americans responded with force.

Conclusion

In the last year of the Second World War, Reid had imagined Canada standing apart from the Soviet Union and the United States, or even perhaps standing between them as a "chastity belt." But for most of the government, from Prime Minister King down through the Post-Hostilities Planning Committee, and both the Departments of External Affairs and National Defence, the defence plans and policy of Canada and the United States were intertwined.

The discussion engendered by Reid's 1946 thought-piece led to a confirmation of King's long-standing policy: Canada and the United States were on the same side in peace — and in the Cold War. And while the American political system was odd and sometimes seemed dangerous, it was better that the United States was playing a part in world affairs, as this was more likely to guarantee peace. And yet, it seemed likely that if the United States thought peace was in jeopardy, it was prepared to destroy that threat to peace by resorting to war. It was crucial, then, to find a way of understanding Moscow's true intentions.

2

Agreed Intelligence

In early 1948, Canadian diplomats were growing more concerned by the changes in American strategy they had detected in 1947. Pearson heard rumours of a United States "master plan" for global war and thought the British may have had some knowledge of, and perhaps a part in, the making of this plan. The Canadians, as they had told the Americans in December 1947, were eager to know about any such "global strategy" because Canada assumed and expected to play a role in any future war. But were the British and Americans making assumptions, or even plans, about what Canadian forces would do in a war, without Canadian input?[1]

Even in 1948, there remained some debate about just what shape a future war would take. In Canada, the chief of the general staff, Lieutenant-General Charles Foulkes, assumed that a new general war would follow traditional patterns. "The teachings of military history," he told the other chiefs, "confirmed the view that wars were eventually won or lost on the ground."[2]

But increasingly, and to the contrary, there was an expectation the next war would be nothing like the gruelling Second World War. The chief of the air staff, supported by the chair of the Defence Research Board, disagreed with Foulkes. They believed that the next war would be "won or lost in its very early stages by direct air attacks on ... vital centres."[3]

This view tracked closely with thinking in the United States. The release of the Finletter Report in the United States, the result of a study of military strategy commissioned by President Truman in the summer of 1947, suggested that the Americans would prioritize offensive air power.[4] This is certainly how the Canadians interpreted the American views.[5]

Prioritizing offensive air power had major implications for the planning done by the MCC. The US-Canadian work to date on the Basic Security Plan had been based on the appreciation of 1946. As discussed in the previous chapter, these plans were security or defence plans, not war plans. They did not take into account the offensive strategy the Americans or Canadians would pursue in war. Now, if the Finletter Report showed the future of American thinking about war, and that future revolved around massive offensive striking power, existing plans to defend North America seemed obsolete, even unrealistic.

Members of Canada's Chiefs of Staff Committee (CSC) started calling for a review of the "whole Canada-U.S. Basic Security Plan." If offensive air operations were to be the main effort in a general war, then defensive air operations "should form only a very small part of any overall plan." Future war would call for the best defence: a strong offence.[6]

The Canadians were aware of, and disliked, the unrealism of developing one plan for the defence of North America, and a separate offensive war strategy. These tensions were never fully resolved.

In 1948, Canadian analysts prepared assessments of the threat to North America in advance of bilateral meetings with the United States. These bilateral meetings would result in American-Canadian Agreed Intelligence (ACAI) assessments intended to establish a joint appreciation to inform plans for continental defence.

That year the Canadians also participated in separate trilateral military planning meetings with their American and British partners to establish what would become ABC (American-British-Canadian) plans in case of war with the Soviet Union. It was in these emergency war plans that the Americans and British staked out their ideas for offensive operations against the Soviet Union. Canadian efforts to ensure Ottawa's interests were included in these broader plans led to Canadian efforts to assess Soviet aims and strategy in case of general war, too.

These two types of assessments: one needed for the defence of North America, the other designed to understand Soviet strategy and prepare for a response in war, proceeded simultaneously in 1948, and with only limited connection between the two.

Canadian efforts to insert themselves into the tripartite intelligence appreciations were overshadowed in 1949 by two major events: the explosion of a Soviet atomic device, which threw the American, British, and Canadian assessments into question, and the signing of the Washington Treaty, the precursor to the North Atlantic Treaty Organization (NATO), which signalled a shift from tripartite war planning toward a broader alliance defence policy, strategy, and plans.

The Threat to North America

In January 1948, the Military Cooperation Committee requested that the Canadian and US Joint Intelligence Committees separately review the 1946 joint appreciation. Each JIC was to prepare a list of changes or updates. The request, as it was phrased, raised concerns among DEA officers on the Canadian JIC. The recommendation to review and update the appreciation suggested that the new version was to follow the old form, with only some minor changes. The DEA, however, wanted to scrap the initial appreciation and begin again.

The Canadians wanted the new draft to include an "assumptions" section that laid out the basic ideas that informed the plan. The original US-drafted appreciation "omitted ... any reference to the actual potential enemy, Russia" and, as a result, was "unrealistic." When, in a meeting with the Chiefs of Staff, the senior army officer warned about the Canadians pushing too hard on what was to be a joint paper, Escott Reid insisted that the Canadians should not be held back from "putting forward purely Canadian views."[7]

Unlike the 1946 drafting process, the Canadians were eager to have a role in the "development of a proper intelligence appreciation."[8] The Canadian interest in developing a new joint appreciation led the MCC to cancel the January request and instead issue a new request for both JICs to "meet, and together review and revise" the May 1946 appreciation, and produce "a single document" indicating "those enemy capabilities and probable courses of action upon which a review and revision of the Canada-United States Basic Security Plan should be based."[9]

In preparation for such a meeting, the Canadians prepared their own appreciation, JIC 3/48 (Final). The study, titled "An Appreciation of the Possible Military Threat to the Security of Canada and the United States," aimed to assess "the capabilities of a potential enemy to conduct offensive operations" against Canada, Newfoundland, and the United States.[10] It identified the USSR as the only potential threat.

JIC 3/48 (Final) stated that in case of war, a large proportion of Soviet capabilities would be fighting in other theatres removed from North America. Curiously, however, the paper also stated that it was "considered advisable to appreciate the maximum strategically sound effort which the USSR could direct"[11] against Canada and the United States. This "maximum effort" type assessment had already been questioned in Canada. Presumably, because the Canadians knew the Americans would use this same type of assessment, they felt compelled to stick with it. This would allow the officers at the joint conference to compare apples, rather than apples and oranges.

The assessment considered Soviet naval and military capabilities in two time periods: in 1948 and beyond 1948. In 1948, the Soviet Navy would be capable of destroying shipping and carrying out minor attacks on coastal areas. But the lack of trained personnel and shortage of repair bases meant that a sustained naval effort would be impossible, and the Soviet Navy could not "seriously affect the security of Canada and the United States."[12]

Limited bases in Eastern Siberia meant that the Red Army would only be capable of "isolated airborne operations" of up to a few hundred men against North America, and lack of fighter escort meant resupply would be "impossible." Teams of forty saboteurs might be landed by submarines.[13] Overall, the ground threat to North America was limited.

The main concern, air attacks, would also be limited in 1948. The Soviets were working to increase the production of heavy bombers — what the Canadians and their allies referred to as "B-29-type bombers," as they were comparable to the American B-29 Superfortresses strategic bombers that had dropped atomic bombs on Hiroshima and Nagasaki. But despite the increase in heavy bombers, "the employment of these aircraft in any numbers" against the US or Canada was assessed to be limited by the "lack of suitable bases in North Eastern Siberia" and the difficulty of supply in that region. At most, the Soviets could launch 100 bombers against Seattle, Vancouver, and Edmonton for "a very limited period." If the bombers were sent on a one-way mission, they might attack, from either Siberia or Murmansk, all the industrial areas of North America. In short, the Soviet Union was "not considered capable of materially impairing the war-making potential of Canada and the United States by air attack."[14]

In each of the assessments devoted to the Navy, Army, and Air, the Soviet capabilities were expected to improve after 1948. The Canadians, however, were relatively sanguine about the Soviet development of long-range aircraft. They assumed the Soviets would only bother developing long-range aircraft that could attack North America if the Soviets also developed an atomic bomb for the bombers to drop. And while the Soviets were expected to develop their own bomb, the Canadians assumed that the United States would, for the foreseeable future, maintain a greater stock of atomic bombs than the USSR.

Curiously, the relationship between the likelihood of a Soviet bomb, and the assumption that the Soviets would only build long-range aircraft if a bomb was developed, is not followed through to its logical end. As for the future likelihood of "atom bombing," the Canadians punted, arguing that the "very little knowledge of Soviet ability or plans" meant "no definite date" could be given as to when this capability would be available to the Soviets.[15]

While the Soviets had many ways in which they could strike the continent, none were significant. The "most practicable" course of action was via subversive activity, which was mentioned briefly in the assessment and with sensational language.[16] Ultimately, none of the Soviets' military options posed a threat to the security of Canada or the United States or the continent's war-making potential.

In contrast to the 1946 appreciation, the assessment "indicated reductions in the scales of anticipated forms of attack" against North America. The Canadians were confident in these conclusions and wanted them brought forward to the MCC.[17]

While the Canadians were working on their new assessment, meant to inform a jointly derived appreciation, the US JIC went ahead and produced its own independent revision of the 1946 appreciation. The US section of the MCC proposed to use the US JIC's paper as the basis for revising the Basic Security Plan.[18]

The Canadian paper and the US JIC paper differed considerably in their judgment as to whether the USSR had the capacity to "impair [North America's] war-making potential"[19] by direct attack. The Americans thought yes; the Canadians no.

The 1946 draft appreciation had judged that Soviet attacks on the continent would be "of limited strength." The US JIC's 1948 draft removed this qualifier. The Canadians, having "no intelligence which indicates an increased enemy capability in this regard," disagreed. There was no reason to think there had been a change. Neither did the Canadians accept the American contention that the Soviets could seize objectives in Canada, Alaska, or Labrador by airborne attack, and then use those objectives as bases for attacking vital strategic targets in North America.[20] In the Canadian view, there were not enough bases in Eastern Siberia to support much more than a small airborne operation against Canada, and out of range of fighter escorts, any airborne troops could not be resupplied.[21]

Overall, the Canadians complained, there was a "general tendency in the American paper . . . to credit a potential enemy with greater capabilities than we consider reasonable."[22] While the Canadians had conducted a "full re-appreciation," the Americans had just amended the original document. It was not so much that the US had inflated the threat but that they had not downgraded the threat as time passed and intelligence changed.

War Planning

In August 1947, the US Joint War Plans Committee had prepared a joint war plan, BROILER. The plan assumed that the United Kingdom and Canada would fight as allies of the United States in a war, and BROILER (later renamed FROLIC) called for action to secure bases in North America, the United Kingdom, and the Cairo-Suez region for launching a strategic air offensive against the Soviet Union.

When local Communists staged a coup in Czechoslovakia in late February 1948, war planning moved into a new gear. In April, American, British, and Canadian planners met and used BROILER/FROLIC as the basis for an "outline emergency war plan." The outcome was a series of "unilateral but accordant" plans prepared by each participant state; the US plan was known as HALFMOON, the British as DOUBLEQUICK, and the Canadian plan as BULLMOOSE. Later that year, the plans were revised as FLEETWOOD (US) and SPEEDWAY (UK). But the goal of the Canadian attendees was not only to participate in drafting joint plans, but to try to understand their allies' thinking.

Foulkes attended the meeting in April 1948 with a goal to "secure" from the Americans and the British "some idea of their overall strategic concept" so that the Canada-US Basic Security Plan could be developed in relationship to the Anglo-American war plans. He learned, however, that "no common concept" had been developed or agreed between the Americans and the British, but that they were developing arrangements for exchanging information and reaching agreement.[23]

On his trip, it became obvious to Foulkes that little thought had been given in Washington to the Canada-US Basic Security Plan, and when Foulkes told his US counterparts about the old, heavily defensive plan, they thought it "unrealistic." He also learned, and reported back to Ottawa, that the US military officers he met with were now "more concerned about the possibility of war within the next eighteen months."[24]

To support the Canadian planners participating in the staff discussions, the JIC had tasked the Joint Intelligence Staff (JIS) with preparing a second paper, with the "suggested object" being to "determine the ability of the USSR to wage war, its grand strategy and aims in relation to a future war." The "scope" of the paper was to include military factors, but also political and economic factors.[25]

Before his visit to Washington, Foulkes had been urging the DEA to participate in the JIS' task of developing a paper on Soviet grand strategy in war. Such an effort to examine Soviet aims had been on the JIS' agenda for some months, but no work was done on the paper because the Department of External Affairs refused to participate. The DEA did not think it useful to conduct one large global study of Soviet strategy and war aims, preferring to do several regional studies instead. This was consistent with the general DEA view that if war began, it would begin over a local or regional issue and Soviet aims and strategy would be directly related to the war's origins. Foulkes appealed to the DEA to participate by warning the under-secretary of state of External Affairs (USSEA) that Canada needed an "independent paper" on the subject, or else Canada would be forced to "base our military and strategic planning entirely on United Kingdom and United States estimates of the situation."[26] The DEA came around to participating, perhaps convinced that if they did not assist in the creation of such a paper, Canadian military planners could not represent Canadian interests effectively.

By the end of May, the Canadian JIS had completed its paper, JIC 4/48, "An Outline of Soviet Capabilities and Strategic Objectives in a War Beginning before July, 1949." The Canadian assessment listed crucial factors that would influence Soviet strategy: first, the "enemies of the USSR," [27] as the paper put it, would enjoy naval supremacy and be capable of striking Soviet territory from theatres of their own choosing. Second, there would be no allied air or land invasion of Soviet territory early in a war; the Soviet Union only had to fear strategic bombing, and atomic bombing at that. Crucially, the paper claimed the "USSR would not be in a position to seize or neutralize the main allied base — Canada and the United States."[28]

These factors all added up to an important and nuanced analysis of the Soviets' likely strategy: the only way the Soviet Union could defend its territory from strategic bombing would be "to seize or neutralize those areas from which its enemies could strike." The Soviet defensive strategy, then, would require massive offensives to seize or neutralize:

(a) Western Germany, France, Belgium, the Netherlands, Luxembourg.

(b) The United Kingdom.

(c) The Arab States (including the Nile delta) and Persia.

(d) Greece and Turkey.

(e) Italy (including Sicily).

(f) Spain and Portugal.[29]

The Canadians assumed the Soviets could and would move to occupy all these territories (with the exception of the UK and the Nile Delta, which the Canadians thought less likely). It was not so much an assumption that the Soviet Union sought to conquer the world by military force, but that the imperative to deny its enemies bases on its periphery would require massive offensive campaigns.

While the Soviet Union, the drafters assumed, could move in almost all directions on its periphery, the paper concluded that the Soviets would not cross the Atlantic — or Arctic — Oceans. The paper concluded that "[a]t the present time the USSR does not possess the means either at sea or in the air of carrying the war to the North American continent which will be the main bases of its enemies."[30]

Canadian appreciations of possible Soviet strategy in case of war continued to downgrade the likelihood of major Soviet attacks on North America, and implicitly suggested that there would be no chance of the Soviet Union waging a "maximum effort" campaign against North America. If war came, Soviet strategy would be to focus on denying peripheral areas to its enemies — not on attacking the United States.

In June 1948, ABC military planners met again to prepare a short-range plan to meet any emergency before July 1949. Both the Canadian intelligence appreciations and the meetings with ABC military planners confirmed that there was very little possibility of an attack on North America beyond a diversionary attack meant to panic the population and tie down American and

Canadian forces. In this environment, the "passive defence" of North America was both "wrong and unreal." The obvious conclusion was that the Basic Security Plan "should be examined freshly" with North American defence considered "as part of the broad picture and not as an isolated problem."[31]

As the Minister of National Defence Brooke Claxton told his Cabinet Defence Committee colleagues, the Soviet Union was "unlikely to provoke a planned war in the near future, but the possibility of either a planned or an 'accidental' war due to Russian miscalculation must be taken into account."[32] It was wrong to view war as inevitable, but plans must be made for defence. Current assessments claimed that the Soviets could "overrun all of Europe in under six months," but the stronger the Western defence, the longer this would take. "Time," he said, was "not necessarily on side of USSR."[33]

ACAI (American-Canadian Agreed Intelligence)

The MCC planners still had no agreed estimate or appreciation (the American and Canadian terms, respectively), and by August it had "become essential" to arrive at one to inform the Basic Security Plan. In the first week of August 1948, the joint American-Canadian military planners met in Kingston, Ontario, to set terms of reference for a "single agreed strategic estimate (appreciation)" to be drafted and agreed by the two countries' JICs by October 1, 1948. The planners needed estimates of a date when Soviet leaders might think they had adequate military capacity to attack. This would allow them to divide the "foreseeable future" into chronological periods reflecting a significant change in enemy capability or strategy. The planners also sought an estimate of Soviet capabilities and strategy, and the forms and scales of attack on Canada and the US.[34]

The result was the first American-Canadian Agreed Intelligence (ACAI) estimate, "Soviet Capabilities and Probable Courses of Action Against Canada, the United States, and the Areas Adjacent Thereto, 1949–1956," ACAI 5 (Final), finalized on October 21, 1948.[35]

ACAI 5 was prepared over two conferences in September and October, held in Washington and then Ottawa. The Canadian Joint Intelligence Staff (JIS) met with a team from the US Joint Intelligence Group (JIG) in Washington from September 27 to October 1. At the first meeting, the US team tabled a full draft of a complete paper, and evidently expected to have "an agreed appreciation, based on their draft, within a few days." This was far too optimistic. One of the Canadians at the meeting recalled that it "was soon realized that agreement on the title, problem, assumptions, etc., would be a lengthier task than the U.S. team had envisaged."³⁶

The two teams spent time discussing these "preliminary matters" — essentially trying to set the fundamental objectives of their task — and the "feeling developed" that finding agreement on the "essential framework of the paper" was "time well spent." By beginning essentially from scratch, the American "inclination" to regard the Canadians' role as simply "commenting on their paper was overcome." The JIS reported to Ottawa that the Canadian view was given full weight by the Americans.³⁷

After settling these basic points in Washington, the two teams met for a second combined meeting in Ottawa from October 13 to 21. Both teams tabled draft papers, which were then divided up for discussion and editing, before being reassembled into a combined paper. The US-Canadian teams used the American sections and appendices concerned with ground, air, and naval forces, along with "new weapons," and the Canadian sections that covered the "basic concept, capabilities and probable courses of action." The JIS reported that there were "no differences of opinion worthy of mention" during the drafting, and that combined summary and conclusions were agreed to on October 21. The secretary of the US JIG stayed on two more days to help edit the appendices, and on October 26 the final paper was flown to Washington.³⁸ That the paper travelled by air was likely the result of the physical nature of the document: with its reams of data and appendices, it appeared to the Canadians that the final product "was rather bulky, which is in keeping with normal U.S. practice."³⁹

The Canadian team regarded their co-operation with the JIG to be "a very valuable experience." The US team was "very open-minded and willing to make decisions on its own responsibility." The Canadians noted that the volume of information provided by the US intelligence system on naval, army, and air forces, along with scientific, manpower, and mobilizations calculations, was much greater than that available from Canadian sources.

Ultimately, however, "Canadian intelligence calculations . . . very closely paralleled those of the U.S." This, perhaps, was because of the existing "international exchange of intelligence." As a result, the two sides had "no difficulty" in "reaching agreed estimates." Even though the Americans likely understood the significant mismatch in national intelligence gathering capabilities, the US team never questioned Canadian "sources of information" and always "accepted Canadian intelligence at its face value." The process, then, seemed to be a good one, and the Canadians felt like they had held their own: "[i]n the application of information to a strategic intelligence problem, the Canadian intelligence system at no time needed to fear comparison."[40]

In keeping with their interpretation of the MCC instructions, the combined team had split their assessment into two parts: one dealing with the period 1949 to 1952, and the other 1953 to 1956. Questions about how best to split assessments chronologically, between the present and the future, had dogged Canadian intelligence officials throughout the year, and this particular split raised questions. During the conference, the teams had agreed to the particular split because it matched the timing by which the Americans estimated that the Soviets might explode their first atomic weapon: 1953.[41] Upon reviewing the paper in November, the Canadian JIC challenged the significance of 1953. They did not think that year to be important — perhaps because the explosion of a weapon itself was not as significant as the development of the ability to deliver the weapons en masse — and would have preferred a greater focus on 1956.[42]

This chronological break became such a sticking point in Ottawa that it led the chair of the Canadian JIC, G. G. Crean, to write to his US counterpart and put in train plans for a new conference to revise ACAI 5 (Final). One easy change was required at the conference: it was discovered that the US side had used the wrong year's estimates of Soviet naval figures.[43] More important was addressing the chronological breakdown of the paper. The Canadians feared that having split the assessment into two periods, military planners might take 1953 as a critical date, even though the Canadians attached no particular importance to the year. But 1953 did not, in their minds, represent any strategic appreciation of the likelihood of war, that is, that war would be more likely after that point.[44]

Upon Canadian urging, the teams met again in Washington from December 2 to 10 with the task of finding a way to reconcile their differences over the chronological breakdown of the paper. The US JIG thought there should be two distinct estimates, one for an emergency or short-range plan focused on present circumstances, and one for a long-range plan covering a future date range. The Canadians wanted only one estimate.[45] The two teams ultimately decided to draft the paper with two sub-headings under each subject heading, one describing the situation in 1949, and the other 1956. This would meet the US requirement for having an accessible form of "current intelligence," as well as the "Canadian view that the future must be treated essentially as one period." In addition to producing a revised estimate, now titled ACAI 5/1, the meeting had also cleared up "a fundamental point which might otherwise have continued to confuse both parties in future discussions of Canada-United States intelligence problems."[46]

Just before the Americans and Canadians had agreed on ACAI 5, American and British intelligence teams had agreed on their own American-British Agreed Intelligence document, ABAI 5, "Soviet Intentions and Capabilities." The Canadians received copies of the paper (which, when printed in London, bore the British file number JIC (48)100 Final). The Canadians examined ABAI 5 closely and determined that, as the US team had used the same basic intelligence in both papers, it was "quite obvious that the general approach and conclusions are of a very singular nature."[47]

ABAI 5 was also divided into chronological sections, with Part I covering conditions in 1949, and Part II forecasting 1956–57. ABAI 5 was also significant for the Canadians, in that the American-British document "emphasize[d] clearly the position relegated to Canadian Military authorities by the U.S." in case of war.[48] This seemed to suggest a two-tiered intelligence relationship: the Canadians were still stuck working with the US on ACAI papers focused only on the defence of North America, while ABAI papers were the basis for global war plans.

In February 1949, American officials decided it was time to amend the American-Canadian appreciation. ACAI 5/1, according to the Americans, had been "based on intelligence that has now changed considerably," and they sent a list of proposed amendments.[49] The changing intelligence indicated "a marked increase in the Soviet strategic air ability resulting in greater capability of the Soviet Air Force to inflict physical damage on the North American continent."[50] The Canadians were immediately skeptical.

One amendment, referring to the number of Soviet B-29-type aircraft and transport aircraft, was two and a half times greater than the British estimate known to the Royal Canadian Air Force (RCAF), and so was unacceptable to the RCAF.[51] Wing Commander William Weiser, the director of air intelligence told his colleagues on the Canadian JIC that the American "figures would not bear critical analysis." He connected the newly increased numbers to internal US disagreements between the US Air Force, President Truman, and Congress, and "suspected that the intelligence was coloured by the U.S.A.F. desire for a larger airforce."[52]

Crean refused to accept the list of amendments and suggested instead that a conference would be preferable to trying to update the ACAI document by correspondence. The Canadians wanted to avoid the back-and-forth proposal of unilateral amendments, ostensibly because it would complicate planning, but also no doubt because the Canadians believed the conference approach had led to a far better ACAI 5 and ACAI 5/1 than acceptance of the original US paper proposed in 1948.[53]

When the Canadians complained about the bomber numbers, they got a bit of a shock. US officials told the Canadians that at a recent USAF-RAF conference they had agreed to the higher bomber figures. The US side was essentially using a joint US-UK estimate to rebut Canadian intelligence in an American-Canadian exchange.[54] The Americans suggested that the US and Canadians just list separate national figures in their joint appreciation, but the Canadians refused, believing that this "would lead to an impossible situation as there would be no agreed intelligence on which any joint plan could be acceptably prepared." The Canadians wanted to discuss this and come to an agreement. They pressed the conference idea, believing that "if the basic intelligence on which the aircraft figures had been arrived at was jointly examined by both the Canadian and American intelligence organizations, agreement should be possible."[55]

The Americans agreed to a conference. In May 1949, as the MCC prepared for its second annual revision of the Basic Security Plan, the MCC formally advised both governments that "it would be highly desirable to have available, for comparative purposes, an up-to-date, agreed Canada-United States intelligence document" and requested both JICs to produce such a document.[56]

It was also in May 1949 that Canada made an effort to be included in the American-British agreed intelligence framework that provided appreciations for the ABC planners.[57] Yet it is necessary to understand the evolution of ACAI intelligence in 1949 by examining the period before the first and only ABCI intelligence conference in the autumn of 1949.

The efforts to revamp ACAI 5/1 as ACAI 5/2 suffered "considerable delay" in the spring of 1949 which, in turn, had delayed the agreement of a revised Basic Security Plan.[58] The delay, resulted from the fact that the "Estimate (Appreciation) was not acceptable on the Canadian side because of disagreement with the intelligence data upon which it was based."[59]

Part of the disagreement rested on production figures of B-36-type bombers; the Canadians again thought the US figures high and preferred

British numbers they had been forwarded from London. In preparing ACAI 5/2, the US side had predicated their assessment on the assumption that "the whole weight of the U.S.S.R. would be thrown against this continent [North America]," and ignored the possibility — even likelihood — that the Soviets would deploy part of their forces elsewhere.[60]

This continued adherence to using "maximum capability" figures to inform appreciations led to much discussion and debate in Canada's JIC. It would be impossible to prepare a "realistic paper that was based on Soviet capabilities against the North American continent" when the paper ignored "the employment of Soviet forces against other areas."[61] Quite obviously, ignoring the likely use of Soviet force elsewhere, or even the "effects on Soviet strategy of the efforts of the Western Powers to counter-balance Soviet capabilities," had led to a rather skewed and unrealistic assessment.[62]

Ultimately, the Canadians would agree to many of the American drafting positions. But the JIC forwarded ACAI 5/2 to the Chiefs of Staff Committee with a covering memorandum explaining the "maximum capability" approach: the US-Canadian intelligence team had drafted the appreciation with the assumption "that all the weapons which had the capability of use against this continent would be so used and would not be diverted to other theatres, although it was realized that the USSR would inevitably be engaged in hostilities elsewhere." This approach was accepted by the Canadians, the note went on, because to have done "otherwise would have required an overall, worldwide survey of Soviet course of action beyond the capability of the combined Intelligence teams."[63] With provisos in place, the CSC approved ACAI 5/2, "Probable Soviet Courses of Action Against Canada, the United States, and the Areas Adjacent Thereto, 1 January 1957," in August 1949.[64] By that time, the Canadians were preparing to confront the unreality of the ACAI agreements in a tripartite setting.

Toward American-British-Canadian Intelligence

In the spring of 1949, the Canadians learned that the chair of the UK Joint Intelligence Committee, William Hayter, would soon visit Washington, DC. The Canadians invited Hayter to Ottawa and, ahead of his arrival, secured authorization from the CSC to "raise with him the desirability of Canada taking part in the discussions and writing of strategic estimates which had previously been prepared bilaterally by the U.S. and U.K."[65] These estimates included ABAI 5 that the Canadians had seen earlier that year.

Less than two weeks after the Canadians inquired with Hayter on May 30, the UK JIC passed word that it agreed to Canadian participation in "future Anglo-US intelligence meetings" subject to US agreement.[66] The British JIC also started providing the Canadian JIC with more intelligence papers now that Canada had an increased "need to know."[67]

Shortly after receiving word from London, Crean wrote to Major General W. E. Todd, the deputy director of the US Joint Intelligence Group. Crean, noting that it was "always difficult to participate in bilateral discussions on subjects which concern three parties,"[68] sought to bring Todd fully into the picture by laying out the Canadian interest in participating in tripartite intelligence discussions.

As explained above, the Canadians had participated in tripartite ABC military planning conversations in London in September 1948, and the Canadians had a "natural desire to see the tripartite nature of these arrangements preserved."[69] Since the ABC planners were expecting to continue meeting on a tripartite bases, Crean said the Canadians thought it "only reasonable that all three countries were able to examine the basis upon which the Intelligence Estimates were made."[70] As the Canadians worked with both British and American authorities, "we stand to suffer most from any lack of coordination" between the three countries. This was "particularly true," he wrote, in relation to "something as basic to government policy as an Intelligence Estimate."[71]

On their face, these are reasonable arguments and likely represent the fundamental Canadian objectives for wishing to insert themselves in tripartite intelligence appreciations. That said, there are a host of other reasons why the Canadians wished to participate. In the first place, the Canadians had found British estimates of Soviet air capabilities more in keeping with their own, and yet the US JIG had been able to use bilateral US-UK estimates to rebut Canadian intelligence on air issues. A tripartite estimate would also allow for the Canadians to have another opportunity at assessing the Soviet threat to North America, on which Ottawa and Washington clearly diverged. The Canadians had noted the volume of intelligence information available to the Americans, and while they received vast amounts of information in the ACAI process, an ABC intelligence process might offer even more.

The primary concern, however, must have been ensuring a Canadian role in intelligence appreciations that would go on to inform force planning and the defence budget. By May 1949, the North Atlantic Treaty had already been signed, and work was underway on the military system that would support the alliance.[72] Crean clearly saw — and, as this chapter implies, he was correct to see — US-UK meetings as the basis for what would become NATO planning. As he told the JIC he chaired, "in the event of a satisfactory arrangement whereby Canada would be included in future US-UK intelligence discussions, we might be in a stronger position to deal with discussions on the form of the Atlantic organization."[73]

After sending his letter, Crean met Todd in Washington on other intelligence business and discussed "our participation in ABC Intelligence appreciations." Todd seemed entirely agreeable.[74] In early July, Todd wrote back formally, describing the issue as one of "Canadian participation in future US/UK intelligence discussions." The US JIC thought it "advantageous to all concerned if the estimates we make in collaboration with the British are consistent with those prepared jointly with the Canadians." He expressed American willingness "to conduct our next intelligence discussion on a trial tri-partite basis." The trial effort would help determine "workability of such procedure" and whether "resulting intelligence instrument serves the special needs of Canadian-United States MCC planners."[75]

Todd's letter may not have been a ringing endorsement of tripartite intelligence, but he followed up on September 1 with a cordial invitation for a Canadian intelligence team to visit Washington and join a ten-person team representing the UK JIC led by Brigadier Valentine Boucher, the UK director of military intelligence.[76] The conference would set out to revise ABAI 5, which had been previously prepared in a bilateral American-British conference.[77] The US sent ABAI 5 to Ottawa on September 2, and the Canadian team prepared, on September 10, to write an "agreed appreciation" with the object of estimating "the strategic intentions and capabilities of the Soviet Union in the event of a war in which the United States of America, the United Kingdom and Canada are involved now to the end of 1950, and to project this estimate to 1956-57."[78]

The Canadian team of eight, including and led by Group Captain W. W. Bean, set out for Washington with three instructions from JIC. First, while the tripartite estimate itself would be subject to JIC approval upon completion, Bean's JIS team was "empowered to give provisional, corporate approval" on matters that would not need reference to JIC. Second, the team was to conduct discussions "in such a manner as to negate the possibility of either the British or Americans presuming that the Canadian team is taking sides." Finally, it was "imperative" that "attacks against the North American continent are considered in relation to other theatres, and the form and scales of such attacks clearly emerge."[79] This instruction was, perhaps, the most important element to stress in the conference.

The First and Last ABCI Conference

The first meeting of the American-British-Canadian Intelligence conference was held the morning of September 12, 1949. Rear Admiral Thomas B. Inglis, the director of US naval intelligence, opened the conference by noting that there had been a US-UK meeting about one year before, and also several US-Canadian meetings. This was the first conference, he announced, to be "conducted on a tripartite basis."[80]

It also was to be the last. Very early in the conference, Todd made clear that "[t]his was definitely the first and last intelligence appreciation which would be a combined U.K.-U.S. and Canadian effort." This "dictum" had been handed down by the US Joint Chiefs of Staff and concurred by the British Chiefs of Staff. It was not only the last ABC Intelligence appreciation, but the end of ABC military planning, for this "principle is to be applied to planning also."[81]

It was initially unclear to the Canadians why this "dictum" had been applied. Even by the end of the conference, the Canadian JIC was asking Bean to try and determine the future intentions of the Americans toward both ABC intelligence and ABC planning. If Canada was not to participate in the intelligence appreciation, or planning, "we might find ourselves in the position of being asked to commit forces on the original plan to which we had agreed, although not consulted on any revisions. This might be most embarrassing from our point of view."[82] Only over the rest of 1949 would it be obvious that the winding down of formal ABC conferences was connected to the American and British desire to push planning and intelligence appreciations into the new NATO structure, and the need to ensure that any extra-NATO planning occurred invisibly to the other allies.

That this was to be the last such appreciation did not devalue the appreciation itself, nor the import with which the conference attached to its task. As Inglis noted, the paper "would be the principal paper on which all planning would be based." A previous US-UK meeting had produced the document under review at this meeting, ABAI 5. It had been written in support of HALFMOON. But HALFMOON had been developed, and ABAI 5 written in a different budgetary environment in the United States. Inglis took a moment to express his "personal views" on ABAI 5, explaining how planners thought the Soviet capabilities described in it had "been overrated and that it would not be possible for the Soviets to overrun all of Europe and the Middle East within six months." There were logistical limitations on the Soviet action, and the paper had ignored opposition the Soviets surely would encounter. The result had been "too optimistic from the Soviet point of view." Boucher, in agreement, bluntly said that the British "too had been under pressure with respect to possible overstatement of Soviet capabilities in A.B.A.I. 5." But UK authorities felt it "necessary to present to the Planners the maximum capabilities of the Soviet Union and that caution should be exercised in downscaling those capabilities."[83] Boucher was not being disingenuous, but represented the British efforts to navigate between their own preference for minimal planning and their growing sense that their new European allies would need maximum support from the United States.

On the afternoon of the first day, Todd, in the chair, sought to set an informal tone for the rest of the conference. He urged Boucher and Bean to consider themselves co-chairs of the conference. Both the US and UK teams tabled revisions of both the first and second parts of ABAI 5, and the teams were divided up to allow tripartite representation on subcommittees related to the different sections of the estimate.[84]

The British made a bold bid to push their own paper as the basis for the conference. In ABAI 5, the British and American intelligence teams had assumed that M-Day and D-Day — that is, the days the Soviets began mobilizing and the day they began their attacks — would be the same day. The new British version reflected their assessment that the "possibility of war before the end of 1950 was remote" and that there would be a longer period between M-Day and D-Day.[85] (That is, the Soviets would need some time between the start of mobilization and the beginning of operations.) This would be a sticking point throughout the conference.

In line with the aforementioned JIC instructions to the JIS team, Bean expressed the Canadian desire for the estimate to "contain a full consideration of the forms and scale of Soviet attacks against the North American continent in relation to campaigns elsewhere."[86]

Before the meeting adjourned, an American Army officer suggested that the paper be drafted with the phrase "Anglo-American Powers" replacing "Western Powers." It was important, he said, that the paper reflect that the

Soviet capabilities "had been dealt with only from the tripartite viewpoint." (He perhaps considered the phrase Anglo-American as inclusive of Canada). Bean suggested a formulation that included Canada, and it was agreed at the second meeting the paper should use the phrase "United States, United Kingdom, Canada and their Allies."[87] The issue would remain dormant until the end of the conference, when an American representative would again push for the restatement of the "Problem" section of the assessment without mention of Canada. Bean agreed to this if a footnote were to be included.[88] After some meetings between the co-chairmen, the Canadians, "under strong pressure," realized the other two would not give in and "Anglo-American" would stand against Canadian objections, with no footnote included.[89]

ABCI 15

By the end of the conference in the last week of September 1949, the American-British-Canadian teams had agreed to a provisional document with two parts: an estimate of Soviet "intentions and capabilities" in war against "the Anglo-American Powers" in 1950 (Part I) and in 1956–57 (Part II). Before the end of the conference, however, Part II had been rendered totally useless by the first Soviet atomic explosion.

The Soviet explosion occurred in August, just before the ABCI conference began. It is unclear who, if any, of the officers at the conference knew about the detonation, and when. As late as September 14 during the conference, the Scientific Committee (made up of officials from each state) had estimated that the "earliest possible date" by which the Soviets might explode "their first test atomic bomb" was in mid-1950. The "probable date," however, was "mid-1953."[90] This had been the date pressed by the Americans, and which had been used to mark the chronological divisions in both the previous ACAI and ABAI papers.

Nearly a month after the Soviet explosion, and near the end of the tripartite intelligence conference, President Truman announced news of the test. The explosion of the Soviet device set off a major debate within the US intelligence community.[91] But for the joint teams, it meant that the estimates for Soviet atomic production figures included Part II were far too low, and that the entirety of Part II would need to re-evaluated.[92]

Both Parts of ABCI 15 are significant: Part I for what it revealed about assessments of the immediate Soviet threats, and Part II for the gaping hole it left in intelligence estimates and planning for a future war with the Soviet Union.

Part I of ABCI 15

The first part of ABCI 15 was a large document, sprawling over eighty pages and including eleven appendices. It included, as per its "object" statement, an analysis of Soviet strategic intentions and capabilities in case of war, but also detailed estimates and a map of probable Soviet campaign plans, as well as analyses of the military capabilities of states potentially allied with the Anglo-American powers.

It was clear from the very first page of ABCI 15 that this was something of a compromise document: the first heading, "The Outbreak of War," laid out the separate and unreconciled views between the United States on one hand and the United Kingdom and Canada (mentioned by name) on the other as to whether they would receive warning of an impending attack. The UK and Canadian position was that war was not likely, and that if it did come in 1950 it would be preceded by a three- to four-month build-up and a period of strategic warning. This was in contrast to the American position that the Soviets could launch a war and achieve their objectives without mobilization, thus without warning to the Anglo-Americans. The issue of strategic warning would gain important salience in the coming years, but in ABCI 15 the parties agreed to disagree.[93]

There was also obvious disagreement between the American and British estimates of a Soviet atomic capability in case of war in 1950. The final draft stated that the Soviets would have "no more than 10 atomic bombs by the beginning of 1950 and a maximum of 30 by the end of 1950." The British fought a rearguard action into December of 1949 to amend this section, ultimately getting agreement to add a footnote indicating that the UK JIC thought these were "absolute outside figures" and would have preferred no figures be stated.[94]

Since the appreciation would be used to plan for war, and as the UK was expected to be a target for Soviet atomic bombing, it seems possible that the British wished to downplay the likelihood of Britain's nuclear destruction. If both assumptions were true, that is if the Soviets had these bombs, and they would be used against the UK, then there would be little point in planning for the defence of the home islands.

ABCI 15 was somewhat vague and contradictory in its explanation of Soviet goals in war. At one point, the estimate stated that the "ultimate object of Soviet policy" was "the establishment of communism, directed by Moscow, throughout the world." The intelligence staff assumed that the Soviets would know that "this object can only be attained through the collapse of the two main bastions of democratic power—the U.K. and the U.S.A.," and that in 1950 the "major military invasion of North America would be an impossible task." Given these assumptions, the Soviets could be expected to launch a two-stage war: in the first stage, they would defeat the United Kingdom and dominate Europe and Asia. From there, they would "consolidate . . . an impregnable position from which North America could be gradually weakened by communist infiltration and economic pressure, and ultimately attacked by military forces." The Soviets, in turn, could expect that the Anglo-Americans would not let bits of the world "be overrun singly" and "would attack the Soviet Union from any direction that was possible." As a result, it was essential for the USSR to launch simultaneous full-scale campaigns. The opening stage of a war would be tremendous in scope and size, with Soviet thrusts outwards in all directions from its borders:

> "In the event of war in 1950 the Soviet plan would be to undertake the following operations:
>
> a) Simultaneously
>   i. A campaign against Western Europe including Italy.
>   ii. An aerial bombardment against the British Isles.
>   iii. Campaigns against the Near and Middle East, including Greece and Turkey.
>   iv. Campaigns with limited objectives in the Far East.
>   v. Attacks with limited objectives against Canada and the United States, including Alaska and the Aleutians.
>   vi. A sea and air offensive against Anglo-American sea communications.
>   vii. Subversive activities and sabotage against Anglo-American interests in all parts of the world."
>
> b) As soon as possible, after the occupation of the Channel Port areas, a full-scale sea and air offensive against the British Isles.

    c) As soon as feasible, campaigns against Scandinavia and the Iberian Peninsula. [The UK disagreed regrading this Iberian assessment.]

    d) As necessary, air attacks against Pakistan."

The estimates of Soviet strength and capabilities in the paper suggested the Soviets could launch all of these operations and still keep forces in reserve.

But would the Soviets launch such an attack? And if so, why? Set against this extraordinary list of Soviet capabilities and the list of operations the Soviets could take if war broke out, was a peripheral discussion of whether war would come at all. As the British and Canadians had stipulated on the first page of the report, they considered war unlikely. ABCI 15, in another section, noted that from a "purely economic standpoint," the USSR "would not willingly engage in a major war." In fact, the "Allies possess or hold at their disposal a great preponderance in resources and production in practically every basic strategic commodity, a preponderance much greater than that of the Allies over the Axis power in World War II."[95]

For the purpose of describing likely Soviet military operations, the assessment had filled in Soviet intentions as above: the establishment of Communism throughout the world. But in a subsection titled "Soviet War Aims," there was an important discussion, one that would foreshadow more specific assessments of whether or not the Soviets would, in fact, go to war.

If the Soviet rulers were certain they could achieve, by war, "a communist world order under their own domination," they would not hesitate. Even if the Soviet peoples showed no interest in war, the ABC officers assumed that the power of the Soviet state could whip its citizens into frenzy. But Soviet leaders could have no certainty in 1950 that they would win a war, and so "weighty considerations tend to deter them from this line of action." Somewhat contradictorily, however, ABCI 15 predicted that if the Soviets chose war in 1950, it was because they had "decided that the progressive economic recovery, political coalescence and military rehabilitation of Western Europe pose such an intolerable threat to the Soviet Union, or such an obstacle to the attainment of its ultimate objective, that it could only be overcome by the immediate use of military force."[96]

In this assessment, then, the Soviets would choose war if they were certain they would win; they also might choose war if they felt time was running out. As ABCI 15 was meant to assist military planning for warfare, and thus inform the requirements necessary for fighting that war, it gave contradictory signals: that a weak West might tempt the USSR into attack, but a strong West might also compel them to strike out as a last gasp.

Putting ABCI Part 1 to Use

One of the final acts of the conference was to select a tripartite committee to brief the ABC Joint Planners on "Soviet Intentions and Capabilities up to the end of 1950" (that is, Part I of ABCI 15).[97] ABCI 15 was then used to inform an ABC conference at the end of September and into early October 1949.

The ABC planners at the autumn conference worked off a draft of a new US plan called OFFTACKLE. The results were finally approved in December 1949 as ABC 109. ABC 109 was not a single plan for all three states, but the basis for revisions to each state's existing plans.[98] The Canadian plan was renamed HICKORY.[99]

The conference, however, did not meet its full goals, and the representatives of the three states agreed that "[b]ecause of the divergent views expressed by the representatives of the United States, the United Kingdom and Canadian Planners in the meetings, it was decided that no single agreed plan could be prepared."[100]

The three planning teams, confirming what had been implicit at the beginning of the conference, agreed that in "view of the North Atlantic Treaty planning, further U.S-U.K.-Canadian planning conferences are considered inadvisable."[101] On October 5, the day after the ABC planning conference ended, the defence ministers of the North Atlantic Alliance met at the Pentagon for the first time as the Defence Committee, and instructed NATO's Military Committee to develop a strategic concept and a medium-term defence plan. But because NATO's early strategic guidance and defence plans were based on OFFTACKLE, they were based in part on the fruits of the 1949 ABC Intelligence conference.

The connections between NATO's planning and the ABC Intelligence conference was a closely held secret. Already, the existence of the ABC Intelligence and ABC Planning efforts were subject to stringent security measures, indoctrination lists, and other measures. When, in December 1949, it became clear that ABCI 15 was to be used in connection with NATO defence planning, the Canadians, for instance, introduced "special security measures" to conceal the existence of combined ABC intelligence.[102] It remained "of the utmost importance" that in any discussion of NATO, "no reference whatsoever be made to the existence of any ABC documents."[103] This was to avoid any suggestion in the mind of NATO's other allies — and especially the French — that a tripartite directorate was controlling NATO's destiny.

Aftermath

In autumn 1949, as the Americans and British prepared to use ABCI 15 Part I to guide NATO's strategic concepts, intelligence organizations in Washington, London, and Ottawa considered the fate of Part II of the study.[104] In Ottawa, the acting director of military intelligence (DMI), Lieutenant-Colonel Tim McCoy, summed up the prevailing mood: ABCI 15, because of its mistaken atomic estimates, "cannot be considered an adequate intelligence instrument to place in the hands of the Chiefs of Staff, and thus, irrespective of future international discussions, the need for a revision of the paper is clearly demonstrated."[105] Still, the dissatisfaction with Part II left a gap and, possibly, an opportunity. Even though there were supposedly to be no more tripartite conferences, JIC members assumed that "circumstances will arise whereby Canadian participation in bipartite discussions is inevitable." It was vital, then, that the JIC "give the highest priority to the undertaking of such a programme so that Canadian national intelligence will be able to play its full part by the tabling of its own appreciations in future international discussions."[106] Some, like Bean, even expected that the need to revise Part II might be a good reason for reopening tripartite discussions, which remained desirable for the Canadians.[107] Revising Part II, even if the revisions were not to be formally accepted in a tripartite assessment, were now an "urgent national intelligence requirement." Their preparation would "enable Canadian national intelligence" (this phrase, something of a neologism, was repeated here again) "to play its full part by the tabling of its own appreciations in future international discussions."[108]

In Washington, the Canadian director of naval intelligence, L. L. Atwood, learned that ABCI 15 Part II had "been suppressed" and there were "only three copies in existence" anywhere in the capital. The Americans on the US JIC and JIG were equally critical of Part I, he said, even if they were "prepared to accept it for North Atlantic and planning purposes."[109] The Americans had decided they did not like the approach to assessment used for ABCI 15 (or, clearly, ABAI 5 that preceded it), and were "very definite that intelligence must get out of war gaming and give up trying to time and place campaigns as was done in ABCI 15."¹¹⁰ In the future, the Americans wanted intelligence "up to the point of contact," and planners would handle things from there on.

US officers told the Canadians that the US was studying the issues raised by Part II, and believed that upon completion of their revisions, it would be "desirable to arrange for the production of a joint Canadian-United States long-range estimate."¹¹¹ Todd, from the US JIG, also told the British and Canadian delegations "that there would be no further tripartite discussions" but agreed on the need for revising Part II, suggesting Canadian participation in bipartite discussions.¹¹² This was a road back to bilateral ACAI efforts.

The British JIC, for its part, decided Part II would not "receive the authority" of the JIC and would not be submitted to the Chiefs of Staff.¹¹³ Ultimately, there would be "no joint (ABC) intelligence appreciation suitable for long-range planning."¹¹⁴ But all three states were increasingly concerned about filling the gap left by the ill-starred Part II.

It was the Soviet atomic test that had created the most glaring problems in the product of the ABCI conference. Over the previous two years, Canadian intelligence and, to some extent, military planners, had tended to downgrade the threat to North America from the Soviet Union. A Soviet Union with atomic weapons would change that calculus.

ABCI 15 itself was read to the prime minister and the Cabinet Defence Committee on November 23, 1949 (but went unnamed in the record of the discussion). As the minister of National Defence explained, previous assessments had assumed any Soviet attacks on North America would be "of a diversionary nature." Now, the bomb "could mean that these countries might be subject to raids by aircraft carrying atom bombs." Even one or two atom bombs dropped on Canada would be of devastating consequence. As it stood in late 1949, the Soviet Union did not require long-range aircraft to bomb Europe but would need more and better aircraft to reach North America. If the Soviet Union were to invest in long-range aircraft, it "might imply that the Russians were contemplating long range attacks."¹¹⁵

A few days before Christmas in 1949, Robert MacKay of External Affairs summed up the obvious difficulty of "knowing what to do next." It was not desirable, he wrote, to come to "any firm decision on policy . . . as to the appropriate defence programme for Canada over the next five years." The international situation was still "too fluid," Canada's role in the new North Atlantic pact was undecided, and there was doubt among some Canadian officials as to how seriously the US and UK were taking the North Atlantic Treaty. MacKay warned that "[r]evised estimates of atomic weapons which the USSR may have four or five years hence may well mean that we shall have to concentrate more on the direct defence of North America than we had anticipated."[116]

On December 22, the Cabinet Defence Committee met again and discussed some of the basic findings from ABCI 15: the Soviets would not hesitate to go to war if they believed they could win, but that the new North Atlantic Defence Organization (not yet called NATO) had as its objective building up military power to convince the USSR that "a war would not pay."[117] The prospects for war, it seemed, depended on the Soviet Union.

Soviet Intentions

In light of the gap left by the abandonment of Part II of ABCI, and the growing questions about Soviet intentions, the JIC directed the JIS to prepare an appreciation of "long-term Soviet intentions." The study was to take "a fundamentally new approach" that should "be based upon a logical appreciation of Soviet intentions." The object of the study, however, was not fundamentally new. It was to determine "broad courses of action open to the USSR for a planned war and the length of time it would take to assemble the resources required for each course."[118]

The JIC explicitly noted that the study was *not* to consider "whether the USSR will in fact undertake a world war," but assume "she will resort to war if other methods fail to achieve her aim of world domination."[119] This assessment would, ultimately, lead to a Chiefs of Staff Committee document, CSC 1(50).

Just how to go about such a study led to debate within the JIS. The working draft rested on assumptions similar to that which had guided ABCI 15: that "the aim of the Soviet Union is world domination."[120] There was "heated debate" between the JIS members over what constituted world domination, and the draft asked the rhetorical question of "what, in the Soviet view, constitutes world domination?" The draft answered its own question by listing two conditions: "communist administrations in at least the major capitalist nations of the west; and . . . the control of these administrations by Moscow." Again, and like ABCI 15, the draft concluded that "military courses of action open to the Soviet Union are not likely to be implemented unless these seem likely to lead to the achievement of Soviet aims."[121]

The Canadian drafters, like their American and British allies, were dealing with an analytic problem: the Soviet Union seemed to be preparing, or already be prepared, for war. And yet, in drafting CSC 1(50), the Canadians had concluded (as had the ABCI 15 drafters), that the Soviets were preparing for a defensive war.[122] And while the USSR was preparing for a war that might develop from its bid for world domination, there remained "the possibility that a world war is and will long remain undesirable to the Soviet Union in the achievement of its aim."[123]

The Department of External Affairs, in particular, believed the USSR's military preparation was for a defensive war. Canadian military officers, too, were beginning to question whether it could be assumed the Soviet Union was preparing for an offensive war.[124] After reflecting on the initial draft of the paper on Soviet intentions, the director of military intelligence, Colonel A. F. B. Knight, wanted the "probability of the Soviet Union's going to war debated instead of assumed."[125] He wrote to his fellow JIC members to suggest that "since Soviet military strategy is very closely coordinated with political aims, the political objectives in each case should be determined."[126] And since political aims and objectives, he noted, were the responsibility of the DEA, the DEA should study these issues to support the Joint Intelligence Staff's drafting. Knight insisted that "the answer to the above problems must be found before any attempt is made to decide the format and details to be included in Soviet Intentions as a basis for Long-Term planning,"[127] and that this required input from External Affairs.

DEA officials got to work in February and April preparing a "mature departmental opinion" for JIS.[128] As the officials from External Affairs discussed the best approach, their efforts drifted toward the theoretical, including a "study of war in Soviet theory," or "something along the line of Communist theory as to the function of war in bringing about a Communistic society on a world basis."[129] There were, the officials decided, three questions to answer: whether Communist theory believed war with capitalist states was inevitable; whether war was likely to be initiated by capitalist states, and whether Communist theory would require the USSR, as the leader of Communist states, "to resort to force in bringing about a Communist world order."[130] As part of their work, Canadian officials read, and agreed with, George Kennan's article in the *Reader's Digest* entitled "Is War with Russia Inevitable?" (Kennan had answered, emphatically, in the negative.)

Robert Ford, one of Canada's Soviet specialists, was tasked with drafting the External Affairs paper.[131] But the drafting process was bogged down by increasingly lengthy papers between offices in the DEA debating Soviet theory.¹³² The whole DEA draft became "hopelessly long," and needed to be "put on ice" and picked up again on "a rainy day."¹³³

A Fresh Start

At around the same time the Canadians were engaged in a close reading of Soviet theory, UK JIC put it all much more succinctly in a short paper with a long title: [UK] JIC (50)7 (Final) "The Likelihood of War with the Soviet Union and the Date by Which the Soviet Leaders Might be Prepared to Risk It."¹³⁴

The British reached four primary conclusions. First, Soviet policy was based on establishing world Communism and the Soviets believed their goal could be "achieved without the Soviet Union becoming involved in a major war." Second, and related to the first, it was "not therefore in the interest of the Soviet leaders deliberately to start a world war." Third, while the Soviets would press ahead with political, economic, and ideological warfare, they were unlikely "to force any issue to a point where a risk of war with the Western Powers would arise." And finally, the UK JIC warned that "[a] time may come, however, when the Soviet leaders consider themselves strong enough to counter any military action by the Western Powers and they may then press on with their plans to extend their influence and control regardless of Western reactions." A Western world destabilized by political and economic instability, or a serious lag in rearmament, might lead the Soviets to "disregard possible Western reactions to the extension of Communist influence and control."¹³⁵

The British assessment, then, was not a call for relaxation, but a warning that Soviet policy could change if the Western powers failed to unify. In a meeting of the UK JIC, some officials warned that current British assessments predicted the Soviet Union would not reach war readiness before 1955 at the earliest. But previous assessments, and the previous planning date, had put the year at 1956 or 1957. It was "significant that the danger date was advancing instead of receding."¹³⁶

The British passed their paper and minutes of their discussion to Ottawa through the Canadian liaison officer in London. George Glazebrook found it of "unusual interest," and Escott Reid decided it was important enough to send up to Pearson.¹³⁷

The direct result of the British paper was a Canadian "fresh start" on the problem. It was not a JIC paper but, as the DMI had suggested, a DEA paper that would ultimately bear the title "Political Factors in the Likelihood of War with the Soviet Union." An early draft of the paper set its object clearly and plainly: "Will the Soviet Union go to war? . . . If so, when and why?"[138] This was the question that would consume the rest of the decade. It also represented a fundamental shift from the earlier papers that had focused on what the Soviet Union would do in a war, rather than whether it would start one.

The British model showed that this could be done without the theoretical debates the DEA officers entered into earlier in the year. The Canadians were now ready to conclude that there was "no useful purpose" served in exploring contradictions between Communist theory and the objectives of the Soviet state. It was far better, they concurred, to acknowledge that "[i]n practice Marxism — or communism — is what the Politburo says it is."[139] The "Russians," as the Canadians and British often referred to the Soviet leadership, "do not, however, live in a political vacuum, and are not blind fanatics." While in the long term they were interested in the establishment "of a communist world-order," they were prepared to "compromise between the ultimate goal and the short-term goal: the security of the Soviet state."[140] The Canadians, like the British, concluded that if the Soviet leadership believed the result of a war would be uncertain, the Soviets would not launch a war and would work to strengthen "the Soviet fatherland."[141]

Indeed, the Canadians went one step further, assessing that "[e]ven if the military balance were in their favour, the Soviet leaders would probably not select war as their most favoured method of expansion."[142] While the Soviet leadership often used the threat of a "hostile outer world" to control their citizens, they could not avoid the conclusion that war "would lead to enormous devastation within the Soviet Union."[143]

The Canadians certainly expected the Soviet Union to seek, through political and other means, to "expand its dominion," and that Soviet leaders did believe a clash would come with the non-Communist world. According to the Department of External Affairs, the "inevitability of a clash theory" was, "in Soviet eyes, a very long-term project." The Soviet belief that one day violence would come meant that it could be put off in the meantime. The Canadian assessment was driven by a calculation of Soviet interests, a bit of theory, and some evidence. The Canadians pointed to the often-repeated assertion in the state-controlled Soviet press that Moscow and its declared enemies "can coexist peacefully, and even that a sanguinary clash can be averted."[144]

After several false starts, then, the Canadians finally had an assessment of whether the Soviet Union sought general war: The DEA paper argued that until Soviet leaders "feel that they are adequately prepared for war with the West, they will actively seek to avoid war." But, crucially, even "[w]hen they feel they are adequately prepared, they will not of preference choose to go to war."[145]

The Canadian paper was finally approved for circulation to the JIC on June 19, 1949.[146] Five days later, tanks from Communist North Korea rolled into South Korea touching off a war. Was this the prelude to general war?

3

The Most Important Question

On June 26, 1950, North Korean tanks rolled across the 38th parallel, touching off the Korean War.[1] Months earlier, American, British, and Canadian intelligence assessments had speculated as to when a war would begin, and how. These assessments had been referring to general war with the Soviet Union. In June and into July 1950, the fundamental question was whether or not these two things were the same: was the Korean War the first stage of a general war? Had the Soviets decided the West was weak and thus been tempted into attacking in hopes of an easy victory? Or, had the opposite occurred: had Stalin worried about the growing unity and defence program in Western Europe and launched a war in a bid to break the encirclement? Next to no attention was given to the possibility that this was largely an inter-Korean struggle. All strategic intelligence efforts were focused on judging whether general war was imminent.

At a meeting of the Joint Intelligence Committee (JIC) on July 5, 1950, Group Captain Bean, now the director of air intelligence (DAI), read aloud a draft paper suggesting that the JIC should advise the Chiefs of Staff "of their opinion on the likelihood of war in the near future, as a guide to the preparations that should be made for this eventuality."[2] The DAI paper Bean read was ominously titled "Imminence of War." It would serve as the basis for a JIC paper of the same name, the first of many.

The DAI assumed, like many others, that the North Korean attack had been coordinated in full with the Soviet Union, and indeed had probably been instigated by Stalin. In the DAI's assessment, the Soviets had likely assumed that South Korea would be overrun quickly, and that the Western powers would not intervene. It was also, perhaps, a deliberate test of the United States' reactions and capabilities. Now, with the war nearly two weeks old by the time of the DAI's assessment, the North Koreans had suffered a "tactical reverse," South Korea had not collapsed, and the United States had joined the war.

"The most important question," according to the paper, was "whether the Soviet Union is likely to precipitate a major war in the near future."[3] In early July, there was no evidence that the Soviets were preparing for war, nor was there evidence the Soviets intended to intervene directly. They were "not likely to precipitate a full-scale war"[4] by supporting the North Koreans. But now that the Americans had committed forces to Korea, the DAI assumed that the USSR "can now be expected to exploit favourable situations elsewhere."[5] The paper suggested Moscow might foment unrest in any or all of Indochina, Siam, Malaya, Burma, Hong Kong, Yugoslavia, Iran, and Berlin. But exploiting favourable situations and precipitating general war were two different issues. DAI judged that the Soviet Union would only risk war once it had built enough atomic bombs to wage atomic war and re-equipped its fighter forces to blunt a US atomic attack.[6]

Korea, then, according to DAI, would not be the source of general war, but the American commitment to Korea might increase the possibility of more conflict elsewhere in the world. It was still unlikely the Soviet Union would risk a war before it had built up its atomic offensive capabilities and better prepared its defences for an atomic attack. As a result, "[t]he risk of war though not imminent is progressively becoming more serious."[7]

The JIC met again a few days later, discussed the DAI's draft, marked it up, and agreed that the JIC should take on a study "[t]o examine the imminence of a major war arising from: (a) the situation in Korea, (b) similar situations elsewhere, or (c) other causes."[8]

This study was completed on July 14, 1950. The director of Scientific Intelligence (DSI), A. J. Langley, thought it was "as good an appreciation of the situation as is possible,"[9] and DEA officials thought it was "quite a sound paper."[10] After a round of comments, the study, now bearing the title CSC(20)50, "The Imminence of War," was put forward for consideration at the Chiefs of Staff Committee meeting on July 17, less than a week after the study's objectives had been set in the JIC.[11]

Like the DAI paper, CSC (20)50 discounted the possibility of major war arising from the situation in Korea. The paper restated the DAI's assumptions about the Soviet role in instigating the conflict but pointed out the lack of a direct Soviet role in the invasion. The new paper maintained that "no evidence has come to light which would indicate that the Soviet Union had made advance dispositions and preparations for a war as a result of developments in Korea."[12]

The CSC (20)50 paper, however, went further in suggesting that the invasion of Korea might require an adjustment in assumptions about the risk of war. The attack, the paper warned, might "indicate a new stage in Soviet strategy involving more aggressive action short of a major war whenever opportunity arises."[13] Nonetheless, after again listing a number of potential global hotspots — Formosa, Indochina, Siam, Malaya, Burma, Hong Kong, Yugoslavia, and Iran.— the paper concluded that it "does not seem likely that Soviet inspired activities in the above areas would lead to direct Soviet intervention and to a major war."[14]

CSC (20)50 did offer the possibility that "other causes" — that is, beyond a Soviet decision to start a war — might lead to war. General war might come, the paper argued, due to either Chinese action or perhaps an American strike against the USSR.

There were several scenarios by which the US and China might come to blows. A US-Chinese war might occur if the Soviets encouraged the Chinese to attack Formosa, the last stronghold of Chiang Kai-shek's Nationalist regime, in an effort to take the pressure off the North Koreans. The Canadians also noted that if United Nations forces tried to occupy and unite all of Korea, the Soviets might intervene. At the time, the Canadians thought such UN action unlikely. The Canadian paper also warned that the "extensive United States involvement in the Far East," if combined with a "multiplication and intensification of incidents elsewhere," might strengthen the argument of those in the United States "who feel that preventive war against the Soviet Union is desirable."[15]

In conclusion, the paper stated the "likelihood that the Soviet Union will precipitate a major war is considered not to be significantly changed by the Korean war."[16] The Soviets were still unlikely to launch a war until they could minimize allied strategic air offensives, mount effective atomic offensives, and seriously interrupt allied sea communications. Trying to understand just when the Kremlin believed they would achieve these capabilities was still next to impossible, but the war in Korea itself changed none of these factors. Clearly, however, the Canadians believed that the war in Korea, and especially the American commitment to the peninsula, created other possible avenues to war, either by calculation or by accident.

As the Chiefs of Staff Committee examined CSC (20)50, consideration of the paper led rapidly to a more general discussion "involving analysis of the overall situation in Korea and at large, and study of the possibilities and probabilities of courses which events could take in the next few months."[17]

One exchange recorded in the minutes of the Chiefs of Staff Committee is particularly instructive: Omond Solandt, the chair of the Defense Research Board, wondered if "the U.S.S.R. move in Korea" was an indication that Moscow "was abandoning its policy of Cold War in favour of an eventual hot war."[18] The invasion, he mused, might be "an early military gambit to pin down United Nations forces preparatory to inviting general war." Arnold Heeney, the under-secretary of state for External Affairs, disagreed, pointing out that "[t]here was no more evidence than six months earlier of U.S.S.R. intention to initiate a general war."[19] Heeney, supported by similar analysis from CSC (20)50, saw nothing in Korea that suggested a change in Soviet intentions.

But intentions are not the full measure of possibilities: the war in Korea had created, or would create, changes in military deployments that could create new avenues for war. General Foulkes, chief of the general staff, laid this out grimly in his analysis of the "future progress" of the Korean War. To evict the North Koreans from South Korea, he predicted, the United Nations would require six divisions of combat troops in Korea.[20] Shortages of equipped and trained troops in UN member countries, and the need to maintain existing formations in "trouble and danger spots" like Germany, Japan, and Malaya, meant the combat forces for Korea would have to come from the continental United States. When the US sent these troops, it would "practically denude the country [the United States]" of ground forces.[21]

The results, whether or not the Soviets had anticipated them, would be dire from Washington's perspective. Starting about September 1950, when the US forces left the continental United States for Korea, there would be a period of "maximum vulnerability, and thus of danger," for several months. The war in Korea would weaken the Western position everywhere else in the world, and the Soviets would recognize this and "undoubtedly exploit" other areas.[22]

The chiefs approved CSC (20)50, with an addendum summarizing Foulkes' concerns, and the "Imminence of War" paper made its way up the chain to the Cabinet Defence Committee and the Cabinet. On July 19, Brooke Claxton, the minister of National Defence, described the paper to his colleagues, explaining that the risk of major war as a result of the Korean situation was "slight," that war might come between the US and China, and that the Soviets would try to exploit "favourable situations elsewhere." Claxton concluded by noting that the "Korean incident" suggested an "increased willingness on both sides to take risks involving the possibility of war and that the risk of a major war was correspondingly greater,"[23] especially because, as Foulkes had pointed out the day before, the war called into action the only available reserve forces from the US.

This early assessment of the effects of the Korean War on the likelihood of general war are especially important: Officials in Ottawa clearly discounted the notion that the Soviet Union was seeking general war — and yet the Korean War, by its very nature and location, led to new fears. Pearson, the secretary of state for External Affairs, noted the gap between the initial assessment that the risk of war was slight, and the Foulkes addendum that the US response to the war in Korea created new risks. Pearson warned that "the risk of a major war as a direct result of the Korean situation was somewhat greater than slight."[24] The imminence of war needed to be reexamined.

The Greatest Danger

While the later years of the Korean War were stuck in stalemate, its first weeks and months saw rapid shifts in the fortunes on both sides. On July 28, the United States government, via its ambassador in Ottawa, requested that Canada contribute ground troops to the war effort. This led the Chiefs of Staff Committee to urgently seek a review by the JIC of "the chances of a world war rising out of events marching along with the situation on a world-wide basis since the outbreak of war in Korea."[25] They wanted the JIC to "re-examine the imminence of war" so that the minister could use the assessment in an upcoming Cabinet meeting on August 4.

The chiefs asked for a review of how other UN states reacted to the war, a reassessment of the Soviet satellites and their military capabilities, and comments on the imminence of war. The paper was also to comment on the role "proposed by the U.S. of fighting communism wherever it breaks out,"[26] a reference to a sweeping change to American containment strategy that called for the US to meet Communist aggression anywhere in the world.

The scope of what the CSC asked for was, as had become routine in the postwar world, more than an intelligence assessment. It was neither an appreciation nor a planning document, but a mixture of the two. The resulting paper was the product of a joint JIC and Joint Planning Committee (JPC) effort. The JIC's section of the paper had to be completed before the JPC could finish their parts.[27]

CSC 22(50), "The Imminence of War," was marked "TOP SECRET Canadian eyes only."[28] The "object" of the paper was to "determine the imminence of war, and the effect of it and of other world-wide events arising out of hostilities in Korea on Canadian rearmament."[29] This was an enormously broad remit, but even the specific task of determining Soviet intentions proved frustratingly difficult for the JIC.

As the director of military intelligence, Colonel Knight, explained to the CGS, it was "impossible to be more specific concerning the imminence of war in the face of the existing evidence." Canadian officers in London had canvassed their colleagues in the British DMI, and officers in Washington had done the same with the G-2 intelligence staff in Washington. The Canadian DMI was confident the JIC had "incorporate[d] all material available" to the allies in the Canadian assessment, but the material itself was thin. There were rumours and unconfirmed reports regarding the movement of Soviet troops and their allies in Europe, but nothing reliable. "In the absence of 'inside' information in the capitals behind the iron curtain," Knight said, "Western intelligence cannot be confident of predicting the intentions of the USSR; we can only point out the military capabilities of our enemies."[30]

Given these extreme limitations, the JIC proceeded by essentially establishing a ledger sheet — a list of factors suggesting war was imminent, and a list of factors suggesting it was not. The notable factors that suggested war was imminent included long-standing observations about the size of the Soviet military force and attention to recent Soviet actions around the world.

Since 1945, the USSR had maintained the "largest armed forces in the world" and there "is every indication that they are being prepared for major war." Despite the debates in the preceding year over Soviet intentions, the new assessment concluded that Soviet efforts to build up particular forces, like armour, long-range submarines, and strategic bombers were "too extensive to be merely defensive in purpose," and instead were designed to "ensure that it possess[es] overwhelming military power." The Soviet government had reorganized and rearmed satellite forces with Soviet arms and, in some cases, officers.[31]

The Soviets seemed to be taking greater risk, too: the paper listed the attack on Korea, but also attacks on a US Navy plane in the Baltic, sabotage against the Royal Navy, and the appearance of Soviet submarines in Canadian territorial waters. The war itself had started poorly for the Americans in Korea, with US troops suffering early defeats. The "weakness of American ground forces in Korea, and the inability of the American air forces effectively to influence the fighting" might cause the Soviets estimate of American and Western forces to diminish.[32]

By one reading, then, the Soviets were strong and getting stronger, and this posed a threat. At the same time, and somewhat contradictorily, the paper went on to suggest that Soviet concerns about the weakness of their own position was also a factor for war. The Soviet Union might have realized that its "preponderance in conventional weapons"[33] was being threatened by the mobilization of Western powers, and the "comparative failure" of Russian aims in influencing Western Europe may push the Soviets to embark on war.[34]

On the opposite side of the ledger were factors that suggested war was not imminent. The appreciation pointed out that the reorganization and equipment of Soviet forces might not yet be finished; that the call-up and release of troops was following normal routine; and there was no evidence of a larger mobilization of reservists. Soviet Army forces were being kept at a peacetime establishment of 70 percent. There was no stockpiling in Eastern Europe, and no preparations for mobilization were underway. The balance of forces in Eastern Europe, which included a higher proportion of armoured units as against infantry, did not suggest "a balanced force which would normally be expected to be necessary for operations."[35]

The conclusion to this section was underwhelming. It pointed out the Soviets had the "capability to wage a major war at any time," and while there was "no evidence of Soviet intentions to precipitate a major war immediately," the strength of Soviet forces and their dispositions meant that "advance indications of intention to precipitate a major war may not be discernible."[36]

In the end, CSC 22(50) sidestepped any deep discussion of the American policy of "fighting communism wherever it breaks out." The authors observed that it would be "difficult to see how the United States, in its position as leader of the anti-communist nations, could, without disastrous consequences, have avoided stating the policy and attempting to implement it." Nonetheless, the implications of the US approach were worrying. There remained a risk the policy "may lead to dangerous dispersion of United States forces while Soviet forces remain uninvolved."[37] Whether because it was too difficult to assess US policy, or simply impolitic, the Canadians left the US role in the imminence of war unexamined.

When the CSC met to discuss CSC 22(50), the CGS noted that from a "short-term point of view," the world had entered a period "of intense danger." In the long term, the Korean invasion had so galvanized the United States that the upshot of the war would be an increase in US forces and a "distinct improvement in the overall picture."[38] This "period [of] intense danger" would last over the next twelve months because, as Foulkes had explained in July, the Western world would be "vulnerable to attack because of the lack of forces available to withstand aggression."[39] The only solution was the rapid development on military power in Western Europe and North America.

There remained a "lack of positive evidence of USSR intentions" available to Canadian intelligence. But the chiefs concluded the likelihood of war with the USSR in "the next twelve months was greater than at any time in the past and probably greater than in the succeeding period."[40]

Although the DEA chair of the JIC would have had to approve the document that became CSC 22(50), it reflected the views of the military members of the Chiefs of Staff Committee better than the views of the DEA. In mid-September, one DEA official noted that the continuing "primary question which faces the government is the likelihood of another world war or of another war such as that in Korea."[41] The Government of Canada lacked any agreed idea of whether such a war was likely.

No doubt all the senior leaders had their own assessment of war: "the Prime Minister must have one, the Secretary of State for External Affairs must have one, and the Minister of National Defence must have one; each of the service Chiefs of Staff undoubtedly has his views, and so on." There was "no guarantee," however, that these views were "all alike."[42] This was a curious statement, and an important one, for it reveals the place of the JIC appreciations — even those that were approved as CSC papers. They could not be said to stand in for an agreed governmental view.

In early October, the JIC asked the JIS to review the imminence of war once again, and revise CSC 20(50) in what would become a new paper, CSC 31(50). The revised paper was discussed in the JIC on October 19 and printed as CSC 31(50) on October 24, 1950, in time to inform an upcoming NATO Military Committee meeting.[43] But events would once again leave the appreciation trailing behind changing circumstances. In October, Chinese forces crossed the border into North Korea. The previous appreciation of the imminence of war was out of date, and new factors needed to be considered.[44]

In a meeting of the CSC on November 21 to discuss the implications of the Chinese intervention, the USSEA argued that the Chinese had had two objectives. In the first place, it was a defensive move: the Chinese suffered from "a real apprehension of United States territorial acquisition," and the US drives toward China had worried the People's Republic of China (PRC). In addition, the invasion was a "deliberate move, probably at the instigation of the USSR, to contain in Korea large United Nations and United States forces."[45] The chief of the general staff noted that "military views" were similar: the Chinese intervention was a "purely defensive action" to protect its port and water facilities, was designed to gain time for the North Korean forces to regroup, and was part of a Soviet plan to contain the maximum UN forces in the Far East.[46]

The paradoxical result of the meeting, then, was agreement that the Chinese intervention was defensive in nature but also part of a broader Soviet plan to tie down Western forces in Asia (and thus away from Europe). This suggested to some a more dangerous period: "Time," said the deputy minister of National Defence, "was running out on the military advantages which the USSR had held until recently." They worried that Soviet appreciation of this fact might affect Soviet decisions "as to their military actions in the immediately following months."[47]

The period of greatest danger had been coming closer and closer, and now the Canadians believed it had arrived. It had come not because of a Soviet effort to initiate general war, but a more complicated pattern in which the Soviets seemed to have encouraged a local war, leading to the United States committing resources to the fight that exposed Western Europe to Soviet response. As a result, the course of the fighting had introduced two factors: the possibility of a war with China, and the possibility of the Soviets deciding that they must take broader military action immediately.

In such a dangerous situation, it was prudent to watch closely and regularly for indications that war was about to break out. In early December, a subcommittee of the JIC met to discuss how to find "some means of systematically reviewing the world situation at regular and frequent intervals."[48] They proposed two methods. The first was the production of short "imminence of war"-style papers every two weeks, improving the "imminence of war" papers that had been sent to and approved by the CSC. The second idea was for each service intelligence directorate to forward "any items of information which might indicate new trends or developments having significance in relation to the imminence of war."⁴⁹ The JIS could prepare periodic, consolidated lists of these items. In this second idea lay a version of "indications intelligence" that the Americans and British practised to some extent, and which will be the focus of the next chapter. The JIC directed the JISC to proceed with its first idea: a newly reviewed paper every two weeks, and then to develop an ad hoc system to keep track of indications.

Canada's allies were watching the situation closely, too, and the British were focused on estimating the probability of war. Foulkes visited London and learned that the British were worried about Indochina and Berlin, especially after the "increase in Bereitschaften [East German paramilitary police units] and closing off of secondary roads to Berlin."⁵⁰ The risks in Germany would increase as NATO built up its integrated force, which was to include a Canadian brigade. If the Soviets waited too long, and the NATO forces were in place, they could only attack by concentrating troops, and these concentrations would "provide suitable targets for tactical use of atom bomb[s]."⁵¹ But if the Soviets struck before the NATO build-up was complete, they could avoid large concentrations and succeed. Military logic suggested to Foulkes that if the Soviets were going to launch a war, they should do it sooner than later.

In Washington, there occurred a pronounced shift in American analysis of Soviet intentions since the beginning of the war. In June and July, there had been a firm and sustained CIA analysis that the Soviets were "unwilling to undertake a global conflict with the West at this time."⁵² By September, US intelligence officials seemed convinced that Moscow might be seeking general war.⁵³ A series of US National Intelligence Estimates (NIEs) judged that the Soviet Union might launch a war, and even that it was possible, Moscow had "already made a decision for general war."⁵⁴ The Canadians were aware of the hardening American position, but there is no indication they agreed.⁵⁵

At the very end of December 1950, Pearson and Claxton submitted a joint memorandum to the Cabinet assessing the international situation and the JIC's views. The paper, which served as a spur for an acceleration of the Canadian defence program, pointed out that earlier assumptions about the possibility of general war, before Korea, had estimated the period of greatest danger lay in the future, well into the 1950s. Now, they argued, "the only safe assumption is that the period of greatest danger has already begun."⁵⁶

The Meaning of Korea

It is striking that even by late 1950, the JIC kept being pulled back into discussions of what objects the Soviet Union would seek in a general war, rather than whether or not such a war was likely, or sought by Moscow.[57] Canadian diplomats, especially those with experience in the Soviet Union, would not shake their conviction that the Soviet Union was not seeking war. In January 1951, Robert Ford, head of DEA's European Division, weighed in again on the JIC's "Imminence of War" papers. Such appreciations, he wrote, must place more emphasis on the fact that "a new holocaust would seriously endanger the citadel of Communism." Even if the Soviets were to win a war, which was far from assured, they "must know perfectly well" it "would leave their country in ruins and all the countries which they might over-run."[58] The Soviets, he seemed to be indicating, would not choose war. He worried that the papers the DEA was preparing were being used for military planning talks in which the DEA itself was not playing any real role.

Ford took his concerns to the under-secretary. He noted that he and his division had been asked to contribute to several papers prepared by the Department of National Defence (DND) "on the subject of planning — for a war in 1951, 1954, 1957, long-term and so on." He was not sure what these papers were used for, he said (although they were probably ACAI papers). He assumed they were taken to Washington and discussed with the Americans. What he was sure of was that this was an encroachment by DND on DEA's "field of international political affairs."[59]

The planning papers he had read all began, he said, "with assumptions of a political nature, which seem to me in many cases to be largely false. As military planning is based on these assumptions, it becomes a serious matter for Canada." It was time, he wrote, to "take the task of political star-gazing out of the hands of National Defence, and assign it definitively to External Affairs." Only once the Canadian diplomats, perhaps along with their American and British colleagues, agreed on "what we think the course of the next five years are likely to be," then the militaries could start planning on that basis.[60]

There was recognition by some DEA officials that "[t]he military must plan on the basis of 'if war comes'" and that planners "are some times disposed to transpose 'if' with 'when' and thus to give a misleading impression."[61]

But for Ford, the implications of leaving the assumptions in the hands of "National Defence and the Pentagon," rather than with External Affairs and the State Department, was planning based on the assumption "that there is bound to be a war within a fairly short time, which means that we build up defences against a military threat from the Soviet Union."[62] While a threat "certainly exists," it was "not primarily military, but ideological and economic." If the West put the greatest proportion of resources "preparing for war at the expense of social and economic aid, we may find the Soviet Union has gained its objectives in Western Europe, the Middle East and Asia, without firing a shot."[63] Only by properly assessing the likelihood of war could Canada and its allies determine how to allocate its resources in the broader Cold War.

Now or Later

The Canadian government would ultimately come to its own conclusions on Soviet intentions by triangulating their views with assessments they received from London and Washington.

Throughout 1951, both the US and British JICs prepared estimates of Soviet intentions and capabilities. In October, the two JICs ultimately produced a joint paper to inform discussions of the US and UK Chiefs of Staff in Washington. The Canadians received both the American paper, JIC 531/10, and the British paper, JIC 2533(50), as well as the final joint paper "Soviet Intentions and Capabilities, 1950–1954," which was over 100 pages long.[64]

The US-UK paper was similar to ABC1 15, the document produced by the three powers in 1949. It covered both the likelihood of war and then operations the Soviet Union would conduct in case of war. It concluded that "if the Soviet leaders think war inevitable they may initiate a major war while their strength vis-a-vis the Western Powers is at its maxim[um]."[65] This danger would persist until about 1954, when NATO forces were built up to withstand any surprise attack.

But the Anglo-American paper also revealed continuing transatlantic disagreement on several important matters: The likelihood the Soviet Union would initiate war, the date by which the Soviets would consider war feasible, and the probable Soviet stockpile of atomic bombs. The British did not think the Soviets would be willing to embark on a war until 1955, when their economy might be capable of withstanding the strains of a long war and air defence was more adequate. The US continued to argue that "in output and stockpiles of war material the Soviet Union will be superior to the West until 1953 and in relative air strength the Soviet superiority will increase until 1952 and then decline."[66] The US analysts assumed the Soviet leaders were willing to take significant risks, and that as a result "the danger of a deliberate war is much closer."[67] For the British, the issue was the absolute strength of the Soviet Union: they would be stronger later. For the Americans, it was relational: the Soviets "may well consider themselves in a better relative position for war now than they will be in 1953 or later."[68]

To External Affairs officials who compared the US and UK estimates, it was "plain" that the Soviets "are increasingly willing to conduct or instigate operations which contain the risk of war."[69] Both London and Washington agreed that the "risk of general war exists from now on." But, curiously, the "main risk" of war would "arise from Soviet or Soviet inspired operations which are not intended to lead to general war."[70]

A Canadian review of the British and American assessments concluded that the prospect of war "may be now or later, since to some extent Soviet policy must be opportunistic and dependent on a number of factors now incalculable."[71] The Canadians thought the present situation carried great danger and warned not to count on the diminution of that danger after 1952.

The Politics of Danger

The war in Korea dragged on. By mid-April 1951, Pearson and Claxton decided that it was necessary to update their Cabinet colleagues on the world situation that had seemed so precarious the previous December. The JIC was once again directed to "record particularly their views on the imminence of war." The driving questions should be: "Has the danger of general war changed materially since the end of 1950? In what degree? With what implications?"[72]

The resulting paper, which was prepared for Cabinet ministers, was not titled "Imminence of War" but instead bore the blander title of "The International Situation." It concluded that "the risk of a deliberate resort to war by the Soviet Union in pursuit of its long-term objectives is unchanged since December 1950." There were no indications that Soviet leaders were seeking general war, but their military build-up continued and the global situation was slightly more worrying than in 1950. "Danger of war," according to the appreciation, "will persist over a very long time, failing some radical and unforeseen diplomatic rapprochement."[73]

The drafting process for "The International Situation" is enormously instructive for what it reveals about the preparation of intelligence appreciations for Cabinet consumption. Some officials in the DEA thought the overall tone too pessimistic. John Hadwen of Defence Liaison (1) Division, or DL(1), thought it incorrect to leave the impression that the prospects of war were increasing, especially as there was no evidence of Soviet preparations for an attack. His colleague Thomas L. Carter of Defence Liaison (2), or DL(2), wrote in the margin: "[n]o evidence necessary." When Hadwen wrote that "war is not necessarily inevitable and yet this Memorandum as a whole seems based on a premise that war is coming either before 1952 or afterwards." Carter penned in the margins: "risks persist even if war doesn't come."[74] The exchange indicates the challenges that had been present in drafting these appreciations for months, that the risks of war had seemed to increase even though it was difficult to find any state that wanted war.

But the April memorandum was the result not only of an intelligence puzzle but a political one: officials in the Department of Finance warned that Douglas Abbott, the minister of Finance, was preparing the annual, high-profile budget speech that "might contain an appraisal of the international situation which was . . . too optimistic."[75]

To ensure this did not happen, the Finance officials suggested External Affairs prepare a submission "emphasizing that the basic situation and the basic danger today is substantially as great as it was three or six months ago."[76] Pearson was apprised of this warning, and by the time the draft memorandum reached him, the report's "general conclusion is that the likelihood of war is just as great as it was in December and in some respects there has been a change for the worse."[77]

In the short term, then, the tone of the April assessment was calculated to impress on Cabinet the continuing international dangers. But this calculation, in turn raised more questions. Intelligence appreciations had now, for months, been warning of danger, and, as one official put it, a danger "that in all likelihood will be with us for many years to come." If Pearson and Claxton were not careful, their consistent invocations of danger might "build up a resistance in the minds of the [other] Cabinet Ministers to our repeated warnings."[78]

Pearson decided not to send "The International Situation" paper to Cabinet, but only to the Prime Minister, Abbott, and Claxton, perhaps hoping this limited distribution would influence Abbott's speech without the possible negative implications of another frightening but inconclusive report for Cabinet.[79]

The Canadian View from Abroad

Pearson did send "The International Situation" to the Prime Minister and some Cabinet colleagues, but he also had drafts of the paper sent to Canadian diplomats around the world, in hopes of gaining some reactions and to keep the answers regarding the "imminence of war" up to date.[80]

One response, a paper prepared in the Canadian embassy in Washington, pointed out the obvious: the imminence of war paper that was distributed did "not answer the question as to the 'imminence of war.'"[81] It did not lay out the conditions in which the Soviet leadership might go to war, whether these conditions existed or not, or when they might in the future. The assessment did lay out just what action the Soviet Union could "conceivably" take, but the paper would be more useful if it assessed what Moscow was "likely to do."[82]

Hume Wrong, the ambassador in Washington, wrote a letter emphasizing this point: any assessment of the imminence of war should "concern itself more fully with the probable intentions of the Soviet leaders."[83] Incidentally, Canadian diplomats in Washington also learned that the Soviet desk at the State Department was of the "private opinion" that the Soviet Union was "unlikely to embark on a world war now," and that the Soviets had made a "tremendous mistake" in Korea.[84]

Arthur Menzies, writing from Tokyo, agreed with this assessment. He was confident that the United Nations' determination and success in Korea, "once more on a shoe string, as in Berlin and Greece," had sobered the Soviet leadership.[85]

Menzies pointed out that US Secretary of Defence George Marshall's recent senate testimony, in which he explained that the US could not support Douglas MacArthur's aggressive policy in Korea because the United States was too weak, implied that if the United States was stronger, it would, in fact, force a showdown with Moscow. This was another example of US policy raising the chances of war.[86] Maurice Pope, now ambassador in Brussels, took this point further, insisting that he did "not believe in the imminence of war, save perhaps that rash action on our part might well prompt the Russians to march against us."[87]

Pope was by far the most critical of the paper, which he said "smacks more of the work of a Ministry of War than that of a Ministry of Foreign or External Affairs." He may have been the most outspoken respondent, but he was hardly the only one who complained the paper spent too much time counting divisions and tanks of the Soviet Army rather than "the attitude of mind of these who direct its destinies."[88]

Pope assumed this emphasis on capabilities, rather than intentions, was the mark of an American influence on Canadian intelligence, and that there was no good reason to think Moscow wanted war: "I have never once heard of a single shred of good evidence pointing to the conclusion that the Soviets mean to make offensive war."[89]

In Washington, Hume Wrong continued to be skeptical that the USSR could want war. In the aftermath of two world wars, it was obvious that in modern war "victor and vanquished alike undergo terrible destruction." Surely, he thought, the Soviet leadership would have "grave doubts" about their ability to control their country in case of war — and that war might break apart the Soviet state.[90] R. M. Macdonnell, writing from Paris, agreed. The Soviet leadership was "intelligent and well-enough informed," he wrote, to realize that any war would be "long and immensely destructive."[91]

The fundamental question surrounding these debates revolved around the Korean War. Bill Crean argued that the analyses of the Soviet policy had been too ready to assume that Korea proved "the spread of Communism was henceforth to be conducted principally on the points of Soviet bayonets."[92] He did not accept the notion that "the Russians thought they were risking a major war when the campaign began."[93]

Macdonnell, supporting Crean's point from Paris, thought the Soviets had shown a "healthy prudence" and been willing to accept "local setbacks," for instance in Greece or Berlin, rather than risk general war. In fact, Soviet action in the Korean War, and in particular the limitations on assistance from the USSR to the North Korea or Chinese "suggests forcibly that the Kremlin has had just as many fears and hesitations as we have." Any suggestion that Korea showed a willingness of the Soviet Union to pursue objectives, even at the risk of major war, should be called into question.[94]

If war was imminent — and the Canadian diplomatic corps did not think it was — it was not because Moscow wanted it. These observations would come to play a significant part in future assessments of the imminence of war.

The End of Imminence

In June 1951, a year after the outbreak of the Korean War, the Chiefs of Staff Committee directed the JIC to once again review the standing "Imminence of War" paper. The first draft was the collaborative work of External Affairs and the directorate of air intelligence. It maintained the fundamental assumption that Soviet leaders held two goals: the long-term aim of establishing "world Communism under Russian domination," and the short-term aim of establishing the USSR "in an impregnable position."[95] The second was an essential ingredient for completing the former goal. But crucially, in this assessment, war was not considered to be an essential stepping stone to either aim. In fact, the External Affairs/DAI draft established war as a possible impediment to Soviet goals.

The draft assessment drew on and reflected, to a significant extent, some of the letters that Canadian missions had written in response to the request for comment on the last "Imminence of War" paper. In particular, it included the point, made by several diplomats, that given the obvious costs of modern war, the Soviets would far prefer to seek their objectives short of war.[96]

The draft appreciation suggested that the Soviet leaders did "genuinely fear an attack"[97] by the Western powers, and might conclude that the Western Powers had decided to destroy Soviet power. It warned that "[c]ertainly the unprecedented preparations for war now being urgently pressed forward by the democratic countries in NATO could be construed as supporting such a theory."[98] Again, building on thinking within the DEA and from missions abroad, the Canadian assessment acknowledged that Western rearmament was a factor driving Soviet preparations for war.

In keeping with previous Canadian assessments, the drafters punted on the question of whether Soviet leaders might decide to initiate a war: "[i]t is not possible to appreciate at what point such a decision would be made."[99] But the argument made elsewhere in the paper about the costs of war provided important context for this non-appreciation.

Also in keeping with previous assessment, this paper noted that the Soviet Union's military strength suggested it was capable of war. But the assessment also made clear that Moscow would still have to make "some 'last minute' preparation" before launching operations. None of these preparations had started, and this was evidence "Soviet leaders have not decided to start a general war in the next few months."[100]

The world was still a dangerous place, and war might develop "from some local operation,"[101] but this draft paper reflected the view, long building in the Department of External Affairs, that war was not imminent.

The External Affairs/DAI draft was altered, somewhat, before it was sent to the Chiefs of Staff Committee. The changes resulted in a more polished but less sanguine paper, presented to the CSC in July 1951 as JIC 20(51), "The Imminence of War."[102] The new version had been made somewhat starker. The suggestion that Western rearmament might reasonably be understood by Moscow as a prelude to an attack was excised. And while JIC 20(51) pointed out "certain weaknesses" in the Soviet position, it maintained the argument that the Soviet Union could embark on a massive war by waging simultaneous campaigns around the world. The draft's suggestion that the Soviet leadership understood the costs of modern warfare had been deleted, although the new draft did include the observation that "Soviet leaders will prefer . . . all other means short of war" to achieve its goals.[103] The JIC paper concluded that "the long-term danger of war remains the same, but that there is no evidence that either deliberate resort to war, or war arising from local operations, is likely in 1951."[104]

Still, the CSC thought JIC 20(51) painted far too rosy a picture. The chief of the general staff sensed an unacceptable "air of optimism." Charles "Bud" Drury, the deputy minister of National Defence, was also troubled by the paper. From "various other papers [he] had read," Drury said, "[he] had gained the impression that the period of greatest danger to the free world was at present." And yet the paper suggested "war was not imminent during 1951."[105] The deputy minister's observations are striking in that they indicate an obverse relationship to how the JIC was supposed to work: instead of the JIC sending an intelligence appreciation up to the CSC, the CSC seemed to be telegraphing an intelligence appreciation down to the JIC, and asking them to write it up formally. Foulkes himself demonstrated some of the futility of the exercise at hand when he pointed out that while "we had no available information suggesting that the Soviet Union intended to precipitate a war during 1951, it was equally true that we had no information which suggested that Russia did not intend to suddenly open hostilities during the period in question."[106]

To the chiefs, it seemed that the dangers of war as assessed months earlier remained the same. Those earlier assessments had helped reinforce the Cabinet's decisions to accelerate the rearmament of Canadian forces. They likely, and reasonably, wondered whether an assessment of lesser risk would slow Canada's defence build-up. And yet, from the view of External Affairs officers, the fact remained that war — either launched deliberately by the Soviets, or the result of an accident — "does not appear likely in 1951, where six months ago we probably could not have made such a positive statement."[107]

JIC 20(51) was not approved by the CSC but instead sent back to the JIC for redrafting.[108]

From "Imminence" to "Risks"

A redrafted "Imminence of War" paper would come before the Chiefs of Staff Committee in September 1951, but it would bear a new name. On the advice of the DEA members of the JIC, the "Imminence of War" title had been changed to "The Current Risks of War." This was done purposefully, the USSEA told the committee, because the very word imminence "tended to prejudge international developments."[109]

During the August revision, Charles Ritchie had directed George Glazebrook to ensure the new draft accounted for the reports made by Canadian missions abroad, as well as "the impressions gained by the Minister to the general effect that the danger of war this year was less."[110] After all, as the secretary of Cabinet reminded the CSC, the Cabinet had received a paper in late 1950 indicating that the next year would be the "most critical." Now, with a year having passed, it was time to present the government with "a clear picture of the risks of hostilities."[111]

External Affairs officials continued to worry about the effects of seeming to cry wolf. If "too black a picture were painted," Heeney told the CSC, "and nothing serious transpired the effectiveness of these preparations would be considerably lessened."[112] Simply changing the title was important for the reasons the External Affairs officials indicated.

Beyond the title change, the updated draft did contain a new and important feature. It made a distinction between a "deliberate Soviet resort to war and a war arising from miscalculations by either side or the acceptance of risks in a local operation."[113] But ultimately, the drafters of the "Current Risks" paper reflected the views of the CSC and deleted one of the lines from JIC 20(51) that had so bothered the chiefs: the seemingly benign statement that "no available information suggests that the Soviet Union intends to precipitate a war during 1951."[114]

External Affairs officials still grumbled about the "Risks of War" paper. The appreciation's drafters had been looking for evidence of war — evidence that war was imminent. This had always struck External Affairs officials as the wrong way to go about the problem. An appreciation, they thought, should consider whether war was likely or not, and not just look for evidence of imminence.

External Affairs officials continued to see nuance in Soviet policy. Max Wershof pointed out that general war would only cut against Soviet goals of achieving Communism.[115] Similarly, J. A. McCordick thought the document did not go far enough to describe limits on the Soviet Union and that the Soviet satellites provided a source of weakness, not strength. Problems within the Soviet Union — especially the unpopularity of collectivization and the opposition of the churches to Communism, were problems that existed now but "would be more acute in wartime."[116] Fundamentally, the appreciation ignored the reasons the Soviet Union would not wish to go to war.

The Likelihood of War

In 1952, DEA officials sought to re-write the "Current Risks of War" paper with the deliberate goal of offering an assessment of the likelihood, rather than imminence, of war. They were inspired, perhaps, by a similar British assessment. The previous November, the UK JIC had sent the Canadians a copy of their JIC (451)103 (Final), entitled "Likelihood of Total War with the Soviet Union up to the End of 1954."[117] The paper matched very closely with DEA views. It noted that there was a danger that the Soviet Union might start a war, and that it had the military power to do so. The Soviet leaders might view Western actions, especially the growth of NATO to include West Germany, as evidence of an upcoming Western attack that Moscow might choose to pre-empt with war. But, overall, the UK JIC believed that the "Soviet Government will wish to avoid a total war in the period under review."[118]

Glazebrook read and largely concurred with the British paper and, in January 1952, determined it was time for a new study of the risks of war.[119] Dana Wilgress, the former Canadian ambassador to Moscow, led the drafting process in DEA's DL(2). He read both the UK JIC paper and a contemporaneous US National Intelligence Estimate.[120]

The Wilgress paper would end up being discussed at length in the Joint Intelligence Committee, and re-drafted multiple times. However, it kept its main argument from Wilgress' first draft: the Soviet Union could undertake a war by launching simultaneous campaigns, but the growth in Western strength would result now in a war of attrition — "a war in which the weaknesses of the Soviet position would be evident."[121] General war, then, would not be a likely choice for Moscow.

Wilgress could imagine two scenarios in which the Soviets might "resort to general war and launch without warning an attack on the West as the

Germans did against the Soviet Union in 1941." First, Moscow might "feel" it had "reached the limit of expansion by methods short of general war" in Europe.[122] But, he pointed out, these limits would not be felt in Asia, where the Soviets could continue to try and expand their influence short of war. It would seem that "[t]here appear[s], therefore to be various alternatives open to the Soviet leaders for expansionist moves other than general war."[123]

The second scenario would be the result of a "conviction that the United States would lead the Western coalition in an assault on the USSR when the coalition is strong enough." The Soviets may well think this, especially given "the bellicose statements of various service chiefs and politicians" in the US, which mixed potently with "communist dogma about eventual clashes between capitalism and communism." The UK and Western European countries, however, clearly had no such aggressive intentions; any such war of the West against the USSR would require the United States to "force her reluctant partners to agree to such an attack or . . . drag them in without agreement."[124] Fundamentally, despite the atomic power of the United States, the Western powers did not have the conventional forces to hold Europe, much less to advance east against the Red Army. Such a scenario, even in the minds of paranoid Soviet leaders, was unlikely. Using both possible cases for why the Soviet Union might launch a general war, Wilgress had effectively explained why they would not make this choice.

But war could still come about because of miscalculation. Wilgress was convinced that the Soviets had not expected the Greek Rebellion (or Greek Civil War, 1946–49) or the Berlin Blockade (1948–49) to lead to general war, and had no doubt hoped that the North Korean invasion of South Korea would be limited to fighting between Korean forces. None of these actions had gone according to plan.

Stalin backed down on Berlin. The Soviets did not officially join the war in Korea. And when the situation in Korea became "very explosive," they proposed an armistice. All of this seemed "to indicate that the Soviet leaders would not persist in local operations which became too risky." But the Soviets could make miscalculations, assuming, for instance, that operations in Yugoslavia, or Chinese intervention in Indochina, could remain localized, when in fact both might lead to Western reactions that could "set in train a series of developments leading to general war." [125]

Wilgress' draft would be rewritten by the Joint Intelligence Staff. The JIS pushed back against efforts, likely led by the DEA member of the JIC, to include a paragraph "dealing with 'war mongering' by leaders of the Western Powers"[126] — surely the Americans. But in the end, the fundamental point, one consistently raised by members of the DEA, was ensconced in the conclusions of JIC 42/2(51): while the Soviet Union had the capability to "embark on a major war at any time," the JIC "do not consider that it will do so deliberately during 1952."[127]

Senior DEA officials were pleased with the document, describing it as "a very cool headed and realistic assessment of the current dangers of a war." They hoped that the Chiefs of Staff would "not try to 'hot it up.'" They remained on the lookout for the chiefs' efforts to "over-emphasize the risk of war."[128]

The DEA's concern was not, or not only, about the impropriety of "hotting up" an assessment. They had bigger worries: that if the risks of war were emphasized too greatly, and there was no Soviet aggression in the next two or three years, "[p]ublic opinion may then swing dangerously in the opposite direction of under-estimating the risks." The DEA was worried that exaggerated "public statements about the risk of war" made in 1951 already had this effect.[129]

Comparison with the US & UK

Throughout 1952, the Canadians continued to assess their appreciation of the likelihood of war with similar assessments made in London and Washington. The Canadian JIS and JIC members reviewed the British Chiefs of Staff paper COS (52)285, "The Likelihood of Total War up to the End of 1954," and the US National Intelligence Estimate 48, "Likelihood of the Deliberate Initiation of Full-Scale War by the USSR against the US and Its Western Allies Prior to the End of 1952."[130]

The British paper was striking for its forthright statement that there had been "no new aggressive action of the part of the Communists" nor "any intelligence which would suggest that action of an unambiguously aggressive character is imminent."[131] It outlined Soviet efforts to relax tensions, noting that the goal of these "conciliatory words" (if not deeds) was to "embarrass the Western Governments, to weaken their resolution to rearm, and to delay their defence preparations," while the Soviets continued their own defence preparation at a high rate.

The result, in British eyes, was "a difficult and dangerous" period: in Europe, the Soviets might react strongly to changes in West Germany; in Korea, the Communist forces might start a major offensive. Ultimately, however, the

UK JIC (with approval by the UK Chiefs of Staff) concluded that the "Soviet Government will not wish to start a total war in the period under review."

The American NIE marked a change from the alarmist tone of similar US documents since the last quarter of 1950. In the first sentence of NIE 48, the report noted that "[o]n balance we believe it unlikely that the Kremlin will deliberately initiate general war during 1952."[132] Instead, the NIE suggested that the Kremlin preferred "to pursue its objectives through methods short of deliberate resort to war."

As a result of actions by the US and its allies, the NIE concluded, the Kremlin was "deterred from a deliberate resort to war," and by "certainty of extensive destruction in the USSR as well as by the risk that the Soviet system might be destroyed."[133] There was also a belief that the Soviets might attack if they felt the balance of power shifting against them, but in 1952, the Soviet leadership had thought such a shift had occurred and war had not come.[134] The Canadians noted that the US NIE was different from the Canadian one, but the parts that were comparable "are identical."

It was intriguing that Americans and Canadians reached the same conclusion but by different means, especially when they both considered circumstances in which the Soviet Union might choose war. In the NIE, the US intelligence machinery identified conditions that might induce the Soviets to war, and compared these against those conditions deterring the Soviet Union. They decided, on balance, the deterrent to be stronger. The Canadian paper, in contrast, attempted "to show that the necessary sets of circumstances are unlikely to exist during 1952."[135] Through different routes, the Canadian and American assessments agreed that the Soviets would not seek general war in 1952.

While likely unbeknownst to the Canadians at the time, the CIA conducted an internal critique of previous NIEs. The results offer an explanation for why American and Canadian assessments had differed at the beginning of the Korean War. One cause of the CIA's alarm had been due to an emphasis on Soviet military strength, rather than its political and economic weakness. The CIA report also suggested that previous American documents had led readers to "assume that the Soviet leaders are trigger-happy militarists anxious to lunge their empire into general war." Canadian assessments in both the pre-Korean War era and during the war itself had avoided each of these errors, often emphasizing the Soviet caution that the CIA reviewers faulted earlier CIA analysts for having ignored.[136]

Evidence

By June, a final revision of the Canadian "Current Risks" paper, now JIC 42/3(52), was prepared for a Chiefs of Staff Committee meeting in early July.[137] DEA officials were prepared for some of the chiefs to disagree with the paper because it was "somewhat more optimistic than its predecessor."[138] But by now the Korean War was two years old and had been mired in stalemate for a year. The CSC approved the paper, and also approved its distribution to the UK JIC, the US JIC, and CIA.

In discussion, the CSC members acknowledged that "a great deal of the information" used to develop the Canadian appreciation had come to Canada from the United States or the United Kingdom. And yet the CSC thought it important to send the paper to Washington and London to "keep up the reciprocal exchange of intelligence information." The CIA had suggested they wished to receive Canadian appreciations to test their own estimates, calling the Canadian input a "useful means of assessing their own work." But they had also made it "quite obvious that the U.S. placed great importance on the quantitative supply of intelligence information from Canada."[139]

Before the paper could be distributed to allies, however, revisions had to be made: the sentence "provocative statements by certain service chiefs and politicians" had to be changed to read "service personnel" rather than chiefs — no doubt in a bid to avoid identifying US officials too narrowly.[140] Intriguingly, then, while the Canadian assessments had identified American policy as contributing to the risk of war, this was never put neatly to the Americans.

Only months after the final draft of the "Current Risks" paper was approved by the CSC, it was time for a new revision. The Chiefs of Staff requested the JIC review the last paper "and determine whether or not any decrease in the likelihood of war can be foreseen."[141] Even this phrasing suggests a more balanced and less leading question for the drafters.

The result of this review was JIC 58(52), "A Review of the Risks of War." It upheld the conclusions of the previous risks of war papers: that the Soviet Union was unlikely to go to war in 1953, but there remained a danger of war through miscalculation or local operations.[142] Discussion of the paper in the CSC revealed that the broader question (and the chiefs' worry) of the relationship between intelligence appreciations and the Canadian rearmament program was still alive.

Foulkes started off the CSC meeting making plain his frustration with DEA's approach to judging the risk of war. He argued that from the information available, the Chiefs of Staff could find no evidence to show that Moscow had given up the quest for world domination. As long as the Western powers continued to oppose Soviet expansion, the risk of war would continue undiminished.[143]

Privately, External Affairs officials thought Foulkes was coming close to a "deliberate misrepresentation."[144] DEA's view, quite simply, was that the "risk of war had diminished." The rearmament of Western Europe and especially the growth of the US atomic arsenal, "provided a strong deterrent and Stalin, unlike Hitler, was unlikely to commit the Soviet Union to a full-scale war when there was any doubt as to its outcome."[145]

Heeney, representing External Affairs in the CSC, told Foulkes that "nations appeared to assess the risk of war to suit their particular circumstances, and it was, therefore, hard to come to a firm conclusion."[146] Heeney's comment was a general one, but it had relevance for the Canadian position, too. The chiefs seemed to worry that any assessment of a declining risk of war would not suit the particular circumstances of National Defence and its goals of increased defence spending. Despite the JIC assessment that the risk of war was not as high as it had been, the general views of the Chiefs of Staff were that "insofar as it affects military requirements the Canadian military opinion is that the risk of aggression has not diminished."[147]

This unsatisfying stalemate led to renewed effort in the JIC to make an accurate appreciation of the risks of war. As Ivor Bowen, director of Canada's Joint Intelligence Bureau (JIB), told the committee, there existed in Ottawa "a great many opinions on the likelihood of war." Some were based on the logic of risk, or, perhaps, the needs of departments. The "very strength" of a JIC appreciation, however, "is that it derives from an examination of evidence." What followed was an effort to assess the risk of war with a longer paper that gave "considerable treatment of the evidence which is examined in arriving at the conclusions."[148]

A new paper was drafted in late October 1952. It came in for major criticism from DEA officials because it did not take account of possible American actions that could risk war. One official complained that the assessment "ignores completely the implications of a Republican victory which might occur in the United States on November 4th."[149] There was real concern in Washington that if Eisenhower won the 1952 election, "the 'Neanderthal' wing of the Party will dominate Congress"¹⁵⁰ and the president might give in to those advocating preventive war. DEA officials worried that the Soviets would share these fears, and that a Republican victory might "encourage the Soviet Union to resort to direct aggression," touching off a "a general war resulting through miscalculation on either side." A JIC assessment of the current risks of war that focused only on potential Soviet actions, and did not include potential American actions, or, to take it one step further, Soviet reactions to American reactions, was "unrealistic."¹⁵¹

By February 1953, the JIC had put together a new full draft of "The Current Risks of General War," JIC 64/1(53). This draft marked a significant change, and one made in response to the frustrations of 1952. JIC papers were to have a new format, with the conclusion placed at the beginning of the paper, rather than at the end.

As a result, one of the first things readers saw was the conclusion "that it is unlikely that the Soviet Union will deliberately precipitate a general war by attacking the West during 1953," with a caveat that this possibility of conflict could not be excluded. The "main risk" of general war in 1953 were Soviet actions "known to entail risks of general war; or from genuine miscalculations or errors of conduct on either side, or from accidental occurrences."¹⁵²

While war could still be brought about in a number of ways, JIC 64(53) and its later revisions were explicitly concerned with the "likelihood of war resulting from action by the Soviet bloc." The paper stated unequivocally that "Western actions may involve risks of war," but it was assumed the "West will proceed with caution." DEA officials concerns about US decision-making, a point so often raised in correspondence and in committee, did not appear in JIC papers going forward.

The new "Current Risks" paper also spent more ink than earlier iterations in describing why the calculation of risk was so complex. In noted the "difficulties of obtaining intelligence on the Soviet bloc," a challenge enhanced by the difficulty in estimating how Soviet leaders themselves might "weigh a situation and choose between alternatives." The JIC considered Communist doctrine, Soviet statements, and intelligence and published statistics on Soviet capabilities. But all three sources of information, they determined, were ultimately "unsatisfactory."¹⁵³

Going forward, this appreciation and those that followed gave much more consideration to External Affairs' position that the Soviets would not make a deliberate choice for war. The paper clearly stated that "on the basis of capabilities alone, general war in 1953 would thus very probably appear to the Soviet Union as an uncertain gamble, with very serious risks that the Soviet Union would suffer extensive damage, and the possibility that the Soviet system itself might be destroyed."[154]

The real threat, the paper stressed, was not a deliberate Soviet resort to war but a mistake. The Soviets had miscalculated, badly, in Berlin and in Korea. And it was possible that they might make a miscalculation again. The document's strong statement of the risk of miscalculation or misunderstanding was considered an achievement in DEA, for it "gives the reader a clearer idea of where the risk of war lies."[155]

The "Current Risks" paper was expected to "to remove the impression" given to readers of earlier estimates "that the Soviet Union had a great deal to gain and little to lose in a general war." But in place of the caricature of a bloodthirsty Soviet Union champing at the bit for global military operations was the "obvious but not unimportant concept of human fallibility" and the idea that leaders who did not want general war could bring one on by accident.[156]

The World Turns

A month after the "Current Risks" paper was completed, the world changed again. In March 1953, Joseph Stalin died. Five months later, the Soviets exploded their own hydrogen bomb, demonstrating that they were capable of waging not only nuclear but thermonuclear war. The Canadians began their revision of their appreciation of the risks of war, as did their allies.[157]

Canadian thinking in mid-1953 mirrored the conclusions of the British JIC's "Likelihood of General War with the Soviet Union up to the End of 1955" (JIC (53)79 (Final))[158] While acknowledging Stalin's death and the thermonuclear explosion, the UK JIC downgraded the likelihood of war, writing that the Soviet Government "will be more cautious in the conduct of their cold-war struggle against the West."[159] The "Soviet Government still wish to avoid starting a general war."[160]

The Canadians agreed, if for slightly different reasons. The new Canadian "Current Risks" paper concluded that it might appear to the Soviets that "time is on their side, in the sense that their capabilities (especially in the nuclear field) will increase, while Western military development and unity will continue to be impeded by political and economic strains." This was "an added reason why the likelihood of deliberate war during at least the coming year seems remote."[161]

With the Soviets keeping up with atomic developments, Moscow might estimate that the "balance of power in the long term must be favourable to themselves." The Soviet leadership would work to break the unity of the West and increase its influence around the world, but not with recourse to war. The "likelihood of a general conflict in the immediate future," the Canadians judged, "is remote."[162] In February 1954, the British and Canadian assessments were echoed by a US Special National Intelligence Estimate (SNIE11-54) that concluded "Communist rulers will continue to consider general war a hazardous gamble" that would result in widespread destruction in the USSR and perhaps the collapse of the whole Soviet system.

The world, in the eyes of the American, British, and Canadian intelligence communities, had settled into a Cold War. Intelligence appreciations in all three countries had supplemented their studies of what the Soviet Union would do in a general war to assessing whether the Soviet Union would launch such a war. As the UK JIC put it in 1953, NATO and the Soviet Union were reaching "the point when either side could destroy the other and when war might well result in the annihilation of both," and that "neither will risk a deliberate war and neither will allow itself to be drawn into war by a process of 'chain reaction' in a time of crisis."[163]

General nuclear war would serve no state's goals. And yet, the British paper continued, the very elements that had made war so undesirable had significant consequences: "As the atomic power of both sides grows, so will the temptation to strike the first blow, and that this will increase the dangers inherent in any such crisis."[164] Nuclear armament and improving delivery capabilities made war unwanted, perhaps even unlikely, but it raised the stakes of a war to an existential level. The potential for such a general war — general war that the Canadians believed would only come by miscalculation and mistake — meant Canadian intelligence officials had a new task: to identify, and if possible prevent, any such miscalculation.

PART 2

Indications of War, 1954–1966

4

The Origins of Indications Intelligence

In the early days of the Korean War, Canada's Joint Intelligence Sub-Committee (JISC) recommended two possible methods for tracking any change in the likelihood of war. The method that was ultimately accepted (and described in the previous chapter) was a series of papers, or appreciations, titled "Imminence of War."

The JISC's preferred option, however, was to develop a system for tracking indications intelligence. Instead of a regular appreciation, this would instead be a method of tracking and cataloguing specific indicators that war might be imminent. The Americans had an advanced indications intelligence system, and the British had a much less-developed version. The American system was premised on a series of "check lists" — that is, a list of things to watch for that, if observed, might indicate preparations for an attack. The items on such a checklist or "indicator list" developed over the Cold War, but they could include observations of the recall of reserves and mobilization of troops, the movement of forces out of regular barracks areas, the readiness of aircraft, and any of the other steps the Soviet Union would have to take before waging war.

In the JISC's 1950 plan, the services' intelligence directorates would track, and then forward, "any items of information which might indicate new trends or developments having significance in relation to the imminence of war."[1] JIS could then prepare "periodic, consolidated lists of these items, add any remarks or recommendations they might wish to make and forward them for the consideration" of the JIC at regular meetings. But in 1950, the Canadian JIC rejected the idea. A few years later, however, the search for indications of war would become an important component of Canada's efforts to determine whether the Cold War was turning hot.

The development of indications intelligence in Canada was connected to and built on the shoulders of the American indications system. In fact, as will be evident in the next chapter, Canada's indications intelligence system was purposefully integrated and inseparable from the American and British systems. To understand what developed in Canada, it is essential to understand the origins of the indications rooms and Watch Committee in the United States.

US Origins, 1948–1950

Amid the Berlin Blockade in 1948, President Harry Truman received a swirl of competing reports seeking to identify Stalin's goals and what the Soviet Union might do next. "Who," he asked, "is keeping track of all these indications?" While the story may well be apocryphal, 1948 seems to mark the origins of "indications intelligence."[2]

The beginning of indications intelligence is perhaps more closely connected to the period after the March 1948 coup in Czechoslovakia and in the weeks before the blockade, when British intelligence analysts passed on a "check list" of indicators they had developed as a means of assessing Soviet intentions in East Germany.[3] The coup in Prague had led both British and American analysts to look for signs the Red Army was moving to seize Berlin. While the checklist was a British tool shared with the Americans, it seems that American officials then developed a much lengthier list of 112 different indicators. They passed this list on to the JIC (London) which, after trimming down the list of indicators to eighty-one, approved its own paper on the subject "Indications of Russian Preparedness for War."[4]

In early 1949, State Department officials suggested maintaining an ad hoc committee as a Watch Committee "to form a pool for interdepartmental consideration of Soviet intentions for war."[5] The CIA resisted the idea because this was the Agency's task.[6]

While no formal "Watch Committee" was created then, there was some movement to ensure communication of indications intelligence between agencies in late 1949. Member agencies of the Intelligence Advisory Committee (IAC) were asked to designate two members of their staffs as "Check List officers" to "follow evidence bearing on the various indicators in the Check List." The IAC's hope was that the newly appointed Check List officers would "form, ex officio, an informal ad hoc 'network'" that would meet regularly to consider and report on Soviet intentions.[7] Fundamentally, this network was — in Director of Central Intelligence R. H. Hillenkoetter's words — to "provide timely warning, through the use of certain indicators, of impending Soviet military action in the *near* future."[8]

By January 1950, however, the Department of the Army had determined that the Check List Group was not enough.[9] The Army proposed that the Department of State's proposal for the establishment of a Watch Committee be reconsidered.[10]

In anticipation of an upcoming debate over the meaning and value of indications intelligence, Hillenkoetter noted that the name "Check List Group" conveyed "connotation of merely a collection and file" system and so "Watch Committee" was more appropriate.[11] The State Department supported this idea, arguing that a committee was required not simply to exchange information but to provide "a mechanism whereby all such items of information be juxtaposed, compared with each other, discussed, and jointly evaluated by the members." The value of such a committee was that it would ensure a joint effort was made to answer one critical question: "What are the proper and significant categories of information (indicators) having a bearing on Soviet intentions to make war in the near future?"[12]

An operating procedure for a Watch Committee was drafted in February and March of 1950, "for the purpose of providing timely warning of Soviet military action"[13] and a charter for the Watch Committee was being negotiated when North Korean tanks crossed the 38th parallel in June 1950.[14] By November 1950, the Watch Committee had established its "Watch Room" in a closed area of the CIA's Que Building. It was staffed twenty-four hours a day, seven days a week, by a representative who could communicate via teletype with representatives from other agencies.[15]

In autumn 1950, this existing Watch Committee was disbanded and its efforts fused with the US Army Joint Indications Intelligence Committee. The IAC formally established a new Watch Committee with a mission "to collect, evaluate, analyze and report indications of Soviet-Communist intentions of hostile action and it is responsible for issuing a weekly report on Indications of Soviet-Communist Intention of Hostile Action." Going forward, this Watch Committee was "the intelligence body charged with the responsibility of alerting the US Government of Soviet-Communist intention to initiate war."[16]

The early years of Watch Committee work in the US were revealing. The need to operate across departments and agencies was recognized as essential, but it was also difficult to achieve in practice. Those looking for indications intelligence had to consider how far forward they should look: were they preparing estimates or situation reports? And if they were only to report on the current situation, how far back should they look to identify trends and change?

The early days in the US also saw creeping concern that indications intelligence would be subsumed by an instinct to graph, chart, or otherwise mechanically track intelligence. But how else might a watch committee track and measure indications? Officials, especially those in the State Department, worried that any attempt at "selection, formulation, and approval" of so-called "indicators" of Soviet intentions "might lead to a mechanical handling of the watching process." At the same time, they recognized the value of lists for making the "watching process in general 'more systematic.'"[17] The Canadians would share these concerns as they learned more about the US system.

United Kingdom and Canada (1950–1953)

The development of indications intelligence in Canada and the United Kingdom proceeded on a much smaller scale and at a much slower pace than in the United States.

In 1950, the JIC (London) began its regular "Review of the Situation Round the Soviet and Satellite Perimeter," what would come to be known as the "Perimeter Review." This would later become the "Weekly Review of Current Intelligence" discussed below. The weekly review had four primary purposes, but the first was to "identify and evaluate immediately any indicators of Soviet preparedness for war."[18] Thus, as the historian of the JIC, Michael Goodman, has pointed out, the review "included a warning function, something which the JIC would be repeatedly accused of failing to perform effectively."[19] Indeed, as we will see below, this criticism came from allies, too, especially Washington.

By the end of 1951, the Canadian process (if it bears the name) for considering indications intelligence was roughly similar to the British: any crucial intelligence, "including indications of attack" were to be reported at the weekly JIC meeting, and if thought necessary, an emergency meeting of the JIC could be called. This was considered adequate.[20]

In early 1952, the directorate of air intelligence pushed for change. The director suggested that an "organization should be set up to collate and evaluate" any indicators of war, or if no central organization was created, then one service intelligence agency should be given the responsibility. If the agency revised sufficient indicators, they would alert the JIC, who would in turn alert the Chiefs of Staff.[21]

Between 1951 and 1953, there had been discussions in the JIC and elsewhere as to whether Canada should establish a "War Room," but such a room's function was ambiguous and vague. In May 1953, there was finally discussion of just what function a "War Room" would service in peacetime. A paper prepared for the JIC suggested that the "main intelligence requirement is for arrangements to ensure that information concerning indications of war is centrally collated and displayed."[22] The room, then would be an "Indications of War" room for intelligence use in the Department of National Defence.

A Model for Americans and Canadians (1953–1954)

Separate visits by American and Canadian intelligence officials to US Air Force facilities served as a major impetus for the establishment of a central "indications center" and "indications room" in Washington and Ottawa, respectively.

There is no evidence that Canadian officials knew much about the development of the American Watch Committee and indications system until their visit to USAF facilities in 1953 (described below). They would later learn some of this history from their American allies, and the American system developed in this period had important ramifications for Canadian developments.

Complaints about the US Watch Committee led to a search for new solutions in Washington in 1952. The CIA, sensing a shift in Soviet tactics toward political and economic warfare, urged the Watch Committee to move beyond its military-focused legacy and extend "indications coverage to include the economic, industrial, and political fields."[23]

The issue of tracking indications remained, however. One senior CIA official thought it was time to use "a mechanical device for keeping track of indicators" and displaying the indicators visually. He had been partly inspired by a visit to the US Air Defence Command at Colorado Springs where he had seen the Air Force's "indications board" — a wall-mounted display of indications intelligence. In keeping with the existing concerns about mechanical assessments, he thought the "board alone was incipiently dangerous," and that the key was well-trained people.[24]

A 1953 National Security Council (NSC) report detailing defence and intelligence programs 1953 advised the president that the Watch Committee had made improvements but that "current information on the Soviet Orbit is partial and inadequate. Accordingly, conclusions concerning Soviet and Communist intentions to initiate hostilities at any given time must be tentative generalizations drawn from inadequate evidence." The report stated starkly that there existed "*no guarantee that intelligence will be able to give adequate warning of attack prior to actual detection of hostile formations.*"[25]

By the end of the year, the top echelons of the CIA were concerned that the Watch Committee had not adapted to the new Cold War. In October, Director of Central Intelligence (DCI) Walter Bedell Smith told the IAC that the world had changed since the outbreak of the Korean War. Now the "probabilities of economic and political aggression, at least for the next few years, overshadow the possibility of military aggression." No longer was "the disposition and movement of troops the only vital question" and the Watch Committee needed to adapt. The DCI proposed the establishment of a high-level committee to examine the issue and nominated Huntington "Ting" Sheldon as the CIA representative.[26]

Sheldon would chair the Ad Hoc IAC Committee (Watch), called the "Sheldon Committee," in an effort to adapt the US watch system. The Sheldon Committee's deliberations were thorough and lengthy, ranging from 1953 to '54. All the IAC agencies participated fully, knowing that the outcome might well, as one analyst put it, "affect future balances of bureaucratic power within the intelligence community."[27] The Sheldon Committee visited Colorado Springs and saw the "elaborate command post and warning center" there. In its final report the committee recommended the establishment of a worldwide indications centre modelled on the Air Defence Command at Colorado Springs.[28]

The Sheldon Committee's work coincided with another significant change in Washington. In October 1953, President Eisenhower signed NSC 162/2, establishing a new Basic National Security Policy for the United States. The policy required, and NSC 162/2 directed, the development and maintenance of an "intelligence system capable of . . . [c]ollecting and analyzing indications of hostile intentions that would give maximum prior warning of possible aggression or subversion in any area of the world."[29] For the first time, the "watch function," was considered "a major intelligence objective."[30]

The year 1954 then saw the establishment of a centralized official Watch Committee (as part of the IAC) and the development of the National Indications Center. This was the end of the beginning, rather than the beginning of the end of the US watch function. It would continue to evolve. Only months after the terms of reference had been established for the Watch Committee, CIA officials pointed out that they needed more information, and not only about the enemy. To provide effective "warning of hostile action," watchers must not only have intelligence regarding their adversary, but also have "knowledge of US or allied operations." Without knowing what action the US and its allies were taking abroad, there was bound to be "false warning" that could be "seriously misconstrued (in either direction)."[31] This was a contentious issue that made it all the way to the president and the NSC. It was also an issue that the Canadians of External Affairs had worried about in the "Imminence of War" discussions: that American action could lead to Soviet reaction.

Ultimately, the NSC agreed to "make fully available to the IAC Watch Committee all significant information and intelligence pertinent to its mission and function . . . without restriction because of source, policy or operational sensitivity." It was to be kept informed of all "significant diplomat, political, military, or other courses of action by the U.S.,"[32] with the president serving as final arbiter in case of disagreement. The US NIC, then, was privy to information not only about hostile action but also about American action abroad. The Joint Chiefs of Staffs' sensitivity about protecting war plans was assuaged, but operational actions were to be passed to the Watch Committee. This would have important ramifications for future co-operation with allies.

Also in 1954, a Special National Intelligence Estimate (SNIE 11-8-54) assessed that the US watch system could expect to provide "as much as six months and not less than 30 days warning of Soviet preparations for a full-scale ground, sea, and air attack in the event of prior mobilization." This amount of warning time was expected to shrink quickly in the coming years. The US was almost entirely dependent on radar and forward observation stations. Having been stymied by the Soviet counterespionage system, the US had no "adequate penetrations of the Soviet Bloc." By 1957, the estimate warned, there may be "only a few hours or in some cases no specific warning, other than that provided by early warning radar" in case of attack.[33] In an effort to keep the warning window open, all IAC committee members signed a memorandum warning of "serious gaps" in US intelligence of the Soviet

Union, especially "in relation to our ability to determine the capabilities of the Soviet Union to launch nuclear attack against the US," and called for the use of "aerial reconnaissance and photography."[34]

By the end of 1954, the US intelligence organizations had overcome bureaucratic infighting to establish a watch and indications system with access to all source intelligence and information about US operations abroad. In a bid to keep open the rapidly closing warning window, they were preparing to develop new methods of intelligence collection.

It is a curious quirk of history that both American and Canadian visits to USAF facilities sparked a new phase in indications intelligence. In early 1953, members of the Canadian Joint Intelligence Staff visited the USAF Indications of War Room and Command Post. They learned that the USAF directorate of Intelligence had established its own section to deal exclusively with "indications of war" to obtain "all possible early indications of any impending Soviet attack." The JIS staff, impressed by what they saw, urged the JIC to run a "small-scale trial" of a similar effort in Canada to "determine the possibilities of a scheme which was both original and interesting in itself, and possibly of extreme potential importance to the defence of Canada."[35]

The JIC's members responded with mixed enthusiasm in March 1953, with the representatives of the director of naval intelligence (DNI) and director of military intelligence (DMI) the least enthusiastic. The DMI's representative noted that "the amount of original Canadian intelligence" was so limited that any Canadian effort would be of limited value. He assumed that "US co-operation with Canada in this field was questionable."[36] Ivor Bowen of the JIB, however, thought the United States would be willing to co-operate with Canada on any issue related to the defence of North America. Director of Scientific Intelligence A. J. Langley warned that the "difficulty of obtaining intelligence of any type" was so considerable that anything that might "increase our knowledge of the USSR and its possible intentions should be thoroughly explored."[37]

A spring 1953 visit to the USAF Indications Room seems to have influenced both the DNI and DMI officials. They warned, however, that the American project was an "elaborate one which we should not attempt to parallel." Still, the DMI representative suggested that Canada should consider "establishing exchange arrangements with the US" in the indications field.[38] The RCAF representative, who was far more enthusiastic, emphasized the value of the information the US authorities "appeared prepared to provide us." Group Captain Edwards told the JIC, "We should attempt to obtain this material as it was the essence of all the intelligence obtained by the US intelligence agencies."[39]

Bowen, again, spoke out strongly for co-operation with the Americans in this field. He thought it essential to establish routines for transmitting intelligence, because in a true crisis there remained "the likelihood that, at the critical time, the US authorities would be so occupied that they would overlook keeping us informed."[40] Bowen's argument, that routines and habits of intelligence sharing were crucially important to ensure Canada received information from the US in times of crisis, would play an important role in shaping Canada's approach to indications intelligence going forward.

No decision was made on a Canadian indications program in the spring or summer of 1953 as JIC representatives investigated the American system along "individual channels."[41] By the end of the year, General Foulkes, chair of the Chiefs of Staff, showed "considerable interest" in the idea, and was especially attracted to the idea of an "intelligence briefing room" and exchange and liaison arrangements with the United States.[42] On the CSC's directions, the JIC "undert[ook] a project concerned with 'indications intelligence.'"[43]

The JIS prepared a lengthy memorandum titled "The 'Indications' Project," JIC 89(53) of December 8, 1953.[44] It proposed that every research officer in each of the intelligence directorates and agencies be issued a "master list of indicators." When, in the course of his work, the officer noted any item concerning a subject on the list, he would enter the information on a specially prepared index card and send it on to the JIS marked "urgent." The JIS would screen all incoming cards and prepare a periodical report for the JIC and, if necessary, the CSC. According to the initial plan, the JIS would request researchers to make two copies of each itemized card, one for use in Ottawa and one to be dispatched to the indications room in Washington. The cards received by the JIS for Canadian use would be filed until methods for "visual presentation" of the data were settled upon.[45]

Attached to JIC 89(53) were two master lists of indicators, one entitled "Possible Indicators of Increased Soviet Preparedness for War" and another listing the "Indicators of the Imminence of the Outbreak of War or of Attack on North America." These were lengthy lists detailing hundreds of indicators. Also attached was a template that could be printed on 5 x 8 inch filing cards that the JIS would provide all agencies (if the plan were approved).[46]

Discussion of JIC 89(53) revealed continued suspicion and skepticism of indications intelligence in the JIC. DMI representatives pointed out the "lack of original Canadian sources." They suggested that the delay in receiving, let alone evaluating, intelligence from the US, along with the duplication of work would make a Canadian effort "ineffective."[47] George Glazebrook of External Affairs warned that any Canadian effort would grow to be much more work than expected. But despite a host of concerns, G. G. Crean, the JIC chair, thought the JIC should "go ahead with its Indications Project and thus be prepared to handle any information received from the US National Indications Room in the future."[48] The JIC adopted JIC 89(53) on December 22, 1953.

In March 1954, Crean visited Air Defense Command (ADC) at Colorado Springs to see the indications intelligence project directed by Brigadier-General Woodbury M. Burgess. This was separate from the USAF indications room other JIC members had seen in Washington, DC, but it was the project that had inspired the Sheldon Committee during its contemporaneous work.

Crean noticed that the intelligence staff at the ADC took every item they had evaluated as an "indication" and represented it on a wall-mounted board against an appropriate indicator. Various colours on the board represented the degree to which indications intelligence showed an increased readiness for war: "if there are enough indications plugged in against a particular indicator it will change its colour from yellow to red to black." After six months the board was photographed, and a new board is started, thus achieving what had been described in some quarters in Washington as "memory in depth." Burgess conceded to Crean that his system had certain weaknesses. It was, for instance, "extremely hard to represent visually a political or propaganda situation." It was much easier, however, to represent, visually, increased capabilities of the Soviet armed forces and certain physical items like new airfield construction. On the board, however, "no particular weight was given to any individual 'indication.'"[49]

Crean reported on two principal weakness he saw in the ADC system. In the first place, it simply "does not seem possible to represent by a plug on a board a given political situation and, indeed, a board only lends itself to representing a physical fact."[50] Second, the system whereby indicators were added to a board, seemed to limit "a continuous system of revaluation of given items of intelligence." Indicators might continue to pile up, but not be re-evaluated. The "system could lead to the ridiculous situation where the entire board turned black in colour, thus showing that a war should take place, but one might well discover that war did not take place because, of course, the board cannot reflect in the final analysis Soviet intentions." Crean echoed the "undesirability," previously voiced by American and Canadian officials, of "falling back too heavily on mechanical aids to intelligence." Before he left the US, Crean met with both Sheldon, who was in the midst of his study, and Park Armstrong of the State Department. Neither of them thought the Air Force's project a "satisfactory method for dealing with the problem of war."[51]

Crean briefed the JIC on his report and told his colleagues that his feelings had not changed: it was "impossible to reduce all items of intelligence to some mechanical system." Nonetheless, he suggested the JIS proceed with establishing its list of indicators and filing systems to be ready for when liaison arrangements were made with the United States.[52] In the spring of 1954, the JIC continued to consider how it might establish an indications project while the JIS reconsidered JIC 89(53).

Bowen, in a March JIC meeting, urged that plans for any indications project should stress the importance of speed. He wanted any procedural documents to be clear that "items of urgent importance should be processed rapidly and, if necessary, discussed at special meetings of the Committee."[53] There may be occasions when it was not wise to wait until the next regular meeting to discuss an indication of war.

By April, the JIC was finally prepared to begin its indications project on a trial basis starting in May. The key component of this trial program was a weekly briefing for the JIC on important "items of current intelligence." The JIS would hold a pre-briefing meeting on Wednesday mornings and then brief the JIC that afternoon, submitting a weekly summary of information bearing on "subjects covered in the lists of 'indicators.'"[54] The JIC would discuss and agree, forming what they called (using the British parlance) "a form of 'perimeter review'" for the chair of the Chiefs of Staff (CCOS) who would be briefed on the Thursday.[55]

A few months after the Canadians established their indications project, the Sheldon Committee reached its final conclusions. The Canadians learned of the significant changes in the US Watch Committee and the establishment of a twenty-person Indications Center.[56] Even before the changes inspired by the Sheldon Committee and NSC 162/2, the Canadians received some copies of both the Watch Committee's report and its special intelligence supplement. The reports, however, were passed directly between American and Canadian cognate partners, for instance the US Army G-2 to the DMI, and the supplement from NSA to Communications Branch, National Research Council (CBNRC).

Now that the Canadians had their own indications project, and the US Watch Committee had expanded with the establishment of the NIC, these products became more important. Crean wrote to Allen Dulles, the newest director of central intelligence, to make sure, first of all, that the US allowed the distribution of these reports to the full Canadian JIC (that is beyond their initial recipients) and also hoped for more copies.[57]

Dulles kicked the can down the road, noting that the establishment of the NIC had led the US to re-examine "the entire dissemination of the Report and Supplement." He provided Crean with information about the NIC and invited him to visit.[58] This was the first hint that, just as the Canadians were establishing their own system for exchanging indications intelligence with the United States, changes in the US would make that exchange more difficult.

At the same time as Crean was asking Dulles about the exchange of the Watch Committee reports, he was growing concerned about the exchange of intelligence in a crisis.[59] When "C," the head of the UK's Secret Intelligence Service (SIS), Sir John Sinclair, visited Ottawa in the autumn of 1954, Crean raised this matter with him.

Crean pointed out that Canada received a significant flow of intelligence from the United States through COMINT channels only. The communications intelligence (COMINT), or signals intelligence, relationship between Canada and the United States (and the United Kingdom) was so deep that this was the one area in which Canada received a regular and direct flow of intelligence information. The extent of the information received through these channels raised concerns for Crean, because he realized that Canada frequently received information from the United States via COMINT channels that it did not receive from any other US source. The quantity of COMINT information, in a roundabout way, caused Crean to worry that the exchange of other intelligence information and analysis between Canada and the United States, and especially between Ottawa and Washington, was quite thin.

Crean was worried that, in a crisis, the United States might choose to act on intelligence information that had not otherwise been sent to Ottawa. He gave the example of air defence: Canada's Air Defence Command at St. Hubert, Quebec, was linked with the American command at Colorado Springs. It seemed possible, even likely, that Colorado Springs might call an air defence alert "without the J.I.C. ever receiving the intelligence information upon which the 'alert' was based."⁶⁰ Crean was clearly concerned that there was no channel for passing time-sensitive intelligence of a non-COMINT nature between national capitals.

It was a matter of "considerable importance," Crean told C, that Canada receive this information "so that we could make our own assessment before operational units were made ready for combat."⁶¹ Crean understood that Canada was already receiving "a great deal of important highly classified information" but much of it was not of an urgent character. It now seemed possible that Canada might "not receive a 'hot' piece of information which might lead to a state of 'alert.'"⁶²

This seemed to pique C's interest. He urged Crean to write to his counterpart, Sir Patrick Dean, chair of the JIC (London). Crean sent a letter to Dean, to be passed "by hand of officer only," asking Dean how he viewed the operation of the US system, and how London "would yourselves act with respect to the Ottawa J.I.C. in the event of receiving 'hot information'" in London from non-COMINT sources. Crean intimated that he thought that if the UK JIC were to receive information that led it to hold a "crash" meeting — that is an emergency, unscheduled meeting — it would be appropriate to also send along that piece of intelligence to Ottawa immediately, even before the meeting ended. If there was information "which would indicate that we are on the brink of war," Crean wrote, our systems "should be geared to exchange such information without having to wait for our respective Chiefs of Staff or Governments to inform the other."⁶³ Dean wrote back to say the British had not considered these points, and "will now do so as soon as possible."⁶⁴

Crean had just described, in brief but in principle, what would over the coming years develop into the Tripartite Intelligence Alerts Agreement. The road to agreement would be a slow and meandering one, but the idea of such a system would receive a major boost from the British in the weeks after Crean sent his letter to Dean.

5

The Tripartite Intelligence Alerts Agreement

In December 1954, NATO adopted a new strategy that relied heavily on nuclear weapons. The new strategy raised thorny questions about who would make the decision to launch nuclear weapons, and the British, with the Canadians, scrambled to find a way into the American nuclear decision-making process. The main effort lay in coordinating national and international indications intelligence programs, which led directly to the Tripartite Intelligence Alerts Agreement of 1957.

In early 1954, the NATO allies embarked on a study to support the development of a new strategy "in light of the effect of new weapons." The resulting strategy document adopted at the December NATO Ministerial meeting, MC 48, was based on the assumption that "Soviet aggression will take the form of a surprise atomic attack aimed at the sudden destruction of NATO's atomic capability."[1] To prepare for this possibility, MC 48 directed NATO authorities to "plan and make preparations on the assumption that atomic and thermo-nuclear weapons will be used by the NATO forces from the outset" in any future major war.[2]

In the lead-up to the December Ministerial meeting, British foreign secretary Anthony Eden feared that the allies might consider "the difficult question of the authority for Saceur to use nuclear weapons."[3] There was, in fact, nothing in MC 48 that would allow NATO's Supreme Allied Commander, Europe (SACEUR) to use such weapons on his own authority. Yet in 1954, NATO's Standing Group had also written a paper detailing a proposed series of operational alerts which would delegate specific powers to commanders upon the declaration of different stages. Eden and his officials were concerned by the draft alert system (which they seem to have mistakenly believed had been approved), which made "it theoretically possible for NATO Commanders to begin a thermo-nuclear defensive war on their own authority." According to the British reasoning, NATO might adopt, via MC 48 and the NATO alerts system, a system that would create "great political difficulty." If Ministers were asked in the House, they would have "to admit that circumstances existed under which atomic warfare could be launched without governmental sanction."[4] The British, unwilling to "abdicate their responsibility on so grave an issue as this,"[5] requested a meeting on the periphery of the Ministerial meeting with Secretary of State John Foster Dulles and invited the Canadian secretary of state for External Affairs, Lester B. Pearson, to join.[6]

On December 16, Dulles, Eden, and Pearson, along with advisers, met to discuss Eden's concerns.[7] During the meeting, in discussion over just how SACEUR would come to be authorized to employ atomic weapons, Dulles said that the "three or four governments who would carry the main load in war"[8] — he obviously intended to include Canada among these — might try to find a formula; and he hoped that discussions would be held outside the council.[9] None of the records of the meeting identify any specific agreement to coordinate an intelligence indication system, and none mention "intelligence alerts," as the phrase was not yet in use in 1954. Nonetheless, this was the crucial conversation that would begin the diplomacy that led to the implementation of the Tripartite Intelligence Alerts Agreement. Based on later references to the meeting, it is clear that Dulles was reiterating earlier US pledges to Canada and the United Kingdom to consult before use of atomic weapons.[10] Following the logic of US strategy — that those weapons would only be used if a Soviet attack seemed imminent — there seems to have been some suggestion of the three establishing a system to communicate any indication of impending hostilities.

A few days after the meeting, Eden followed up with Pearson, alone. Eden wished to once again "express his anxiety over the steps which should now be taken to work out 'alert' procedures by which action could be coordinated in an emergency." (Eden used "alert" in the sense of an operational alert.) He told Pearson that he was going to ask Sir Norman Brook, the Cabinet secretary, to think about the problem and then discuss with Washington and Ottawa "in the hope that the three governments could agree on plans." Pearson told Eden that the Canadians had already "worked out some technical arrangements with the United States in regard to 'alerts' and emergency action" for continental defence, and that this might offer a way forward.[11]

Injecting Words of Caution

Eden wasted little time following up. The JIC (London) met on December 23, 1954, and the chair, Dean, explained that, in light of the Paris discussions and MC 48, it was "necessary at the earliest possible stage to examine the machinery whereby an agreed U.S./U.K./Canadian evaluation of urgent indicator intelligence could be reached and passed to the highest political levels in all three countries."[12] After the holidays, on January 4, a "high level meeting in the Cabinet Office" led to the UK JIC being tasked with studying a "system of evaluating urgent indicator intelligence."[13] Dean cabled G. G. "Bill" Crean, the chair of Canada's Joint Intelligence Committee, to tell him Eden had put in motion a program to draw up requirements for more "expeditious handling" of "indicator intelligence," and "linking up what you might call our indicator centre with corresponding organisations in Ottawa and Washington."[14]

Before the British could consider linking up centres, however, they needed to carefully consider their own indications and watch system. The British system, built around the pre-existing schedule of weekly meetings, was very similar to the early 1950s set-up in Canada. In standing procedure, any and all "significant intelligence" items were reviewed on Tuesdays by the heads of sections meeting in their regular place, the Joint Intelligence Map Room, on the fourth floor of the Ministry of Defence. The product of this effort, the "Weekly Review of Current Intelligence," was then considered by directors of intelligence at the Thursday meeting of the Joint Intelligence Committee before being passed to the Chiefs of Staff and the ministers.[15] There were provisions for urgent intelligence received both during and after working hours, but the British system was "not at present designed to meet a situation in which a surprise attack develops in a matter of hours."[16]

At a JIC meeting in early January meant to fully examine the current practice, Ralph Murray of the Foreign Office questioned whether the existing machinery "was capable of operating fast enough under the circumstances envisaged by the latest thoughts on global strategy." In the worst case, he noted, warning of an attack might precede an attack itself by only thirty minutes. London might likely get more time; several hours of warning, perhaps, and in more favourable circumstances, "a period of mounting political tension extending over days or even weeks." A brigadier from the War Office agreed that the current system was unlikely to operate "really rapidly in an emergency."[17] After business hours, the War Office staffed a Duty Officer but not an intelligence officer who could respond and evaluate a warning. The RAF, on the other hand, had an intelligence officer on duty all day and night, but the RAF system was meant to deal with "an attack of which the first warning would be the appearance of hostile aircraft on UK radar screens."[18]

Indeed, a Soviet attack in which complete surprise was achieved would "probably first be noticed on an Allied radar screen." In such a situation, with an attack in the offing, the British would consider this to be an "operational matter" and so there would be no need for an intelligence alert.[19] In a case where warning of attack was received with less than an hour, the "question of obtaining a Ministerial decision as a result of such a warning was, anyway, entirely academic."[20]

The British could imagine other scenarios, however, where there might be an advanced "indicator" (which they defined, using the same root, as "a measure which may be a significant indication of Soviet precautions for war"). There were three possible categories here: Soviet preparations meant to bring "operational units and facilities to immediate readiness for war," those indicating that "the whole nation [was] being prepared for war in the very near future," or those "indicating long term preparation for war."[21]

The JIC (London) agreed that they required "accelerated evaluation machinery" which could enable Ministers to make decisions "within a few hours" in case indicators appeared. The machinery could be initiated, perhaps, by the "issue of a codeword." They decided it should be possible for directors of intelligence at their Thursday JIC meeting "or in between meetings if necessary" to be authorized to call an "intelligence alert" by which "pre-planned arrangements should come into force" — i.e., the "Heads of Russian Sections," officials responsible for the Soviet Union — would remain in office day or night, ready to evaluate and analyze.[22] Ultimately, the British decided to avoid a codeword system as the group was so small, but they did implement a series of procedures by which special meetings could be called, offices staffed, and notice passed on to ministers.[23] (They would suggest a codeword for the tripartite system developed years later.)

It was for such a time that warning was available — not Soviet bombers on radar screens, but indications of preparation for war — that the British procedure was meant to evaluate. This desire seemed reasonable at face value. But discussions in the JIC make clear just why the British believed they needed to understand and *evaluate* early warning. These warnings would mean nuclear war.

In discussion, the JIC agreed that one of the most important decisions was *when* such "warning of attack" would be passed on — "expressed laterally" — to officials outside of the "intelligence machine." The crucial question was whether it could be "emphatically ensured" that passing on an "intelligence alert" did not lead to "precipitate operational action" before ministers had so authorized.[24] Unlike operational alerts, the "calling of an 'intelligence alert'" was to be a "purely a precautionary measure."[25] It was in these conversations in London that the notion of an "intelligence alert," separate from the operational alerts previously discussed, was coined.

British concern with indications intelligence and the need to differentiate intelligence alerts from operational alerts was directly connected to co-operation and interaction with the United States. The British knew that the Americans had built their own "Indications Center," and it was precisely this that was so important to the British. The British needed their own system and machinery for evaluating indications intelligence if they "wished the Americans to allow [them] to maintain a working liaison with their Indications Centre." And the British desired this very much, specifically "in order that we might inject words of caution into its [Washington's] counsels."[26]

The Canadians, for their part, had sought to build relationships and reach agreements with the Americans meant to constrain any nuclear impulse in Washington until the Canadians could weigh in and agree on US decisions.[27] As Crean, chair of the Canadian JIC, explained to Dean, chair of the UK JIC, what the Canadians were "really concerned about is whether we shall receive expeditiously 'hot' items of intelligence, which might lead to an 'alert,' before we actually receive the 'alert.'"[28] The Canadians did not want to be told by the president, let alone told by the US Air Defence Command that an "alert" was necessary, "without slightest knowledge of the information upon which their decision has been based." Because an operational alert was so tightly coupled with the authority for nuclear war, the Canadians needed to find a role for themselves in the process leading to an alert. Crean, of course, as chair of the Canadian JIC, had his own parochial interests, too. For the JIC to have any real meaning and use in a crisis, it should "have the opportunity of making an assessment of all information which might lead to an 'alert' before the 'alert' actually takes place." This was an important issue for JIC on its own, but also a larger problem, "one of principle involving the Government."[29]

For the Canadians, it was clear that the US Air Defence Command had been calling operational alerts (which, because of coordinated air defence systems resulted in alerts at Air Defence Command in St. Hubert, Quebec) "without telling us precisely the information which has led them to take such action."[30] This was a problem strictly in the sense of continental defence. The adoption of MC 48 and NATO's plans for an alert system magnified the issue for the Canadians, just as it had for Eden and the British. As Crean wrote in January 1955, it was not the "alert" system itself that was of greatest consequence. No matter how good the system was for implementing operational alerts, the "procedure depends fundamentally on an assessment of the information which leads to an 'alert.'"[31] It was now "more than ever important" that JIC (Ottawa) have from both London and Washington "by the most rapid means possible all information of a kind which might lead to an 'alert' so that an intelligence assessment of the information may be made here." Without any such arrangements, "we shall, of course, be at the mercy of the operational commands" in the UK and the US.[32] NATO, similarly, would be "at the mercy of... the United States and United Kingdom."[33] If, however, Britain, the United States, and Canada could reach an agreement "tripartitely," it would "go a long way to ensure that NATO commands receive properly evaluated intelligence from national staffs."[34] Crean's point, implicit but important, was that Canada should not leave these decisions up to others, even its closest allies.

At the 1955 Conference of Commonwealth Prime Ministers in late January and early February 1955, Eden passed on to Pearson the results of the UK Working Party that Sir Norman Brook had been chairing, and in particular a paper on "Possible Stages of Action when Indications of Major Russian Aggression are Received in Good Time." The paper set out "the stages which ought to be completed if time allowed" if there were evidence of impending Soviet aggression specifically against the NATO area.[35]

In the first stage described by the British, a proposed "London Indicator Centre" (what would be, the paper assumed, an adapted version of the current Joint Intelligence Committee organization) would receive a piece of information that might mean the USSR was making preparations for war. The London Indicator Centre would then contact its counterparts in Ottawa and Washington, ensuring "'indicator' experts of the United Kingdom, United States and Canada are fully in touch with each other on the matter."[36] To be effective, new physical communications systems, especially across the Atlantic, would need to be used. In addition, to discuss the information between the three nations' indications centres, relevant ministers, secretaries, and prime ministers and president would be consulted. If the three governments came to the "conclusion that war probably cannot be averted," the British would approach Commonwealth governments while the British and Americans, with Canadian agreement, would approach the French — thus allowing the three Standing Group nations to approach the rest of NATO. The British paper noted that if the French "fail to make up their minds" the British and Americans would go straight to NATO without the French. The result of any approach to NATO would be a meeting of the North Atlantic Council and the approval of NATO's operational "alert" measures.[37]

The Canadian JIC not only found the British ideas acceptable, but advised the Chiefs of Staff Committee that "unless Canada takes part in some arrangement of the kind suggested, the Canadian Government may not receive the intelligence information on which to base conclusions regarding NATO alerts, answers to urgent requests concerned with Strategic Air Command action and with continental defence or other arrangements, or decisions required in other situations."[38] The chair of the Chiefs of Staff Committee took the issue to the minister of National Defence, who agreed that "an indicator system as suggested in the United Kingdom paper should be set up in Ottawa for the exchange and evaluation of 'Hot' information with both the United Kingdom and the United States."[39]

The Canadians had some quibbles with details. The British paper was limited to major Soviet aggression against the NATO area. The Canadians thought there was a good case to include "the whole question of aggressive action by all possible enemies." This was partially a function of the fact that Canada would serve as a base for SAC operations against the Soviet Union even in a war begun elsewhere, say in Asia. The Canadians also warned the British to scrap the reference to Commonwealth countries.[40]

Ottawa relayed its interest in the British paper and suggestions for its improvement back to Dean, in London. The Canadians in London were instructed to make explicit that "the consequences of failing to take part in such a procedure might leave us [Canada] in the position that the Government might have to take a decision without full knowledge upon which such a decision should be based," and that Canada would "be left in a worse position on the exchange of intelligence than we are at the present time."[41] Crean noted the Canadian interest in adapting the procedure to a global scope, and in particular Canada's interest in "possible communist aggression anywhere, including possible Chinese communist aggression."⁴² Were the British limiting their scope for tactical reasons, given US sensitivity to discussing Asia?

Dean explained that, indeed, the focus on NATO was tactical: that the British would start with NATO and then consider adapting the system to cover the Middle East and Asia. He thought that if the paper was "presented to the Americans as something springing directly, as it in fact did, from the last Ministerial meeting in Paris, it should be possible to restrict discussion to the NATO angle."⁴³ What was more, Dean said, the NATO context was actually the most complicated of all global scenarios, given the role and authority (however unclear) of the SACEUR. If the three could find a solution for the NATO context, surely they could solve any other problem later. The Canadians and British were concerned about how they would staff any such organization to implement the procedure, as both ran rather threadbare intelligence establishments relative to the US. They hoped to solve that problem later (while assuring each other that not too many extra officers would be required to set up such a system). Dean agreed to scrap the reference to the Commonwealth countries while not, "of course, regard this as limiting our right to consult and inform Commonwealth Governments."⁴⁴

Dean next considered how to approach Washington. He worried that a joint approach to the Americans would imply that London and Ottawa had come to conclusions without the Americans. Instead, he proposed that the British and Canadian ambassadors make separate approaches to John Foster Dulles. The British ambassador would present the corrected paper seen by the Canadians, and both the ambassadors would suggest the time had come to follow up on the discussions in Paris.⁴⁵

At this stage, Dean assumed the result of these approaches would be a political-military discussion involving British Ambassador Roger Makins, head of the British Joint Staff Mission (BJSM) in Washington General John Whitely, and officials from the CIA and the Pentagon. Makins could present the British paper as a basis for discussion and also mention that the Canadians and British had taken advantage of the Commonwealth Conference to discuss intelligence matters.⁴⁶

The Canadians ultimately agreed with Dean's limitation to the NATO area, allowing that the first goal should be a "practical and speedy procedure preliminary to and in support of the NATO alert system" upon which could later be built "a parallel procedure for other areas of the world."⁴⁷ They agreed that the British Ambassador would go first, and that Arnold Heeney, the Canadian ambassador, would follow up (he did so on April 29, 1955).[48] Optimistically, Dean hoped to have discussions before the next North Atlantic Council ministerial meeting.[49] In fact, discussions would continue for years.

A Canadian Indications Room

Throughout the first half of 1955, the US Watch Committee had been "materially stepped up as a result of a constantly increasing danger of devastating damage to the U.S. in the event major aggression caught us flat-footed."[50] Nonetheless, there was still pessimism about the ability of the US to gain warning of a Soviet attack. Estimates of growing Soviet air capabilities made the National Security Council "somewhat more pessimistic than we were last year regarding our ability to give advance intelligence warning of surprise air attack."[51] If the Soviets were to attempt a major surprise attack from forward bases, it might be detected with a general warning of several days and a specific warning of a day or less, eighteen to twenty-four hours. A smaller attack, if carefully planned, could be launched in 1955 "with no assurance of specific advance warning to U.S. Intelligence (apart from that provided by early warning radar)."[52] The race for indications continued: Soviet security and counter-intelligence measures meant there was no improvement in human intelligence collection capabilities within the Soviet Bloc — a place next to impossible to run spies — but the US had seen "considerable improvement in the collection of intelligence data through technological means . . . together with increasing use of aerial reconnaissance."[53]

Also in 1955, JIC members in Ottawa remained ambiguous about the value of indications intelligence. In February, the DNI, for instance, remained skeptical of paying "too close attention to 'indications' intelligence factors which can be fed into a machine to produce a mechanical answer" which "may well be misleading." An "indications of war display" would only be effective if "the enemy is planning a deliberate war for an established date, when the progressive build up in armaments and in political tension could be watched and a danger point agreed on." What Canada needed in peacetime, he thought (somewhat contradictorily), was "a well-equipped map-room with an adequate supply of relevant and up-to-date charts and diagrams."[54]

The DDNI, for his part, told the DNI that he did not think it was the right time to decide on an indications room for Canada. He knew the JIC (London) was studying the issue but was "undecided as to whether a list of indications is of much value" except in a gradual build up like the DNI had noted. Now, however, the Americans had an indications room "in actual operation" and since information in the Canadian room would "largely derive from UK and US sources," Canada should postpone discussion until "the US room can be seen in operation and the UK make up their minds."[55]

The US room was, of course, up and running and it was impressive to outside observers. Just as the British were reviewing their set-up, the Canadians were trying to learn more about the US National Indications Center that had been in operation since January 24, 1955.[56] The NIC was essentially the staff of the Watch Committee. While the USAF had kept their "Indications Board," there was no other indications staff in Washington, DC — the NIC was it.[57]

The Canadian JIB Liaison officer in Washington visited the NIC and was briefed by its Director, J. J. Hitchcock.[58] Unlike in Ottawa and London, space did not seem to be an issue for the NIC. It occupied a suite in the basement of the Pentagon, which included a conference and briefing room for the Watch Committee, a reception room, and offices for the director and clerical staff, including cubicles for representatives from all the various US intelligence agencies assigned to the NIC. The salaries of representatives were paid for by their respective service, and "Rations and Quarters" were provided by the Air Force, even though the NIC itself came under control of the IAC.

The NIC itself received information from all agencies as well as ticker tape updates from the Associated Press and the United States government's Foreign Broadcast Information Service (FBIS). Certain incoming cables from collectors in the field were also automatically copied to the NIC. The service officers were charged with maintaining links to their home agencies so they could receive assistance in evaluating incoming material. The links also ensured they received any raw intelligence that should have been sent to them in the NIC but was not.

The officers worked twenty-four hours a day to evaluate incoming material, and the NIC could call an unscheduled Watch Committee meeting in a "tense" situation. The Watch Committee then would agree "on a joint interpretation of events to be disseminated to the proper authorities."[59] During the First Taiwan Straits Crisis of February 1955, in which the US Navy evacuated Chinese nationalists from the Tachen islands, the Watch Committee had been called and agreed to a joint appreciation in two hours.

The NIC, ostensibly, was to be responsible for monitoring indications intelligence from around the world to study long-term indications of war. But in its early stages, Hitchcock explained, it was impossible to begin a wholesale indications program, and so the NIC was focusing on two crisis points: conflict between the People's Republic of China and the Republic of China over islands in the Taiwan Strait; and Berlin. This would help the NIC establish an efficient system, and starting so small was safe, Hitchcock said, as "it is a general appreciation that a major war is unlikely to occur in the near future."[60]

The JIB officer noted that the Watch Committee's room in the suite was "elaborately equipped with visual aids." Hitchcock assured him, however, that he was more concerned about collecting, evaluating, and disseminating information than "developing any mechanical mathematical or other alleged foolproof system for measuring the temperature of international tension." Hitchcock's major problem, he said, was getting the co-operating agencies to pass him only the "right kind" of material, rather than "swamping him with irrelevant documents." He hoped that field collection would improve, because attachés and others were not currently looking for indications intelligence — or at least not the right kind, as he saw it.[61]

Hitchcock himself disparaged the regular Watch Committee report, which he thought simply a survey and "not a barometer of the imminence of war or an indications report at all."[62] He hoped to convince the Watch Committee to include an indications annex that might one day overtake the survey itself. This was news to the Canadians who received the Watch Report. It was obvious that the exchange of regular intelligence products would not be the best source for providing indications of war. These things would be detected and then made manifest in an emergency or "crash" meeting of the Watch Committee — and Canada did not receive reports of these meetings. Just as Crean had written to Dean about "crash" meetings of the JIC (London), it was obvious that what really mattered for understanding US indications detection was information about "crash" meetings in the Pentagon. Hitchcock could not provide such information on his own authority. He suggested that Canada could only receive such warning if Allen Dulles and Crean could reach a new agreement, one that would provide the NIC with instruction to release material not currently sent to Ottawa.[63]

In March, the chair of the Chiefs of Staff asked the JIC to describe just how a Canadian system for handling indications intelligence would work.[64] Less than a week later, the JIC had approved a new paper, JIC 135/1(55), "Indications Intelligence," advising of the JIC's conviction that an indications room should be established in Ottawa.[65] The paper sketched out how such a system would operate: the new Canadian Indications Room would be responsible for passing intelligence received from allies to the directorates of Intelligence for evaluation, and, if necessary, call a "crash" meeting of the JIC. There was no twenty-four-hour watch suggested, as the JIC assumed none would be necessary unless there existed an obvious escalation of tension. Nonetheless, an indications room was necessary, they argued, as "Canada must develop its opinions as to the significance"[66] of items of intelligence that the US and UK believed worthy of action.

The JIC expected that Canada could avoid having to "duplicate the scanning of the bulk of United States and United Kingdom source material" and focus on assessment or analysis. While both the US and UK were sensitive about "third nation" information — that is, information from another state — the Canadians assumed that in any new system, they could expect to see third-nation information if Washington or London thought the intelligence "to be of indications significance."[67]

The system, as envisioned in JIC 135/1(55), would require consideration of only a "small volume" of information. Contradictorily, and cutting against the Canadian assumptions that the primary work would be done by the other allies, the JIC noted the "increasing probability that an indication will turn up in Canadian source material."[68] This was likely an allusion to Canada's responsibility for collecting signals intelligence in the Soviet Arctic.[69] This all added up to mean Canada would need its own system for detecting and referring indications intelligence it collected.

The JIC expected that the current "Hydra" system would solve the problem of communication. (For more on the Hydra communications hub, see Chapter 6.) The system had been in place for years, had agreed reservations on its use for specific users, and was "designed primarily to carry intelligence traffic." If the Hydra link in the UK at Government Communications Headquarters (GCHQ) was extended to the Ministry of Defence, and either the Hydra link at the National Security Agency (NSA) or the Canadian link at the Ottawa Wireless Station (located in Leitrim, just south of Ottawa) could be extended by line to the Pentagon, all three indications centres could be linked directly.[70]

Waiting for an American Response

The year ticked away with no response from the Americans to the British and Canadian overtures made in April 1955. In early July, UK foreign secretary Harold Macmillan and Patrick Dean visited New York and met with John

Foster Dulles. They asked American officials about the alerts issue. While Livingston Merchant of the State Department was "hopeful" the US might come to an agreement, a CIA official let on that the CIA "was not very favourably disposed."[71] A few weeks after the New York conversations, Makins checked with the State Department, who explained the delay had been caused by the slow response of the US permanent representative to NATO, George Perkins, who had been asked to comment on the British proposal.[72] Canadian intelligence officials like Crean continued to hear nothing about alerts when they co-operated with the American colleagues on other matters.[73]

Philip Uren, the Canadian liaison officer in Washington, asked Robert Amory, the deputy director of the Central Intelligence Agency, where things lay, but Amory knew nothing about even the initial "high level approach" by the ambassadors. After hearing from Uren about the proposed plan, Amory said he expected the answer would be "unfavourable," partially because of a Pentagon-CIA spat. Amory also criticized the way the British and Canadians had gone about achieving their goal — that is, by raising it on a government-to-government level. Amory blamed the "British tendency to carry matters to the highest level unnecessarily." Had Crean, as head of JIC, simply proposed the solution to Allen Dulles of the CIA, Amory said, "an effective liaison system with the NIC would now be in operation."[74]

As Amory came to understand the Canadian concern — that Ottawa might be left out of the analysis and decision-making process in Washington — he told Uren that the Watch Committee would never hold an emergency meeting on "a subject important to us [Canada]" without Amory personally informing Uren. And if the situation was "sufficiently serious," Amory said, he was "personally prepared to over-ride rules concerning Officials" and, by implication, tell Uren what Canada needed to know. If the Canadian JIC held a similar meeting, Amory said, he hoped he would be informed in kind, "as the Canadian action would effect [sic] his attitude to the problem in Washington."[75] The conversation is instructive, for it suggested the close relationship between Canadian and American intelligence officials. But it clearly relied on trust at the personal level. What could the Canadians expect with a different cast of characters? If Amory were absent? In a real crisis, would any American think of the Canada? The Canadians were seeking a system and a habit, rather than personal guarantees.

By October 1955, neither the British nor the Canadians had heard back from their approach in April. C. Burke Elbrick, the deputy assistant secretary of state for European Affairs, said that the matter was stuck up with Defense. All that the Canadians heard were "rumours and they are generally to the effect that the Pentagon does not like the tripartite scheme" probably because of the "usual conservative attitude of some military officers in relation to what they regard as sensitive intelligence."[76] While this may explain part of the delay, it seems that neither the Canadians nor the British understood the full backstory of the formation of the Watch Committee (and thus the NIC), let alone the theoretical powers of the NIC to be informed of US operations around the world.

The Canadians, like the British, had expected the discussion to move quickly after their first approach to the Americans in the spring of 1955. While Ottawa had an "intrinsic interest in obtaining tripartite agreement in alerts procedures," the Canadians also wanted to use discussions "as a point of departure for further talks on the broader questions of the circumstances under which nuclear weapons might be employed, tactically and strategically, not only in the NATO area but in any other part of the world."[77] In particular, they had thought the tripartite discussion would connect with separate efforts to seek an agreement with the US on a system of bilateral alerts regarding North American defence. They had also not given up their concerns about precipitate American action in Asia, which would almost certainly end up involving Canada given the integrated nature of North America's continental defences.

In late September 1955, in planning for regular high-level US-Canadian consultations, the Canadians considered whether to try and bundle these matters for discussion with the Americans, or to approach them individually.[78] Jules Léger, the USSEA, thought it "important to get on with" US-Canadian discussions regarding operational alerts in North America, "the exchange of indications intelligence on the Far East."[79] But he also did not want to "prejudice" the stalled tripartite system that the British had proposed, with Canadian support.

As the Canadians were deciding how to move, Admiral Arthur W. Radford, the chair of the US Joint Chiefs of Staff, told the Canadians that the Pentagon had already "turned down" the proposal for a tripartite agreement but not yet told the State Department. Radford said that the Joint Chiefs of Staff were reluctant to agree to any form of consultation with foreign powers — the word "consultation" is important. It was already hard enough, Radford said, to obtain "co-ordination inside the United States Governmental machine, in particular between the Pentagon and the Central Intelligence Agency."[80] Radford's comments raised a host of concerns, but one effect was for the DEA to suggest that the Canadians begin discussing a bilateral alert system with the US and seeing how the conversation developed from there.

As the Canadians planned to move forward on bilateral issues, the US replied to the British paper on tripartite indications. On November 18, 1955, British and Canadian embassy officials were called to the State Department, separately, and given an aide-mémoire.[81] This was a curious development because the Canadians knew that opinion within the US government was split. The Air Force and the CIA supported tripartite arrangements. However, the Army, Navy, and Joint Chiefs of Staff were opposed, and rumour had it the IAC had given a "unanimous negative answer to the proposal." Crean assumed that "somebody higher up the line modified the position taken by the IAC."[82] Amory of the CIA let on that he thought the IAC had not understood what the British and Canadians were asking for: IAC members had variously interpreted the British memorandum as a request for more intelligence sharing and consultation.

No matter the process that led to the aide-mémoire, Glazebrook (now at the Canadian embassy in Washington) observed that it was "much more encouraging than all the gossip indicated it would be." Despite the document's lack of clarity, it "seems to add up," Glazebrook thought, "to some kind of acceptance of the original United Kingdom proposal endorsed by us."[83] The American reply also suggested that discussions could move forward on a tripartite basis between the State Department and the British and Canadian embassies in Washington.[84]

The American aide-mémoire was a "rather confusing" document as read in London and Ottawa, seemingly hastily assembled. While it noted American concerns and errors in the British document, it also seemed to suffer from sloppy drafting.[85] The Canadian JIC considered the aide-mémoire paragraph by paragraph, and were put off by the very first paragraph that seemed to declare an American authority to defend Canada without consulting the Government of Canada.[86]

The greatest concern to the Canadians was that the US aide-mémoire suggested that the existing system for the exchange of intelligence was suitable. This was a sticking point for the Canadians. They were not convinced that the ad hoc arrangements that had been established for sharing intelligence across the border were "clearly established or expeditious."[87] This was important to the Canadians for both bilateral and trilateral procedures for intelligence warning. Canada had no "direct liaison" with either the Watch Committee or its Indications Center."[88] The aide-mémoire seemed to suggest the Americans thought there were effective procedures for getting in touch with Canadians in a crisis. However, what the Canadians really sought was to be able to see "the essential intelligence"[89] that the Americans were considering. What the Canadians wanted was a system of "direct contact" — including a direct line of communication — between Canadian and US intelligence (be it the NIC, Watch Committee, or IAC). The establishment of such a system, they expected, "should produce the assurance in a time of crisis."[90]

The Americans had clearly misunderstood parts of the British paper while the Canadians and British were less than enthusiastic about the US aide-mémoire. Although the Americans agreed to talks, just how to move forward was unclear. A simultaneous US-Canadian meeting and subsequent follow-up on continental defence issues would provide the solution.

Bilaterals and Trilaterals

Around the time the Canadians received the American *aide-mémoire*, they were considering how to approach the discussion with the US regarding bilateral alerts in support of North American continental defence. A Canada-US agreement signed in 1952 that allowed ministers to approve US overflights of Canadian territory was of "limited usefulness given interdependence of air defence." What was needed now, wrote Léger, was "an arrangement for the exchange and evaluation of strategic information of a kind which might lead to a decision to take emergency measures or even to go to war." Any such agreement would have to be accompanied by "a firm understanding of the necessity for consultation at the highest political levels of the two governments on the action to be taken as a result of that information."[91]

Ultimately, this boiled down to the need for the Government of Canada to ensure it had "the information it would need to arrive at independent conclusions in an emergency regarding the operation of the continental air defence system and the deployment into or over Canada of the Strategic Air Command."[92] This was a matter of continental defence, but the notion of continental defence and general war were largely indivisible.

Now that the Americans had responded to the British paper with their aide-mémoire, Léger thought it a "propitious" moment to raise the matter of alerts on a bilateral basis with the United States. The Canadians would keep the British in the loop by telling them they were going to discuss alerts with the Americans. But the Canadians would press for "a firm understanding"[93] on procedures in the air defence field and separate from the connection to the NATO system of alerts on which the British paper had been based.

As a starting point for the discussion with the US on bilateral alerts, the DEA drafted a formula of four points by which this process might work, and they shared it with the Americans. According to the proposed formula, if the US or Canadian intelligence authorities concluded that "there was a likelihood of hostilities occurring in which North America would likely be attacked," the Governments would "automatically pass to one another all relevant information," including background information and assessment. This would ensure that if consultations "at a higher level" were required, "Ministers would be fully in possession of the necessary facts." [94] This formula, the Canadians assumed, "might usefully be applied, and probably later, to the tripartite scheme."[95]

The formula, however, did not dispel the cloud of confusion in Washington. When Glazebrook tried out the bilateral formula on State Department officials on January 24, he found them on the defensive. The Americans — C. Burke Elbrick, Outerbridge Horsey, Park Armstrong, and H. E. Furnas — began pushing back by outlining the present exchange of "alert type" or "indicator" intelligence between the United States and Canada: The United States passed its Watch Committee reports to the Canadians immediately upon printing. The RCAF officers at Colorado Springs had access to intelligence, and a special telephone line linked the Joint Air Defence at Colorado Springs with Canadian Air Defence Command. The radar screens that would provide alert intelligence in the north were jointly operated, and the NSA and CBNRC exchanged intelligence. Where, the Americans asked, were the gaps?

Glazebrook sensed that the Americans believed the Canadians were asking "for a more complete exchange of intelligence."[96] He denied this immediately and recognized the misunderstanding — not only in the State Department, but no doubt this was the source of confusion in IAC, too. He explained that, "leaving aside the normal exchange of intelligence, there did not exist, in our opinion, a defined arrangement by which the United States and Canadian intelligence authorities could quickly correspond on an agreed channel and, where necessary, exchange views."[97]

Armstrong replied that if there was enough time for the Watch Committee to meet and appraise the situation, the results would be passed to Ottawa "by the quickest means." But this was the sticking point. Glazebrook noted that "the 'quickest means' were at the moment uncertain and not necessarily quick." The Americans just assumed they would pass the information to the "Canadian liaison officers."[98] By this, they must have meant Uren — but he was not on duty 24/7, and he also had no ready channel of communication to Ottawa.[99] Furthermore, as the Americans acknowledged, some types of intelligence could not be transmitted over regular channels. The State Department men seemed to recognize that there was not an effective system in place, and Glazebrook believed Armstrong would now champion the issue within the IAC. Armstrong promised to speak with Director of Central Intelligence Allen Dulles, and the Canadians would wait until State had spoken with the CIA. It seemed to Glazebrook that the State officials were seeking to leave the American military out of the process, since bringing in service officers "would mean endless comings and goings with the Pentagon."[100] Ultimately, the meeting served to identify "the bogey man lying behind the United States Aide Memoire on the tripartite scheme." If the Canadians could make more headway on the bilateral plan, "there may be some hope of sorting out the tripartite scheme later on."[101]

A month later, Crean travelled to Washington where he had several meetings each with Amory of the CIA and Park Armstrong of the State Department. Crean continued to make the case for a bilateral system between Canada and the US, pressing for a direct line between the NIC and the Canadians Indications Room. Ottawa, he told his interlocutors, was "anxious to eliminate from the system any built-in delays such as getting cypher operators or officers out of bed before a piece of information could be passed in either direction."[102]

Amory, who did not seem to have discussed the issue with his State Department colleagues, was less sanguine than the officials Glazebrook had met with a month earlier. He warned that the IAC was unlikely to accept the formula as it stood. The president, he said, would "almost inevitably initial it," indicating his initial agreement. But then the services will "see all sorts of objections and advise him differently."[103] Amory again advised that the direct link between the NIC and Canadian Indications Room should be dealt with as a matter for Crean and Allen Dulles on their own, to be treated as a "nuts and bolts" problem between their two offices rather than a government-wide matter (which would bring in the military in Washington).[104]

Armstrong, too, seemed to backtrack from the earlier meeting. He hypothesized about the difficult case where a "delicate item" of intelligence that might be "difficult to pass" along a communications channel that ended in another state. He urged the Canadians to increase the liaison staff, but Crean rejected this idea, not wanting to staff the Washington embassy with officers waiting around for an emergency. Crean explained that he knew there might be information from "double agents and that type of thing"[105] that the US could not pass, and "obviously, one would not put on the link what one freely wished to trade."[106]

The most crucial lesson Crean learned from his trip was Amory's observation that the formula as it stood now seemed to combine the issue of "consultation between governments" on one hand, and on the other, "the problem of exchanging information during a period of crisis which might lead to a Declaration of an Alert by either government."[107] Amory asked: Did the Canadians expect to receive the Strategic Air Command's operational plans? (Amory's question, likely unbeknownst to Crean, mirrored the earlier discussion in the US about the relationship between US operations and indications intelligence.) Amory suggested that if the Canadians could separate these two issues, there may be room to move forward. But "consultation" was the main point of contention. It would ultimately stand in the way of easy agreement on exchange of information, as the United States government was unlikely "to bind itself under any formula which required it to consult another government before taking action itself."[108] This would have important implications for the tripartite approach, too.

By April 1956, the Canadians decided that the informal discussions with the Americans on the bilateral issues had essentially run their course. In March, the Canadian director of air intelligence met with the US Air Force director of intelligence Brigadier General John Samford. The American warned he was "not optimistic that early agreement would be reached to exchange indications." The problem was that within the US Watch Committee itself there were significant problems, including "considerable reticence" by agencies to "table all indications available." Several agencies preferred only to table their evaluation of indications, rather than the data itself. Facing "this difficulty at home," Samford "could not see how a free exchange of indications with Canada was possible."[109] The Canadians were not sure whether to take these comments at face value or as a hint that a request would be rejected.

Nonetheless, the Canadians decided they would make their formal approach on the bilateral issue.[110] In the Cabinet Defence Committee, Pearson and the Minister of National Defence Ralph Campney argued that the "main purpose" of such an exchange was "to ensure adequate consultation before a recommendation was made in either country for the calling of an [operational] Alert." Such an alert was synonymous with imminent war; in the event an alert was called, the United States would "evacuate the principal government activities from Washington." There was, the Cabinet Defence Committee agreed, "very little that was more important than the actual calling of an Alert." As a result, "everything should be done to ensure that this step was taken only if the necessity was clearly demonstrated."[111] Ultimately, the Canadians were seeking to build a system to ensure that the Government of Canada was a) "in a position to decide whether an alert should be called" and b) to ensure that Ottawa was "consulted by the United States Government."[112] While the ministers' statements dealt exclusively with bilateral Canadian-American relations, the Canadian thinking paralleled the tripartite issue and mirrored the earlier British thinking about inserting wisdom into American counsels.

The Canadians took Amory's advice to heart and drafted two formal letters, splitting the issues: one suggesting an agreement on the exchange of intelligence, and the other on consultation.[113] The Canadians were prepared to argue that the United States should consult with them because Canada was willing to agree to joint operational control of air defence in North America.[114] (Intriguingly, as will be seen, the Canadians did not make the same push for "consultation" when it came time to negotiate the tripartite agreement.) The letters progressed through the Cabinet Defence Committee, and Heeney presented the letters to John Foster Dulles in May 1956.[115]

The Canadians learned their letter on the exchange of intelligence had been approved relatively quickly, but discussion on the consultation issue dragged on inside the US governmental machine.[116] While they were waiting for a response, Dean approached the Canadians about taking up trilateral issues again.[117] The Canadians would have preferred if the bilateral problem were solved first, but ultimately decided it was better not to delay the tripartite issue because it was unclear when the US would respond to the bilateral letters. More importantly, as Glazebrook noted, the bilateral discussions both he and Crean had with US officials had "removed some serious misunderstandings which had clearly existed in the minds of United States officials"[118] and should help move the tripartite discussion along.

In the summer of 1956, Dean visited the National Indications Center and discussed alerts in Washington. The NIC's director explained to Dean that the "Americans had been rather frightened by our original approach [in spring 1955], because it had included suggestions for high-level policy discussions as well as exchanges of information through intelligence channels."[119] Upon his return to Washington, Dean, clearly influenced by both the Canadian experience and his visit to the NIC, suggested to Crean that the British and Canadians approach the Americans for tripartite discussion "on the exchange of intelligence only."[120]

It seems the matter was dropped by all governments in August 1956. The obvious reason is the Suez Crisis of 1956. Dean played a significant role in the US-UK minuet before the crisis. But in the aftermath of the Suez Crisis, the need for such a system became even more pressing for the British. Harold Macmillan became the British prime minister and US-UK relations experienced a significant rapprochement, including plans for the US basing of Thor missiles in the UK.[121] Macmillan seems to have pushed hard for an agreement, and he used key meetings with Eisenhower in 1957 to force movement in the US bureaucracy. Crean knew that the British were willing to move forward on an intelligence-only basis but expected they may wish to return to the issue of "consultations" later. As the British were going to allow US bases in the UK, Crean expected "they might have a strong point and one which is in some measure comparable to our own position with respect to continental alerts."[122] The upshot of the Suez Crisis then, or at least the following rapprochement, was a stronger British interest in, and case for, a formal agreement to exchange indications intelligence.

In February 1957, Crean travelled to Washington for more meetings with Allen Dulles and other intelligence officials. In his meeting with Dulles, Crean asked about the tripartite issue and Dulles was unwilling to commit himself, saying only that he saw "no reason why the present time would be unsatisfactory" for resuming talks.[123]

In a meeting with Charles P. Cabell, deputy director of the CIA, Crean suggested "an informal tripartite talk confined to civilians, for example, Dean, Allen Dulles, and himself." Cabell, however, was resistant. He said that the British and Americans had their own agreement, as did the Canadian and Americans. There was "[n]o necessity to complete the triangle in a single document."[124] Crean disagreed, pointing out that the US-Canadian agreement focused on continental defence only. Cabell responded that the United States did not interpret the agreement that way. Crean himself seems to have wondered whether it was all looked after under present arrangements, including the informal expansion offered by Americans. But, he asked, "are informal arrangements likely to work in a crisis?"[125] The trip to Washington only raised more questions.

Following his trip, Crean drafted a new formula to serve as the basis for a tripartite discussion. It was based on the US-Canadian bilateral intelligence-sharing formula, but applied to the NATO area.[126] If any of the three governments received information and concluded "there was a likelihood of hostilities occurring in the NATO area . . . it will keep the others informed."[127] The intelligence authority that reached such a conclusion, be it IAC or one of the JICs, "will pass to one another automatically and by the most expeditious means all intelligence information"[128] used to reach the conclusion, as well as background information and assessments.

Crean passed his draft to the high commissioner in London, Norman Robertson, who in turned would pass it to Dean. Robertson's comments on the draft formula are instructive, for they preview future Canadian concerns with the proposed system. The formula Crean sent was restricted (as had been the British working paper) to aggression "occurring in the NATO area." Robertson thought this was problematic and wondered what would happen if there was information "suggesting that the Chinese Communists were preparing an attack on Formosa or even the off-shore islands." Either scenario might result in a Soviet attack on North America "as a result of the operation of USA Defence arrangements with nationalist China on the one hand and the Soviet-Chinese Communist Alliance on the other."[129] Furthermore, the British action at Suez, "without prior notification to the American or ourselves, illustrates the actuality of this problem. It is not inconceivable that such unilateral action by one or other party could if repeated lead to hostilities which might spread to the NATO area." Ultimately, Robertson conceded, "perhaps there is no satisfactory cure for the problem" other than trying to consolidate "co-operation and confidence between gov[ernmen]ts."[130]

Dean received the new Canadian formula and also Crean's report of his meeting with Cabell — including Crean's assessment that the "CIA were very dubious about the desirability or necessity of a tripartite agreement."[131] Dean, who thought he had reached agreement with Dulles was "rather put out" by this "shift in American thinking."[132] Dean's political masters, too, were "disturbed" and "very anxious to get on as fast as possible with establishing an agreed speedy three-cornered arrangement for exchanging intelligence."[133] The ministers agreed that the issue should be raised, and officially entered on the agenda, when Macmillan and Selwyn Lloyd met with Eisenhower and John Foster Dulles at Bermuda in March 1957. As the British had begun their quest for a tripartite arrangement "largely on the suggestion of Foster Dulles himself," they no doubt expected that if the issue was raised at the highest levels they could cut through "misunderstanding" of lower levels of the United States government.[134]

Dean proposed that Crean and Allen Dulles meet immediately following the Bermuda conference.[135] The Canadians liked this idea because their earlier informal discussions in Washington had helped them prepare their formula and letters related to bilateral arrangements. Still, the Canadians agreed among themselves that this was "certainly not our proposal."[136] They were ready to let the British take the lead, associating themselves with any meeting that came out of the British request.[137] For his part, General Foulkes was relieved that the British would not be sending an air intelligence officer, because otherwise he would have to send an officer and "no doubt that the Pentagon would insist on having three intelligence representatives."[138]

But Foulkes wanted to be sure the discussion kept to intelligence exchange rather than consultation. Radford had told Foulkes he was "not at all enthusiastic about United Kingdom – United States consultation on alerts." Foulkes thought that any effort to expand the tripartite discussion to include consultation, rather than intelligence exchange, would negatively affect bilateral US-Canadian relations. The Pentagon, if "faced with trying to arrange a suitable mechanism for consultation on a tripartite basis they might raise so many difficulties that they may call off the arrangements for consultation on a bilateral basis."[139]

Given Cabell's comments, Robert Bryce, the clerk of the Privy Council, thought the meeting might be useless. Still, he could not see "any objection to an informal discussion" between the three intelligence directors, if "only to discover precisely how effectively the two bilateral agreements may be expected to work." He endeavoured to find Crean a seat on the government plane headed to Bermuda.[140] The British were successful in having tripartite alerts added to the agenda for Bermuda, but did not expect any decisions by Eisenhower or Dulles beyond confirming that representatives of the three states should meet again in Washington to discuss things further.[141] Crean then found a seat on the British plane returning from Bermuda to Washington, DC, where the Canadian and British representatives would meet with Dulles.

The British, for their part, thought the Canadian efforts had "set a useful precedent for a tripartite procedure" and had taken on board the Canadian suggestions of focusing only on intelligence rather than consultation. The British committed to concentrating, "in the first place" on "agreed procedures for exchanging intelligence on Soviet intentions to attack the NATO area." They would leave consultations — what they explicitly referred to as "the question of the political decision to authorize the NATO military commanders to use nuclear weapons" for later settlement.[142]

Building a Canadian Indications Room, Part 1

During the tripartite diplomacy, the Joint Intelligence Committee had been giving attention to Canada's ability to handle indications intelligence. In November 1955, the Americans had provided their response to the initial British and Canadian approach in an *aide-mémoire*. Glazebrook, in Washington, had heard rumblings about the Ottawa JIC's plans to improve the Canadian Indications Centre. He thought the Americans would be watching these developments closely. Glazebrook knew that the Canadian indications effort was a "spare-time operation," with rotating staff who had little training. If the Americans were to realize this, "there would be a good deal of puzzlement here [in Washington] as to why we had made a fuss about the thing at all."[143] If the Canadians were to participate in a network of indications centres, they would need a properly functioning centre of their own in Ottawa.

Although the JIC had taken steps to try an indications project, the US aide-mémoire confirmed for the JIC that unless there existed "joint machinery ... to exchange 'hot' information" with the Americans, the "whole basis of political consultation with the US in an emergency would be jeopardized." This was a matter of "some urgency" and the Canadians agreed to put their "indications project" on a twenty-four-hour basis for a three-week trial basis beginning January 3, 1956.[144] Building on Amory's advice to keep the connections between the US and Canadian indications centres on a "nuts and bolts" level, Crean wrote a letter to Dulles suggesting the "existing link between N.S.A. and C.B.N.R.C." be used to connect indications centres.[145] Dulles then cabled A. J. Steele, the CIA representative at the US embassy in Ottawa, and agreed, saying that the terminal link for the US will be in the CIA, not in the

NIC.¹⁴⁶ (This was to connect to Cabell's office in the CIA, for Cabell was in charge of the Watch Committee.)

By May 1956, the JIC was convinced it was "essential to run a Joint Indications Room into which all Directorates and Departments represented on the J.I.C. will submit on a timely basis items which may lead to the opinion that war was imminent or in preparation."¹⁴⁷ Throughout the month, the Chiefs of Staff Committee discussed terms of reference for a Joint Indications Room (JIR), considered the challenge of passing British information to the US and vice versa, and made plans to staff and support, administratively, a JIR that was established that month.¹⁴⁸ In July, JIC established a routine for "action in event of special message from Washington." Including during off-duty hours, the routine essentially consisted of a lengthy list of who should call who to ensure a quick emergency meeting of the JIC.¹⁴⁹

By the end of 1956, the JIR was drafting a Weekly Indications Report, though its purpose was still debated. Bowen, from JIB, was pressing for "Indications" to be interpreted "in a broad sense to include developments which would have a significant bearing on the likelihood of war, e.g., to include changes of political leaning or military capabilities which would encourage or discourage parties to a dispute from the use of force."¹⁵⁰ Bowen, who seems to have given the most thought to the theory and purpose, rather than just the technical arrangements, of indications intelligence, was "firmly convinced that by far the most important task confronting the J.I.C. is that of keeping senior levels of the Government informed about the imminence of hostilities on the best possible and most current basis."¹⁵¹

Agreement

Ahead of the Bermuda conference, Macmillan wrote to Eisenhower to ensure that "Tripartite Alert Procedure" would be on the agenda for their meeting. In Bermuda, Macmillan and Eisenhower agreed that "[a]n effective machinery should be established for the rapid exchange of intelligence between the Governments of the United States, Canada and the United Kingdom on any sudden threat of Soviet aggression against the N.A.T.O. area. For this purpose a meeting between intelligence experts of the three Governments will be held in Washington immediately after the Bermuda Conference."¹⁵²

After flying back from Bermuda, Allen Dulles, Dean, and Crean, along with advisers, met in Washington on March 28, 1957, for the first substantive discussion on how to achieve a tripartite agreement.¹⁵³ Dean began the meeting by describing the Paris meeting in 1954 and noting that current arrangements were not tripartite. While the British "had their letter from Allen Dulles to Mr. [Alan] Crick," the UK's liaison to the CIA, the procedure was "not really adequate for an arrangement of such importance."[154] A tripartite arrangement, Dean went on, "should cover expeditious exchanges not only of information but also of assessments" (though he was careful to make clear he was in no way proposing tripartite agreed assessments). Dean presented the "draft formula," which was the Canadian formula from the bilateral arrangement, suitably adapted and with slight modifications made by the British. This was to serve as the basis of an agreement between all three states.

Crean made clear that he supported the British position and noted that the bilateral arrangements confused things: it was unclear to one ally what the other two knew. He mentioned that any tripartite arrangement would augment but not replace the existing bilateral systems, which now included "direct line communications from C.I.A." to the new Canadian Joint Indications Room. This was supplemented by liaison officers in Ottawa and Washington.

In a pointed interjection, Dulles said it might help if London had a "designated Indications Centre on the lines of those in Washington and Ottawa." Dean "undertook to look into this."[155] (Clearly, it was a good thing that Glazebrook had earlier pressed Ottawa to get to work on its own centre.) The meeting then shifted to discussion of how to physically pass intelligence and assessments among the three capitals. All agreed that "radio communications might be unreliable when most needed" and that intelligence should have its own channels, rather than having to compete with traffic along lines used by the services. Dean suggested that London might rent a channel in the new transatlantic cable, but that this was expensive; Crean suggested that Canada might pay half the cost. The details would have to wait.

Park Armstrong of the State Department pointed out that a "formal tripartite agreement" would be "breaking new ground" for the Department of State. He also worried about exclusion of other NATO allies. All the representatives agreed that informality was, in fact, helpful here: Crean and Dean both agreed that an exchange of letters between the Canadian and British ambassadors with the secretary of state would be all that was necessary.[156]

By April 2, both the British official level and the IAC had agreed to the proposed arrangements. The State Department suggested that London and Ottawa proceed to send their formal letters.[157] Léger, in Ottawa, was "favourably surprised by the speed and receptiveness of the United States officials to the United Kingdom/Canadian proposal," and assumed the speed was due to President Eisenhower's direction to Dulles to "review the exchange of intelligence between the United States, United Kingdom, and Canada."[158] The British foreign secretary, Selwyn Lloyd, approved the proposed agreements on April 8. Prime Minister Diefenbaker was shown the letter and had "no objection" by April 12, 1957.[159] The formal letters were given to given to Park Armstrong on April 16, 1957.[160]

Less than a month later, on May 6, H. E. Furnas of the State Department gave advanced, if unofficial, notice that the US Government would approve the letters, with one major change of wording: "a likelihood of hostilities immediately threatening the NATO area"[161] (the addition pertaining to immediacy). The British and Canadians also learned that the Americans would make their agreement contingent on an expectation the allies were operating their indications organizations on a twenty-four-hour basis (something that the Canadians assumed was "probably directed" at London where the British "do not maintain anything equivalent to our Joint Indications Room here or the National Indications Center in Washington").[162]

On May 8, Deputy Under Secretary Robert Murphy formally replied to both the British and Canadian ambassadors. On May 22 and May 31, the British wrote to the Canadians, and the Canadians replied to the British, respectively, "to complete the triangle."[163] All parties agreed that the "arrangement should not repeat not be registered with the UN."[164] The Tripartite Intelligence Alerts Agreement was in place.

6

The Alerts Agreement in Action

The Tripartite Intelligence Alerts Agreement had been agreed with only a vague sense of how it might work in practice. The most pressing issue after the agreement was finalized was to set up a communications system by which the three governments could, in fact, alert each other to indications of war. But substantive questions about the whole indications program were still being posed throughout the rest of 1957.

For instance, both the Canadians and British had received and read a copy of US NIE 11-3-57, "Probable Intelligence Warning of Soviet Attack on the US." The document raised eyebrows in Ottawa and London. It revealed that the Americans understood their own military and intelligence activities could trigger Soviet reactions that would look like indications of war.

In a vaguely phrased paragraph, the NIE noted that, in a crisis situation, the volume of intelligence reports could be expected to increase dramatically. Furthermore, in crises there "is also an increase in the number of reports from sources of known reliability, some of which sources come into play as a result of a crisis situation." This, the NIE explained, might include "[p]hotographic and electronic reconnaissance over Soviet controlled territory." It might also involve "[a]gents held in reserve for such a situation and equipped with special means of communications [that] could be activated."[1]

The reconnaissance was clearly a reference to overflights by the Americans' new high-altitude aircraft, the U-2. Increased activities of this type, and "in particular air penetrations, could have the effect of increasing tensions or even of provoking Soviet attack." Given the possible upshot of these actions, they would "probably require policy decisions."[2]

The director of Canada's JIB noted that the measures referred to in the NIE "would be subject to very strict security protection, both because of the nature of the job they are intended to perform and because of the political sensitivity surrounding their use." As a result, the information would be "controlled by code words and ... a very limited number of specially indoctrinated personnel would be involved."[3] These would be among the closest guarded secrets in the American intelligence community.

While Bowen had no doubt about the "willingness" of the Americans to "discuss such things in times of great crisis," he did question "the functioning of the machinery at such times if entirely new decisions have to be taken." As a result, Bowen suggested that the chair of the JIC work with Allen Dulles to ensure that "the staffs concerned will have the necessary authority to transmit to us information from these sources during times when the risks of war appear to be very great."[4]

Crean agreed and went even further, believing that "it would be most desirable if we were told of such operations prior to their taking place, especially since they might be of a provocative nature."[5] Here the Canadian concerns echoed the point in NIE 11-3-57 about the effect of US actions on the Soviet Union and the possibility of American operations resulting in Soviet responses that could be interpreted as indicators of preparation for war. The Canadians would pay close attention to this issue going forward, seeking to ensure that they were aware of the activities of "friendly forces," especially Strategic Air Command.[6]

Communications Issues

While the Tripartite Intelligence Alerts Agreement was completed in 1957, the three parties still needed a communications system by which they could meet their obligations under the agreement to exchange information. And although the idea for such an agreement had come at the behest of the British and the Canadians, the Americans were always one step ahead of their allies in implementing the agreement.

In October 1957, Dean and the British were "slightly embarrassed" when an American team showed up in London ready for technical discussions regarding the communications network required to operate the alert system. The British were simply not ready. Neither were the Canadians. The Canadians were invited to attend the discussion with the visiting Americans but had no one in London prepared to attend. Nor could they get someone from Ottawa to London in time.[7]

Despite being caught unready in October, one month later Dean was eager to gain quick agreement from all three parties on cipher equipment. He wrote a letter to Dulles and Crean suggesting that the primary link between the three parties be a recently laid transatlantic cable. The cable connection could be backed-up by a radio system. In normal times, Dean proposed, this cable channel would be used for ordinary diplomatic and intelligence telegrams, but in a crisis the system could be equipped with a "special switching device, with alarm facilities" that would clear the line for "exclusive Alert use" upon activation by Washington, Ottawa or London.[8]

Crean did not like this idea. It meant that any communication lines that were used for the transmission of information in regular (that is, non-crisis) time, would be taken over by the alert system in an emergency. This was unacceptable because the cable already carried "highly important intelligence which had not yet been dealt with by directorates."[9] Switching to exclusive use for intelligence alerts would, at the same time, cut down the overall flow of intelligence.

For the same reason, the Canadians also resisted using the existent Hydra system (although Hydra would, ultimately, be the main conduit for the TIAA communications system). "Hydra" was the name for the transatlantic communication system that had been built at Camp X in Oshawa, Ontario, in 1942 as a training facility for British and American covert agents. It had served as the main communications hub for British Security Coordination during the war and was the centre through which Ultra intelligence was shared between the three governments.[10] In the postwar world Hydra had been maintained as an important tripartite communications link. The Canadian JIC, Crean pointed out, remained "reliant on Hydra to obtain intelligence items rapidly from overseas." The Communications Branch of the National Research Council, Canada's signals intelligence agency (later Communications Security Establishment, CSE) used Hydra, too. If, in a crisis, Hydra were "given over" to Alert messages, "the individual items of intelligence which may be equally vital to us will not be able to pass if there is a radio blackout."[11] The Canadians preferred a system that would not be online all the time, for it would either lay idle or have to be used for something else.

In February 1958, under pressure from Canada's partners to agree to the British communications plan, Crean wrote to Dean and Dulles describing a set of problems "which I suspect arise only in Ottawa" and as a result "do not appear to have been taken into consideration when formulating your proposal."¹² The Canadian concern, ultimately, was that if any of the existing systems for transatlantic communications went "online" as the channel for alert communications, it could not be used for other purposes and would then limit the number of communications channels on which Ottawa received information.

Crean listed the four main Canadian requirements for transatlantic communications: They were, first, the "rapid and continuous passage of raw and finished codeword intelligence" between GCHQ and CBRNC. Second, the rapid exchange of assessments between JICs via the JIC liaison officers in Ottawa and London. Third, the rapid exchange of diplomatic reports from the High Commissioner in London back to Canada. Fourth, and new, was the rapid exchange of assessments on tripartite basis.[13]

To meet all these requirements, Canada had a tape relay centre at the Ottawa Wireless Station in Leitrim (the Canadians referred to the station simply as "Leitrim") equipped with a number of radio channels to the UK. The Canadians and British had also recently added a duplex cable circuit which strengthened the Hydra network. Canada used this system to exchange information with both the NSA and GCHQ, and to exchange British-Canadian diplomatic traffic. Canada had no other transatlantic circuits to achieve its four requirements (while the British and Americans did — they had a direct cable link between GCHQ and NSA).

If the transatlantic link was to go "on-line" for alert traffic, then GCHQ-CBNRC traffic, as well as communications between the Department of External Affairs and Canada House in London would be limited to exchange over radio, which might not work in a radio blackout. This was a drawback because the Canadian JIC relied on these exchanges for its intelligence. While Washington and London would still be able to exchange information via their transatlantic cable facilities, it would effectively leave Ottawa in the dark. No doubt the "scheme you propose looks quite satisfactory to you" in London or Washington, Crean appealed, but it would "leave us in a very awkward, and I believe unacceptable position."[14]

Crean urged his counterparts to "to take another hard look" at his suggestion of an "off-line system" that used the Canadian-developed Rockex cipher machine.[15] Alerts traffic would bear a "special top priority designation" that would see it passed ahead of all other traffic on the Canada-UK cable. The Rockex system would be slower, but everyone who used these systems knew that the biggest temporal challenge was not transmission of messages but assembling the necessary officials to meet in each capital after a message had been received. (The Canadians also pushed for Rockex instead of the American Sigtot equipment because Rockex was available in Canada and Canadians would not need spare parts.)[16]

Despite some grumbling in London, Dean said that the British were likely to accept the idea of off-line ciphers, and Tracey Barnes, the CIA representative in London, said the US was likely to accept too.[17] Dean responded formally to say that he agreed with the Canadian suggestion and that, he "on balance agree[s] with you that the delay of a few minutes in passing telegrams by the off-line system is acceptable."[18]

Crean, on the advice of Drake at CBNRC, also concluded that an off-line connection between CIA and Leitrim was the best answer for the US-Canadian link.[19] Lieutenant-Colonel Paul E. Amyot, the deputy director of signals in the Canadian Army, suggested that there be established a tie-in line from Leitrim to the JIR, and avoid working through CBNRC. A line terminating at Leitrim would also make it easier to resume communications "should circumstances suddenly force a change of venue upon J.I.C."[20]

In 1958, the "so-called direct line" to Ottawa from the CIA actually travelled via NSA to CBNRC and then on to the Joint Indications Room, requiring re-encipherment at both ends.[21] The Canadians and Americans met to discuss the establishment of a truly direct line from CIA to Leitrim. At the meeting, the Americans noted such a line would cost US$1,000 a month. They did not want cost to "hamper or delay" the establishment of an effective system, but they asked the Canadians to consider two separate options: A line from the US embassy in Washington to the JIR or Leitrim, or a line from CIA to the Canadian embassy in Washington. The Canadians pressed for their original plan — the direct line from CIA to Leitrim. While they did not let on to the Americans, they privately concluded that the higher cost was "well justified since in the long term we could look forward to a fair volume of current intelligence passing from the CIA direct to Ottawa."[22]

The Canadians also worried that the staff at both embassies was too small to handle the traffic, and the "trouble with any tie-in-and-switch arrangement is that in a crisis somebody might forget to turn the switch on."[23] On top of the risk of such human error, the embassy's intelligence and diplomatic traffic would have to compete, and working through the US embassy would also give the American embassy "control of the line" which "in certain circumstances" might be undesirable. "Economy at this stage would be false economy" and so if the Americans quibbled about the cost, the Canadians in Washington were to say that Canada would consider sharing the cost of the line, perhaps by paying for the portion of the line running from Leitrim to the border.[24]

In April 1958, representatives of all three parties met in Washington in an attempt to finally resolve all communication matters, including message procedures, tape procedures and supplies, cryptographic systems, and other requirements. The Americans agreed to use the standard operating procedures already employed by the British and Canadians, and a regular type of message heading and classification, with the goal of ensuring faster relay within capitals.

The allies agreed that an "ALE" prefix atop a message would serve as the symbol that the message was calling for, or responding to, an alert. (ALE, of course, being the first three letters of "alert".) Each state would have its own call-sign (LON and OTT for London and Ottawa, respectively, and WAS would be used by the Americans from either Washington, DC, or their alternate location outside the capital) indicating who had sent the message (i.e. ALE-LON, ALE-OTT, ALE-WAS for alert messages from London, Ottawa, or Washington, respectively). They would later establish a pattern whereby non-Alert messages could be sent, with a different prefix, such as JICOTT, JICLON, and CIAWAS. A message with prefix JICOTT, then, was a message from the Canadian Joint Intelligence Committee but of lesser importance than an ALE message.

The Canadians and British already had Rockex equipment, and the British would install three Rockex systems at each of the US sites and provide maintenance until US technicians, trained in Ottawa, were ready to staff their own systems.[25]

While the British agreed that these technical discussions must come first, they knew that next would come a "common doctrine for bringing into use of the system, its operational use, and so on," and began working on those issues.[26] After the communications issues were largely settled, plans were made for a tripartite meeting in June 1958. A month before, in May, CIA representatives met with Canadian and British JICLOs to discuss the implications of the alert system for the liaison officers, to consider "joint indications lists and a common philosophy of indications intelligence" and plans for a test of the communications system.[27] They achieved little and much was deferred until the June meeting.

How and When to Invoke the Agreement

The Canadians learned that Dean was under pressure from his government to achieve substantial progress at the June meeting.[28] The pressure, undoubtedly, stemmed from ongoing negotiations between Washington and London regarding an agreement on nuclear retaliation procedures that would govern the launch of US weapons in the UK.

In April 1958, Dean travelled to Washington and met with Robert Murphy to study "how procedures of the two Governments might [be] concerted for reaching a decision to respond to a Soviet attack by committing nuclear retaliatory forces to the attack from the United Kingdom."[29] In annex B of the agreement listing "Procedures Preceding Attack by United States Retaliatory Forces from the United Kingdom," the US side noted that on "receipt by NIC" of strategic warning indicating "an enemy is likely to launch an attack . . . the intelligence information and the evaluation thereof will have been passed to the Joint Intelligence Committee (London) and the Joint Intelligence Committee (Ottawa) pursuant to the Tripartite Alert procedure agreed to among the Governments of the United Kingdom, Canada and the United States."[30] The TIAA and nuclear retaliation procedures were flip sides of the same coin. The British, in their own internal communications in 1959, described the "Tripartite Alerts Agreement" as one of the agreements "which relate to the mechanics and procedures for using nuclear weapons."[31]

Given the practical and driving need to establish a system to support the Murphy-Dean agreement, the Canadians let Dean's people take the lead in drawing up a working paper that they would respond to, rather than drawing up their own.[32] Thus the British set the pace for the first major discussion of the tripartite system.

The British distributed their paper for use of the "Tripartite Alerts Communication System" in May. The paper suggested the system be used "at all times" for transmitting intelligence information between the three parties, including the British Red Book (a weekly intelligence survey), CIA comments on the Red Book, the BJSM weekly telegram to the UK minister of Defence, the US Watch Committee report, and so on. Dean expected this would keep the channel in "good working order" and the "operators practiced."[33] As for when the system was to be "brought into use for the main purpose"[34] — exchange of intelligence regarding a threat to the NATO area — the British made a series of suggestions: If any capital changed its own state of alert, and if this change was connected with "indications of Soviet bloc warlike intention," they should send an ALE message to its tripartite partners. Also, if what the British called their "special heads of section" called for a meeting to consider intelligence related to the NATO area, others would be alerted of the meeting and its subject.[35] A first message informing the partners should be sent and then followed, as soon as possible, with a more detailed description of intelligence available and "asking for information or opinions."[36]

At the June meeting, Amory of the CIA thought the British plans for passing so much information over the alert communications system was "excessive." He thought it should be restricted only to the US Watch Report and the Canadian and UK equivalents. Any discussion or comments could pass through normal channels.[37]

The meeting also demonstrated the inconsistencies in just what each party meant by the word "alert." The British paper had simply referred to "alerts," but the US officials pointed out they must have meant "intelligence alerts" to differentiate from military or operational alerts. The three states did not have the same system of intelligence alerts, and the Canadians and Americans did not have well-defined alert stages. They would both seek to conform to the British system as far as possible.[38] It was left unsettled, but the plan was to work for a "common nomenclature for stages of alert . . . to ensure that each party knows, for each stage of alert, exactly what it implies for the other two in terms of organisation and state of readiness."[39]

Amory proposed a Command Post Exercise–type test of the system in the fall to test delivery of "an agreed intelligence assessment to the policy levels of government." He suggested preparing fake intelligence.[40] The British and Canadians both tabled indicator lists (the American list having been recently approved by the IAC) that would form the basis of a common indicator list.[41]

To move forward, however, all the allies would need to have functioning indications centres. Here, the British did not have their act together. The Canadians were much further ahead, and of course the Americans already had a well-established centre. Before considering major debates over how to use the system that occurred in 1958, the next section examines the state of Canadian and British Joint Indications Rooms that year.

Building a Canadian Indications Room, Part 2

The Canadian Joint Indications Room and communications systems in Ottawa all experienced growing pains in 1958, but with the pain came growth. After the tripartite communications meeting in April, the Canadians created new lines of communication and procedure within Ottawa, all designed to ensure the connection of the JIR to all necessary facilities.[42]

From April 1958 on, the JIC was hard at work establishing a new set of procedures, entitled "Indications Intelligence: Communications and Watch Procedures" (variously altered, and a sign of the adjustments made, as JIC 278(58); JIC 278/1(58); JIC 278/2(58); JIC 278/3(58)).[43] A study of the speed by which messages were received in Ottawa from abroad indicated some serious delays in intelligence traffic: EMERGENCY messages from Europe and the Far East were sent from the "originating outstations" in fifteen or twenty minutes but then, once received, took a "rather incongruous" two hours "to progress the 100 feet" to the Joint Indications Room. One analysis concluded, perhaps obviously, that "as the indications net develops tripartite-wise the problem of maintaining speedy and efficient communications to facilitate discussion will be of utmost importance."[44] Staffing issues were considered, and the twenty-four-hour watch that had once been in place seems to have been cancelled and then resumed.

The British, however, were having even more trouble. Pat Black, the Canadian JICLO in London (JICLO(L)), wrote that "there is still a good deal of vagueness in L[on]d[o]n as to how a JIR should be run and the merits of having it manned by trained personnel on a twenty-four-hour basis." Part of the problem was no doubt the reorganization of the London JIC's relationship with the Cabinet Office and Chiefs of Staff Committee.[45] Because of a crisis in the Middle East in the summer of 1958 (see below), the British did set up an ad hoc Joint Indications Room that could handle tripartite alerts communications. But once the ad hoc system was closed after the crisis, the British would not be ready to participate in an ongoing tripartite alert system.[46]

London aimed for a start of October 1, 1958, but was unlikely to meet it due to administrative difficulties, lack of personnel, and because the terminal equipment for the new JIR had not been established.[47] At one point it seemed like it might not be ready until 1959 but was in fact working by November 1958 (see below).[48] In addition to the real administrative problems in Whitehall, some in London thought the whole idea of alerts was "just another American 'fad.'"[49] They were perhaps oblivious to the origins of the idea, in which the British had pushed so hard.

It may seem peculiar that the tripartite powers were seeking a system of indications intelligence at a time when the development of Soviet intercontinental ballistic missiles (ICBM) seemed to further limit the warning time that would be available ahead of a war. In spring 1958, Ivor Bowen wrote a lengthy paper called "The Continuing Need for Indications Intelligence."[50] He pointed out that while indications intelligence could hardly guarantee warning of a Soviet ICBM attack, "this lack of certainty is nothing new."[51] Indications intelligence had never been able to guarantee warning against manned bombers, either. And still, proponents of indications intelligence had recognized that launching a major war was such a complex and difficult process that there were many opportunities to compromise surprise.

Even more important, and almost contradictorily, while the Soviet ability to launch ICBMs was coming nearer, global war seemed less likely than it had at the start of the decade. A "global war is at present conceivable," Bowen wrote, "as a result of an accident or of a miscalculation by either side, involving an initial attack mounted in great haste." Hasty preparations would compromise operational security, perhaps resulting in more indications of war. And thus, even in the missile age, there were many scenarios in which a continued indications intelligence effort was necessary and would be so even after 1965, or whenever the Soviets would choose to rely only on ballistic missiles. While it was thought to be no longer possible to wage war early enough to prevent atomic weapons reaching North America, indications intelligence could still "give invaluable warning" and help North American authorities make "survival" decisions.[52]

The Canadians Want to Go Global

Still, despite the obvious importance of the system to all parties, there remained significant work to be done, and confusion to alleviate, after the June 1958 tripartite meeting. The Canadians left the meeting unclear on three things: the procedures for using the system, the agreed indicator list, and the stages of alert. The JIC (Ottawa) had, at first, "no stages of intelligence alerts and no indicator list."[53]

The matter of coordinating intelligence alert stages was unnecessarily complicated. The Canadians adapted the British system of alerts (pre-alert, stage 1, stage 2), while the British simultaneously adopted the new Canadian system of alerts (stages 1, 2, and 3).[54] The two sides finally agreed to both revert to the original British suggestion, beginning with a "pre-alert" stage, followed by stage 2, and then the most serious alert being stage 1. They then moved in 1959 back to the original Canadian system of stages 1, 2, and 3. There were also continued efforts, both nationally and on a tripartite basis, to establish a joint indications list.[55] But just when to invoke the system remained a crucial sticking point.

The Canadians spent the summer of 1958 working on a major paper, JIC 1103/1(58), "Tripartite Alerts System," to guide discussion of the use of the new system. It was to be presented at the next major tripartite conference scheduled for August.[56]

A draft of JIC 1103 makes it clear that Canadians were seeking a nearly global application of the tripartite alerts system. The documents warned that "the likelihood of hostilities in the Middle or even the Far East should be considered as immediately threatening the NATO area," because crises in these areas "through a chain of events" could develop into a major NATO crisis "in days or even hours." And not only did the Canadians want to expand the geography of the agreement, but also for the alert system to cover a range of types of potential conflict, from "one where our armed forces go in with guns blazing, as in Korea" to a non-contested peacekeeping operation like that of the United Nations Emergency Force (UNEF) at the time of the Suez Crisis. On both issues the Canadians were influenced by their "experience in indications matters" during the summer of 1958 when events in both Lebanon and Jordan had escalated into major crises (see below).[57]

Another section of the draft paper also sought to ensure fast and total communication of all indications intelligence gathered around the world. In essence, the Canadians argued that the "agreed tripartite indicators list" must not only be used in the NIC and JIR, but "also at all United States, United Kingdom, and Canadian intelligence collections points around the world." The Canadians suggested that an "agreed codeword, such as MAYHEM," be used and that all MAYHEM signals "will be recognized by all as dealing with tripartite indicators wherever they may originate."[58] There is a hint here of the early Canadian thinking that any indicators recorded on an index card in Ottawa would be copied to the United States. (Later, all three states would push their indicator lists to field collectors, especially attachés, but the indicators collected were never transmitted through the Tripartite Alert System in raw form.)

When the Canadians showed Amory the substance of JIC 1103/1(58) he was clearly alarmed. The proposals in the paper, he said, "go considerably beyond what I believe to be the understanding of the IAC as to the intent of the basic Tripartite Alerts Agreement." As a result, he (and the CIA) would not discuss the paper unless it was taken first to the IAC. But he warned of his own "personal belief" that chances for the paper at the IAC were "dubious at best" and "would almost certainly confuse and delay effective implementation" of the tripartite alert system, "which is already long overdue." Seeking to soften the blow, Amory told the Canadians there would likely be "ample opportunity for negotiations to improve the system" later, so maybe they could raise the issue then, without running the risk of holding up implementation.[59]

The British Embassy officials concerned with intelligence learned of the Canadian paper but had not seen it. They requested guidance from the JIC (London), and so JIC (London) asked the Canadians for a copy of the paper from JIC (Ottawa). There is no record of the Canadians passing the paper to London, though they likely did. JIC (Ottawa) concluded that the British would be "influenced by Mr. Amory's reaction" and assumed the British would support Amory's suggestions that "we delay formal introduction of our more far-reaching proposals until the tripartite alerts system was a going concern within the present context." The JIC instructed the JICLO(W) to withdraw major portions of the document from consideration at the upcoming tripartite meeting.[60]

Hamilton Southam, who had replaced Crean as chair of the JIC, made the decision to withdraw. He recognized that the "new wine of our thinking was too strong for the old bottle of the working group." Yet, he still clung to Amory's suggestion that the issues could be taken up later. "We are all convinced here [in Ottawa]," he wrote, that "we know what we are doing, and that eventually we shall be able to rally our American and British friends to our views."[61]

Setting the Indicator List

The major tripartite meeting scheduled for August was delayed until October 1958, perhaps because of events in the Middle East. But the results of the October meeting, a "Report of Tripartite Working Group on Tripartite Alert System," is a crucial document that set up the key elements of the system. The report included an annex with an agreed list of "Critical Sino-Soviet Bloc Actions."[62] This was a shortened list of crucial indicators. The list, based on an IAC paper with input from JIC (Ottawa) and JIC (London), would serve as the bedrock indicators list for the system and for indications analysts in all three capitals.

The thirty-five indicators identified as "Critical Sino-Soviet Bloc Actions" ranged under nine headings: General, Missiles, Air Forces, Submarines, Naval and Merchant Ships, Ground Forces, Air and Civil Defense, and Logistics. Some indicators were quite straightforward, including "Sino-Soviet Bloc declarations of war or acts of war against the US, UK, Canada or any other NATO member or forces abroad." Others were more nuanced, including the initiation of security procedures, evidence that attack orders were being passed to submarines, or the arrival of specialist units — "especially interrogation and medical units"[63] — in forward areas. For the most part, the indicators were related to fairly obvious preparations, movements, and reinforcements of military units.

The group recommended the list be reviewed semi-annually to reflect new "awareness of changing Sino-Soviet capabilities and operating methods," especially as more information about missiles became available.[64] Going forward, there would be meetings to review the indicator list every March when UK intelligence officials travelled to Washington for an annual Standing Group meeting that occurred at the same time.[65] Later on, the semi-annual meeting occurred less regularly.

The report also contained a chart summarizing the operating procedures of the indications centres in each country. Contrary to both British and Canadian ideas that the system should be used to exchange a whole range of intelligence, the tripartite meeting agreed that the "tripower alert system is to be limited to the transmission of critical intelligence and whatever additional information may be necessary to make proper assessment of the critical intelligence." Critical intelligence was defined as "information indicating a situation or pertaining to a situation threatening the NATO area which affects the security interest of the US, UK, or Canada to such an extent that it may require the immediate attention of the heads of the three governments."[66]

After the important October meeting, there followed a series of smaller and more specialized meetings to discuss watch procedures and clarify prefixes and serial numbers of messages. The British pushed to use the network to share their weekly indications report, ostensibly to keep the system in good working order.[67] On New Year's Eve the British proposed the code word "DRUMSTICK" to give protection to the agreement. The Canadians agreed, and the US agreed in principle, although they needed to refer to their own list of code words to ensure DRUMSTICK was available.[68] Why the British suggested DRUMSTICK is unclear. Perhaps the beat of indications intelligence accompanies the march to war. The code word seems not to have been used going forward.

The Crises of 1958

The years immediately following the establishment of the Tripartite Intelligence Alerts Agreement and its communications network were studded with crises and war scares. Given the delays in London mentioned above, it appears that ALE messages were not sent until late 1958. The crises in the Middle East in the summer of 1958 and the Taiwan Straits in 1958, then, came after the signing of the agreement but before the communications system and procedures were fully established. The crises in Berlin that came and went from 1958 and into the early 1960s, were, however, the subject of ALE messages.

On July 14, 1958, the government of Iraq was toppled in a coup. Lebanon was already in the midst of a civil war, and the Lebanese leader, fearing a similar threat to his regime, asked the Americans to intervene. On July 15, the United States landed marines in Lebanon. The Jordanian king made a request for similar assistance, and two days later, British troops landed in Jordan.

The crises in Iraq, Lebanon, and Jordan appeared to be localized. And yet, behind the scenes, the United States took steps with potentially global implications. On July 15, the United States Strategic Air Command was placed on "improved readiness" to act in case the Soviets intervened, or, perhaps more accurately, as a threat to ensure the Soviets did not intervene. In support of the SAC alert, North American Air Defense Command (NORAD) forces were placed on alert, too. Although NORAD was a bilateral US-Canadian command, the United States did not consult with Ottawa.[69]

On July 15, the Canadian JIC enabled the Joint Indication Room's twenty-four-hour watch. The JIC also requested a Daily Indications Report be prepared, and the report was to include "the movement of friendly forces." There is some evidence that messages dealing with indications intelligence in this period were delayed.[70]

The rapid start to these July crises, then, seemed to confirm for the Canadians that crises outside of the NATO area had the potential to escalate into a great power war. It also emphasized the importance of establishing a swift and reliable system for exchanging information with both Washington and London.

Throughout the crisis, the JICLO(L), Pat Black, liaised regularly with his British counterparts. He also held regular meetings with the Canadian DAI,

DMI, DNI and JIB liaison officers in London to make sure that any information of importance had been passed to Ottawa.⁷¹ In Washington, the USIB set up an Ad Hoc Working Group for this crisis, as well as for crises in the Taiwan Straits and Berlin. In all cases, Philip Uren, the JICLO(W) had been informed of the work of these groups.⁷²

The First ALE Message

By late November 1958, the TIAA communications system was working. In the first month of the Tripartite Alert Communications System, there were "nil" ALE messages and twelve "routine" messages (JICLON, JICOTT, and CIAWAS), exchanging weekly indications reports and discussing the functioning of the system.⁷³

It appears that the first ALE message was sent in 1958, by the Canadians. On December 11, 1958, as a result of "an apparently deteriorating situation in the Middle East," the JIC (Ottawa) called an Intelligence Alert Stage 1. Four days later, on December 15, JIC (Ottawa) dispatched the first ALE-OTT message to London and Washington asking for an assessment.⁷⁴ The alert set off a series of debates and discussion, not over whether war was imminent, but whether the planned procedures worked and whether the Canadians had been right to call an alert in the first place.

The day after the alert, the United States Intelligence Board (which had replaced the IAC) met and held "considerable discussion" as to the "correctness of [the Canadian] use of the alerts system." Sheldon of the CIA thought it was fine, while Cabell was neutral but furious that the United States had not been able to respond as quickly as it had promised. In a follow-up discussion between the Canadian and British JICLOs in Washington, Uren and Paul Jones, and a CIA official from Sheldon's office, Jones thought the use was incorrect because a crisis in the Middle East did not pose a "direct threat to the NATO area." Uren, for his part, argued the Canadian case that this interpretation was "legalistic and would hamper the effective use of the system."⁷⁵ He pointed out that critical situations in the Middle East had previously been used to increase the state of readiness in both NATO forces and NORAD. Uren's point, clearly, was that everyone recognized events in the Middle East might "constitute the beginning of a chain of events" that could threaten NATO.⁷⁶

Both the JIC (London) and its representative in Washington insisted that the ALE prefix use by JIC (Ottawa) was "incorrect." "This prefix should not be used by any of the national authorities for an alert outside the NTO [sic] area and that if this is done it extends the tripartite alerts agreement beyond the area agreed by the three governments concerned." If the Canadians wished to call an alert in Ottawa, and inform the other two states via a JICOTT message they were doing so, that was their prerogative.[77]

The Canadians disagreed with the British, complaining that the UK authorities were "placing an unnecessarily narrow interpretation on the agreement." Did the British really think a war between the United Arab Republic (UAR) and Israel would not affect the NATO area? "This seems to us to reveal not only shortsightedness but a rather short memory, bearing in mind the Soviet notes at the time of the Suez Crisis," the Canadians concluded.[78]

The Canadian told their allies that Ottawa's use of the alerts system was "warranted" and suggested that the Alerts System allow for two stages of alert for various ranges of alert.[79] The USIB rejected this idea, because it "regards the use of the circuit itself as an indication of a need for high level concern."[80] If the message was "not sufficiently important to involve the Chairman of the USA Watch and to invoke the Agreement, then it would be the opinion of the USIB that it did not [repeat] not warrant the use of the circuit." The Americans were concerned about the system being filled with "working level traffic" that would "degrade its value as an alert mechanism."[81]

The Canadians rejected this "overly mechanistic" understanding of the system "as a 'mechanism'" and the "suggestion that the circuit itself is important, rather than the messages passed on it."[82] The tension remained, then, between the function of the alert system as a part of British and American nuclear release procedures, and a Cold War in which both analysts and policymakers had long seen a connection between non-European crises as possible precursors to superpower confrontation. But minds can change. In a matter of months, the British would go from being critical of the Canadian view to championing it.

Ahead of the March 1959 review of indicator lists in Washington, the JIC (London) requested a special meeting of the tripartite alerts working group. The British representative, Antony Duff of the Foreign Office (representing the UK Joint Intelligence Staff), planned to present "views on the use of the tripartite intelligence alerts system for the exchange of intelligence on marginal or developing situations which do not present an 'immediate threat to the NATO area.'" The British brief was essentially a restatement of the Canadian position that consultations on non-NATO areas, including the Middle East, were warranted.[83] The precise reasons for this British about-face are unclear, but it is indicative of a return to early British thinking that had envisioned the ultimate expansion of the agreement (see Chapter 5).

When the British presented their proposals in March 1959, it was obvious to the attendees they were "primarily concerned with providing for consultation on critical areas outside of the NATO area but not repeat not with modifying the levels at which consultation might take place." The British were now pressing for an optional system whereby any of the three states could "ask for the views of the others on a critical situation anywhere in the world."[84] The parties would not use ALE, and would not formally invoke the agreement, but they would use the alerts system to communicate.

The hypothetical offered by the British and recorded by the Canadians was "a critical situation in the Middle East in which the UK might contemplate some form of military action or intervention and might wish to have the views of the US (and by implication, not repeat not, by assertion, those of Canada)." The Canadians said little in the meeting since they agreed with the British position. The Americans, however, gave the idea a "very negative reception," with Sheldon explaining, at length, the difficulty of responding to such requests. The "US could only respond to a request on the system by giving a fully coordinated community view, with all the staff work which that implied." Again, the size and difficulty of managing the US bureaucracy posed a challenge to coordination with others. Despite the US opposition, Sheldon admitted there was "some merit" to the proposal and suggested Dean write to Dulles and John Starnes (who had replaced Southam as chair of the JIC (Ottawa)).[85]

Starnes, who did not attend this meeting but met with Amory a week later, had learned the Americans "probably could be persuaded to extend the tripartite alerts agreement to geographical areas outside the NATO area." They would be reluctant to automatically apply the alerts systems to crises over the Quemoy Islands in the Taiwan Straits, but this could be circumvented if all accepted the principle that "each national authority is free to decide when a developing situation, whether or not it is strictly in the NATO area, warrants the calling of an intelligence alert."[86] Starnes wrote to Dean on March 21 to suggest that the British follow up on their proposals made in the March meeting with a letter to Dulles and Starnes himself as chair of the JIC (Ottawa).

Only the day before, however, Dulles himself raised the matter in a meeting between Dean and Dulles in Washington before Starnes' message reached Dean. Dulles' proposal was to formally amend the agreement itself "to provide for it coming into force automatically in the event of any Sino-Soviet bloc aggressive action" whether affecting the NATO area or not.[87]

While this was a "step forward," Dean told Starnes that it does not "altogether meet either our wishes or yours."[88] The idea pleased Starnes, who recognized the agreement would then come into effect for situations like the Formosa Straits, which, during a recent crisis, the US had "tended to regard as their business alone." Still, Starnes did not like the limitation of attention to the Sino-Soviet bloc, for the "the actions of other states can be equally if not more dangerous. What if Iraq were to take some sudden drastic step such as the seizure of Kuwait?" Starnes admitted this was "perhaps an exaggerated example, but serves to illustrate the point."[89]

Following his conversation with Dulles, Dean wrote him to formally propose amending the agreement and gave examples such as a threatened Soviet move against Iran, the threat of a Viet Minh invasion of South Vietnam, or "serious recrudescence of Communist aggression in the Taiwan Straits." Dean added to the letter "another thought," that of making more use of the "special communications channel which has been established to serve the Tripartite Alerts Agreement."[90] This, Dean told the Canadians, was something they were anxious to achieve.[91]

The Canadian JIC considered the possible amendment. Bowen thought the idea "should be strongly supported by the JIC." Still, there were very few aggressive actions taken by any states outside the Sino-Soviet bloc that would pose a serious threat to Canada. The one Bowen could imagine was "Arab action against Israel, which would involve Canadian forces around the perimeter of Israel." So while Canada would welcome the British effort, JIC (Ottawa) would not "have a case to render strong support."[92]

Some members of JIC (Ottawa), and especially Bowen, wanted Starnes to push the Americans on another issue: those withdrawn passages from JIC 1103/1(58), especially the parts calling for "for the automatic and expeditious passage of all relevant intelligence information," including from field posts.[93] Amory, however, again poured cold water on the issue, and Starnes did not bring it up with Dulles at their next meeting.[94]

Allen Dulles wrote to Dean to explain that the USIB agreed to an amendment to broaden the terms of the agreement. However, he stressed the American position that "traffic passed in this connection be strictly limited to situations of the highest priority in order to avoid diverting this communication channel to uses which might become detrimental to the objective for which it was originally established."⁹⁵ Final wording was proposed by Dulles at the end of August 1959.⁹⁶

Starnes passed the new draft agreement to the chairman of the CSC, General Charles Foulkes. He explained that the JIC supported the change not only because it corresponded with the scope the Canadians wanted for the system, but "also because it is so clearly advantageous from a Canadian point of view in that the Canadian authorities will be brought quickly into the picture on critical situations which may develop outside the NATO area." Foulkes took the agreement to Minister of National Defence George Pearkes; the wording of the revised agreement then went to the Secretary of State for External Affairs and Prime Minister Diefenbaker, who agreed on October 5, 1959, to an exchange of letters that month.⁹⁷

The Berlin Crises, and the Broken Cables

The Berlin Crises of 1958 and 1959 were particularly important for establishing the patterns of habit of the British Joint Indications Room and, as a result, the Canadian liaison with the UK JIR. Pat Black used his experience in the summer of 1958 to establish a practice of meetings with Brits and Canadians to ensure that Canadians were getting every piece of intelligence possible. This included, for instance, a plan to drop in daily on the JIR at a certain intelligence alert level, and especially to seek daily reports from the headquarters of the British Army on the Rhine.⁹⁸

In both Washington and London, the Canadian liaison officers were working to maintain their relationships with American and British counterparts, respectively. It is important to recognize that these relationships continued to be the mainstay of indications intelligence exchange.

And the communications system remained in regular use for the exchange of reviews and reports. During the Berlin Crisis, for instance, the British sent their heads of section and JIC assessments to Ottawa and Washington every Tuesday and Thursday.⁹⁹

In January and February 1959, there were seven ALE messages exchanged between the three powers (along with twenty-eight exercise or test ALE messages, and thirty-three routine JICOTT, JICLON, or CIAWAS messages).¹⁰⁰ But the seven true ALE messages, all sent in late February, were not about the Berlin Crisis. They were about transatlantic cables that had been severed.

On February 25, 1959, the Canadians sent an emergency ALE message to their allies, with a follow-up message the next day. London and Washington both sent back replies. A transatlantic cable belonging to the American Telegraph and Telephone Company (later AT&T), and four Western Union cables had each been broken.

After the first cable was disrupted, American Telegraph and Telephone charted an aircraft to reconnoitre the cables. The aircraft was observing the Soviet trawler MV Novorossisk at the time the fifth cable was broken. The damage had been done roughly 125 miles (200 kilometres) east of Newfoundland, where the cables were 200 fathoms (roughly 365 metres) below the ocean. It seemed at first that the trawler might have cut all five cables during a fifty-mile (80-kilometre) run from north to south.

There was initial confusion as to whether the cables had been cut cleanly, which would have been very difficult at that depth — or whether they had been broken by a trawler dragging its tackle against the cable. It was not terribly unusual for cables to break, and indeed there had been previous times when multiple cables had been damaged in the same short period. But in those cases, multiple trawlers had been in the area at once.

The Canadians and Americans each dispatched a destroyer to intercept and board the trawler.[101] Later, in July, a staff member from the Privy Council Office attended a Joint Intelligence Committee meeting in Ottawa, bringing with him two sections of cables to demonstrate the "difference between a cable which had been broken through tension and one which had been cut."[102] The tenor of the discussions suggest that at least one of the cables had been cut cleanly, but this is not certain given the records released to date.

Future declassifications may shed light on how the cables were severed. But the effect of the incident was dramatic. As the UK JIC realized immediately, "if the Russians cut all the cables and simultaneously jammed the radio circuits, we should have no communications with North America."[103] In addition to the obvious threat posed to the cables themselves, the US "Argus" stratospheric nuclear test explosions had confirmed that nuclear explosions would interfere with radio communications, which were the back-up in case of disrupted cables. The US, UK, and Canada could have all the agreements in place they wanted, but if there were no practical means to communicate, the agreements were worthless.

The three allies decided that the February cable cuts were not indicators of imminent war, even though transatlantic cable-cutting was an item on the indicator list. The UK JIC considered Novorossisk's journey might have been an "experiment" undertaken by the Soviets to see how difficult it was to cut cables in preparation for a "future planned operation."[104]

The British urged a study of transatlantic communications, and the study was launched.[105] An early cursory review by the Canadians included, ominously, that "our present communications facilities are completely vulnerable to Soviet interdiction."[106] Separately, US officials also noted the vulnerability of the transatlantic cables and began exploring the possibility of using circuits of a "USAF Wide-Band Tropospheric Forward Scatter System" — a system that did not require a physical cable link — to connect the three capitals as part of the broader study of possible Soviet interdiction of transatlantic communications.[107] Within a few months of coming online, the alerts communication system was unreliable and obsolete, and the allies would begin looking for new systems to implement the agreement.

The Canadian Indications Procedure

In the time since the tripartite agreement was signed in 1957, the Canadians had continued to develop and improve their own indicator lists and supporting documentation, including JIC 312/2(59), February 5, 1959, "Probable Enemy Activities Prior to the Outbreak of War." In February 1959, while considering the lists, it occurred to Bowen that JIC (Ottawa) had not taken steps to encourage Canadian representatives in missions abroad to report indications intelligence. Obviously, the missions in Moscow, Warsaw, and Prague, if properly organized and briefed on what was occurring in the Joint Indications Room, could be on the "continual lookout" for information listed as "Critical Intelligence Indicators," and also be in a position to respond to requests from the JIR.[108]

As of Bowen's writing, suitable short lists of indicators, and even the stages of intelligence alert adopted by the JIC (Ottawa), existed only as "parts of very highly classified documents relating to the Tripartite Intelligence Alert Agreement."[109] They were thus inaccessible for most field collectors, not because the lists themselves were important but because they disclosed the sensitive agreement. Bowen recommended that these lists be stripped from the larger tripartite packages and issued as separate JIC reports with as low a security classification as possible for distribution in the field.[110]

The Canadians coordinated with the British, who were also trying to bring Foreign Office posts "into the indications picture."[111] Just a month later, the Americans issued a General Indicator List to all diplomatic missions, and included a thorough explanation of how the lists were used by the NIC.[112] (The Americans had sent out a similar message in 1955 after the establishment of the NIC.)

Taking the example of their allies, the Canadians distributed a list of key indicators, JIC 312/2(59), to diplomats posted abroad. It offered a list of "major actions and developments which it is believed may occur prior to the Soviet initiation of major hostilities against the West, and particularly against North America."[113] They also distributed a separate report of the list of Critical Intelligence Indicators, intended to serve as a guide for intelligence reporting officers in the field. Coincidentally harkening back to the late 1940s origins of indications intelligence, the document was to provide "a check list." The list of alert stages was also distributed, and arrangements were made to advise the field when an alert had been declared. In an alert, officers were to review their lists and report anything which might assist assessment in Ottawa.[114]

On September 28, 1960, the JIC agreed to the "Joint Indication Room: Standing Orders," JIC 378/1 (60). This document, which served the purpose indicated by its title, began with an overview of the Tripartite Intelligence Alerts Agreement. It laid out the process and procedures by which Canada would receive and communicate intelligence alert messages with Washington and London. The document would be superseded by updates in 1963 and in 1966: these documents are the best overviews of how the TIAA system was supposed to work. They confirm that Canada's indications intelligence system was built as part of an allied partnership.

In 1962, the JIC planned to update JIC 378/1(60). At first, they hesitated to undertake significant study of the issue until the end of a major NATO exercise, FALLEX 62. The exercise was designed to test all NATO governments' ability to wage and survive nuclear war. (FALLEX 62 did not go well for Canadian intelligence officials. They found out during the exercise that there was no room for the JIC at Canada's National Emergency Headquarters.)[115] Efforts to update the indications procedures were delayed again in October 1962 by a crisis with higher stakes than FALLEX 62.

The Cuban Missile Crisis

In early September 1962 the Joint Intelligence Committee approved a new paper titled "Intelligence Warning of Military Attack on North America," JIC 443/2(62). The purpose of the paper was to assess the length of warning time available in the event of a Soviet attack on North America at any point in the next decade.

JIC 443/2(62) stated plainly that the allies could expect no intelligence with "direct knowledge" of a Soviet decision to go to war, but, as per the fundamental premise of the entire intelligence indications effort, they should expect to receive "evidence of preparations." The main Soviet activity that would provide such a warning would be the "deployment or readying of Soviet nuclear forces for a massive attack on this continent." But the main focus of the paper was on the launch of heavy bombers, and this "would provide little or no intelligence warning."[116]

The same was true for Soviet deployments of missile submarines off the Atlantic or Pacific coasts of North America. As time passed, and the Soviets fielded ballistic missiles that were "permanently deployed and ready," even "radically new sources of intelligence, such as reconnaissance satellites" would be challenged to offer timely warning of attack.[117]

The "clandestine introduction" of nuclear weapons into North America — here the Canadians were referring to early Cold War fears of small weapons smuggled into North America — would also be difficult to detect, even as smaller bombers were capable of offering greater and greater yield.[118]

Overall, the paper offered a grim assessment of the likelihood of intelligence warning. The authors were more correct than the JIC could have realized at the time. In July 1962 the Soviet premier, Nikita Khrushchev, and the Cuban leader, Fidel Castro, had agreed that the Soviet Union would deploy Soviet nuclear missiles to Cuba.

At the time the Canadians were writing the JIC 443/2(62), and noting challenges of both receiving warning about the launch of ballistic missiles and detecting smuggled weapons, the Soviets were clandestinely introducing medium-range ballistic missiles (MRBM) onto the island, about 150 kilometres from the United States.

Canadian intelligence officials did not learn about the missiles in Cuba via the Tripartite Intelligence Alerts Agreement. They learned about them at lunch.

On October 18, 1962, Director of Central Intelligence (and head of the CIA) John McCone invited Ivor Bowen and J. J. McCardle, the chair of the JIC (Ottawa) along with Geoffrey Cook, the JICLO(W), to lunch at his house. The Canadians were in Washington, along with British, Australian, and New Zealander colleagues for a CIA conference on the "impact of a changing world on the conduct of intelligence."[119] But for lunch, it was just the Canadians, McCone, and several other CIA people, including Deputy Director for Intelligence Ray Cline.

It was McCardle who first turned the conversation to Cuba. McCardle explained that Canada was going to refuse Soviet aircraft the right to overfly Canada enroute to Cuba.[120] The Canadians, along with the other allies, were concerned by the increase in Soviet military aid being sent to Cuba. Indeed, over the summer the Canadian embassy in Havana had been reporting on the influx of Soviet personnel and material on the island.[121] But the Canadians had no idea that the aid included nuclear missiles.

McCone told the Canadians that ballistic missile sites had been identified in Cuba.[122] Photographic intelligence — that is, from U-2 spy planes — along with "other intelligence media" had convinced the United States that the USSR had installed about 40 offensive ballistic missiles in Cuba which "directly threaten the Security of U.S.A."[123] This was Canada's first indication of what would become the Cuban Missile Crisis.[124]

At the end of the lunch, McCone asked the Canadians not to share the information of the missile sites with their government in Ottawa. The Americans had made other arrangements for this purpose: President John F. Kennedy has asked Livingston Merchant, an American diplomat who had been the ambassador to Canada until earlier in the year, to visit Ottawa and inform the Prime Minister in person. McCardle made clear he could not keep this information from his government. Upon returning to Ottawa, he reported to Norman Robertson and Robert Bryce, who passed the information to the Prime Minister. When Merchant arrived in Ottawa, Diefenbaker already knew about the missiles.

This exchange between the CIA officials and the Canadians harkens back to the Canadian discussion as to why an alerts agreement and network was important: that the Americans, in a crisis, might be so preoccupied that they would not inform the Canadians of intelligence information without a formal system in place. All available evidence suggests that, at least in the earliest days of the Cuban Missile Crisis, it was personal and working relationships and habit — lunch with the DCI — that got the intelligence to Canadians first. The Kennedy administration seems not to have used the alert system established by the TIAA to share information early in the crisis, and instead relied on a personal emissary, Merchant, who did not arrive in Ottawa until October 22, 1962.

In the afternoon of October 22, at 4:00 p.m., McCardle, as chair of the JIC, directed that a duty officer maintain a "continuous watch" in the Joint Indications Room (JIR). This was the day Merchant arrived, and McCardle knew Kennedy was going to make an announcement of a "serious nature" that night.[125] That evening, Kennedy announced that the United States would quarantine any military equipment being sent to Cuba by ship and demanded the Soviets withdraw the missiles. This dramatically increased the possibility of a direct conflict between US and Soviet forces.

The JIC started meeting regularly the next day, on October 23. The committee reviewed a "Cuban Situation Report" that would become, over the next week and a half, a daily document with the new name "Special Intelligence Report." This daily report developed over the crisis to contain information about the states of allied intelligence and readiness, Soviet motives in placing the missiles in Cuba, and the US and USSR positions at the United Nations. The committee also agreed on October 23 to declare a "Stage 2" intelligence alert, but it is not clear whether the alert took effect on the 23rd or the 24th.[126] While the alert level is not definitive, it does suggest that Canada had not received ALE messages from the US or UK, nor had Ottawa sent such a message by this date.

The minutes of the discussion in the JIC on October 23 is instructive.[127] The director of air intelligence was tasked with investigating "the matter of providing air service to Alert" — that is, the Alert Wireless Station in what was then Alert, Northwest Territories (now Alert, Nunavut). The place name for Alert, the northernmost continuously inhabited settlement in the world, is simply a coincidence. But this discussion point suggests that Canada was gathering signals intelligence on the Soviet Union from Alert with an eye to gaining indications intelligence.

At the same time, the communication system that supported the TIAA had recently been tested, and so the JIC agreed not to send any further test messages, presumably to keep the line clear and reduce any confusion in case of a true alert message. The DNI was tasked with investigating and providing "ways and means by which knowledge of cable breaks would be made rapidly available to the JIC," and the Air Force was to notify the JIC of any "communications interruptions considered to be due to deliberate action." The JIC agreed that if there were indicators of "sabotage" or "communication interruptions," they would pass messages to London and Washington.[128] There was no mention of any ALE messages having been sent, but the Canadians were clearly trying to keep the line clear and ensure it remained in working order.

The JIC was also concerned with ensuring that Canada was aware of the states of operational readiness of US forces. This stemmed from the Canadian understanding that US actions could result in Soviet responses that would appear as indicators of war. Yet it also seems likely that the Canadians were monitoring the state of US readiness to ensure the Government of Canada had the fullest possible knowledge of American actions.

The JIC continued to meet daily, adjusting its meeting times to the early work hours. This allowed the committee time to prepare briefs for others, including the Chiefs of Staff Committee and daily briefings to the Cabinet Defence Committee. These briefs were usually given by McCardle as chair. Diefenbaker himself was secretly pre-briefed to allow him to ask knowledgeable questions in front of his colleagues in the CDC.[129]

The JIC efforts during the Cuban crisis were, fundamentally, an indications effort. Indications liaison officers from the various service branches met daily to prepare information for the JIC meeting and background material for the prime minister who spoke daily in the House.[130]

On October 24, 1962, Canadian intelligence officials noted that "both sides" — the Americans and the Soviets — "have taken significant precautionary military measures." Still, the "intelligence available does not permit a judgment of Soviet intentions."[131] These precautionary measures might have included indications that the USSR was preparing to move bombers to Arctic bases.[132]

On October 26, 1962, the JIC declared an Intelligence Alert Stage 1. The motive for the decision — whether the result of a Canadian assessment or receipt of an ALE message — is unclear. Later that evening, Kennedy received a private message from Khrushchev backing down to American demands.

October 27, 1962, was perhaps the most critical day of the crisis. Khrushchev sent a second message to Kennedy, seemingly backtracking on a first message he had sent to end the crisis. That day, the US Watch Committee noted that five of the MRBM sites in Cuba appeared to be fully operational.[133] US Navy Growler planes were shot at over Cuba, and a US U-2 aircraft was shot down and the pilot killed. War was imminent.

In a letter in support of a later departmental oral history project, Malcolm N. Bow, the special assistant to Secretary of State for External Affairs Howard

Green, recalled how he shuttled "intelligence information" from Green to Diefenbaker on the evening of the 27th:

> At the most critical hour of the missile crisis on the evening of October 27, I was summoned to the Greens' residence in the Roxborough Apartments. My instructions were to deliver a sealed envelope to the Prime Minister at his residence, to be sure that he read the contents immediately and telephoned his reaction to the Minister. Subsequently, I learned that the intelligence information I delivered concerned a US intention of bombing the Cuban missile sites that evening and that the Soviet assurances of withdrawal which forestalled hostilities were received only 25 minutes before the air strike deadline.[134]

It is unclear just what this "intelligence information" was, or its source. Earlier in the week, the phrase "intelligence information" had referred to McCone's meeting with Bowen, McCardle, and Cook. It is possible, but not certain, that the intelligence information Bow is referring to was received via the TIAA network.

The next day, on October 28, 1962, the JIC noted that Radio Moscow was announcing the Soviet Union's willingness to "retire" the offensive weapons in Cuba. The JIC declared an Intelligence Alert Stage 2, a lesser stage of alert. Over the coming days, it became evident the Soviet Union was, in fact, dismantling some of the missile sites in Cuba.

In the famed thirteen days of October 1962, the world was on the brink of nuclear war. Despite the enormous number of declassified American intelligence records related to the crisis, it remains unclear whether the Tripartite Intelligence Alerts Agreement was invoked during the Cuban Missile Crisis. On balance, it appears the agreement was not invoked.

The crisis, one in which the decision for escalation rested with the United States, was not the type of event that the TIAA had been established to identify. It was, however, in keeping with the Imminence of War papers developed nearly a decade before. War had nearly come not because of a major Soviet offensive, but rather a Soviet miscalculation about how the United States would react to Soviet policy. Canadian procedures and processes had shied away from considering situations in which the United States would choose war — an intelligence challenge with too many political implications for Canada to meet squarely.

CONCLUSION

A Semi-Dormant but Continuing Agreement

In the aftermath of the Cuban Missile Crisis, the JIC finally made the previously planned updates for the Joint Indication Room Standing Orders, published as JIC 471(63) in June of 1963. The new orders took account of the JIR's role in the Cuban Missile Crisis. They underlined the need for more staff in a crisis.[1]

More change was to come. In 1965, the Intelligence Division of the Department of National Defence took over the twenty-four-hour watch function from Joint Staff.[2] A year later, a new document, "The Tripartite Intelligence Alerts Agreement," JIC 543(66) (Final), now spelled out the procedures that the Current Intelligence, Indications and Briefing (CIIB) section, a part of the Intelligence Division, would serve the role previously played by the Joint Indications Room.[3]

Work on indicator lists continued. In 1960, a first "Missile Indicator List" was the subject of tripartite discussions, based on an initial indications list drawn up by the US NIC.[4] Other specific lists included "Intelligence Alert Indicator List: Critical Soviet Bloc Actions" and "Indications of Sino-Soviet Bloc Preparations for Early War." Indeed, by the mid-1960s, there was a "Tripartite Intelligence Alert Indicator List for Critical Asian Communist Actions" with indicators to help determine whether "an Asian Communist power is about to initiate or engage in international hostilities." The growing number of these lists was consistent with the 1959 expansion of the agreement, but it confirms that the Canadian wish and hunch that the agreement would take on a global nature had come to pass.[5]

Indeed, in 1965 the British pressed the American and Canadian allies (who both agreed) to show the "Asian" list to Australian and New Zealander

177

intelligence officials. It does not appear that Australia and New Zealand ever became formal members of the Tripartite Intelligence Alerts Agreement, but documents from 1989 note that if the agreement was invoked, the Australians would also "normally be informed given that it is a member of the CAN/AUS/UK/US intelligence sharing agreement."[6]

And yet, despite the development of indicator lists, sharing of these lists to Australia and New Zealand, and an improvement of the communications network to allow "conferencing," 1966 marks the end of the active use of the system.[7] Tests continued every week. What had begun as bi-weekly tests were sent "thrice weekly" as of 1972, with a monthly report tracking the tests.[8] The allies still had an agreed "Tripartite Intelligence Alerts Indicator List" in the 1980s.[9] But according to a 1973 memorandum, no live alert message had been exchanged after 1966, and a CIA official described it as having entered a "semi-dormant stage."[10]

The lack of live alert messages likely reflected two broader trends. The first was a changing international system. While the Cold War would heat up again, including with major nuclear crises in the 1980s, the late 1960s ushered in a period of détente. The other shift was within the tripartite states themselves, and their growing systems for exchanging intelligence.

Both the UK and Canada were members of the American CRITICOMM network, which let Ottawa and London exchange "flash" messages with the CIA and other USIB members. CRITICOMM was also used on a daily basis to exchange intelligence. In 1970, partially because of this CRITICOMM connection, the US proposed cancelling the tripartite alerts communication system itself. (It should be kept in mind that there is no evidence that any party ever suggested doing away with the agreement; these were discussions instead about communications networks and systems.) But neither Canada nor the UK wanted to switch solely to CRITICOMM, which they feared would be overloaded in a crisis.[11]

In 1973, the British were finally willing to discontinue the existing communications system. The Canadians initially hesitated before agreeing to find a more "efficient way to implement [the] Alerts Agreement."[12] Nonetheless, later that year, Canada still maintained two "TRIAN" — Tripartite Intelligence Alert Network — terminals at National Defence buildings. One of the terminals was to be relocated to the new Canadian Intelligence Advisory Committee (IAC) secretariat offices in the East Block, in the old

External Affairs operations centre (and beside the External Affairs "satellite comcentre," which was staying in place.)[13]

The Tripartite Intelligence Alerts Agreement continued to shape crisis procedures in Ottawa for the rest of the Cold War and into the post-Cold War era. In 1976, the IAC developed a document outlining "IAC Procedures in Crisis Situations." The first page of the document referenced the "Tripartite Intelligence Alert Agreement," and an annex includes a description of the agreement and the instructions for sending and communicating messages with London and Washington. These TIAA procedures, and Canada's obligations under the agreement, are an essential element of all IAC crisis procedure documents finalized in 1978, 1989, and 1991 — even after the fall of the Berlin Wall.[14] As recently as 2013, a "familiarization guide" prepared for the director general of intelligence of the Communications Security Establishment included a description of both the initial Tripartite Intelligence Alerts Agreement and the subsequent expansion to expand the agreement to include warning of aggressive action outside of the NATO area.[15] There is no evidence that the TIAA has been cancelled.[16]

***

The history of the Canadian "imminence of war" assessments is now available in released records. The first chapters of this book examined the diplomacy of these appreciations during the most dangerous period of the early Cold War. As the Cold War continued, the Canadians continued to work with their allies to assess the possibility that war, perhaps regional war, might come to the world. Canada continued to exchange JIC papers with the United Kingdom and the United States, but also Australia and New Zealand.[17] Readers will recognize these states as the "Five Eyes" intelligence community. And while the Five Eyes usually refers to a signals intelligence partnership between these countries, the imminence of war studies and the evolution of the Tripartite Intelligence Alerts Agreement procedures make clear that this intelligence community developed into an assessment-sharing community early in the Cold War.

Despite the recent release of "imminence" records, a large number of records from the "indications" side of the ledger are yet to be released. Chapters four through six of this manuscript provide the outline of the agreement and the communications systems put in place, and examine allied thinking about indications intelligence in general. Some information about when and how alerts were called has been released, but there is more research to be done in this area. As more documents are released, researchers will be able to better understand the role that alerts and the communications network played in how Canada and its allies understood and responded to Cold War crises.

The release of the records to support this project has been a long and tedious effort, filled with frustrations. And yet, the release of both "imminence" and "indications" records has been a success in that it has allowed for sustained scholarship in this area. Canada usually lags far behind the United States and the United Kingdom in declassifying historical records related to intelligence. In the case of the Tripartite Intelligence Alerts Agreement, Canada is ahead of its allies in releasing information. The historical understanding that can be gained from these releases is crucial to better understanding our present.

At the end of the Cold War, it might have seemed like imminence of war assessments and indications intelligence systems were purely a thing of the past. The September 11, 2001 terrorist attacks against the United States led to a surge in intelligence spending in Canada and allied countries, and the search for indicators of attack focused on a more granular level, with attention to individuals and terrorist groups. The 2020s, however, have reminded allied leaders that general war is not necessarily a relic of the past. With the return of war to Europe with the Russian invasion of Ukraine, and growing tensions between the United States and the People's Republic of China, Canada and its allies must think once again about how best to assess the imminence of war.

There was no "War of 196?" like that described in the introduction to this book. That no third world war has yet occurred does not suggest general war will not come again. Indeed, and unfortunately, there is no time like the present to revisit and review the history of how Canada and its allies prepared to identify the imminence of war.

Notes

RESOURCES AND ACRONYMS

Many citations in the following notes include an alpha-numeric Canada Declassified (CD) identifier, for instance CDIW00001. Any document with a CD identifier can be accessed online by visiting *Canada Declassified* (https://declassified.library.utoronto.ca) and searching for the CD identifier. Page numbers that follow the CD identifier reflect the page numbering in the electronic pdf rather than any numbering used in the original document.

As well, the Cabinet Conclusions, 1944–1979 (CC) from Library and Archives Canada are searchable at https://library-archives.canada.ca/eng/collection/research-help/politics-government-law/Pages/cabinet-conclusions.aspx.

ACRONYMS USED IN NOTES

CIA FOIA RR	Central Intelligence Agency Freedom of Information Act Reading Room
DCER	*Documents on Canadian External Relations*
DHH/DND	Directorate of History and Heritage, Department of National Defence
FRUS	*Foreign Relations of the United States*
GAC ATIP	Global Affairs Canada Access to Information and Privacy
LAC	Library and Archives Canada
LAC ATIP	Library and Archives Canada Access to Information and Privacy
LAC CC	Library and Archives Canada Cabinet Conclusions, 1944–1979
NAUK	National Archives of the United Kingdom
PCO ATIP	Privy Council Office Access to Information and Privacy
RG	Record Group

NOTES TO INTRODUCTION

1. What follows is drawn from "Design for Tomorrow – 196?," June 1959, LAC RG 24, file CSC 7-18, part 1. The draft was written "for exercise purposes only." I am grateful to Alan Barnes for bringing this document to my attention.
2. James Eayrs, *In Defence of Canada Vol IV: Growing Up Allied* (Toronto: University of Toronto Press, 1985).
3. See Asa McKercher, "Neutralism, Nationalism, and Nukes, Oh My! Revisiting Peacemaker or Powder-Monkey and Canadian Strategy in the Nuclear Age," in *Nuclear North: Histories of Canada in the Atomic Age*, eds. Susan Colbourn and Timothy Andrews Sayle (Vancouver: UBC Press, 2019), 88–108.
4. For an overview of the postwar intelligence structure in Canada, see Alan Barnes, "A Confusion, Not a System: The Organizational Evolution of Strategic Intelligence Assessment in Canada, 1943 to 2003," *Intelligence and National Security* 34, no. 4 (2019): 464–79, https://doi.org/10.1080/02684527.2019.1578043, and Kurt F. Jensen, *Cautious Beginnings: Canadian Foreign Intelligence, 1939–51* (Vancouver: UBC Press, 2009).
5. Memorandum by Assistant Under-Secretary of State for External Affairs [hereafter USSEA], December 27, 1941, in *Documents on Canadian External Relations* [hereafter *DCER*], vol. 9, doc. 951, p. 1136.
6. Quoted in C. P. Stacey, *Arms, Men and Governments: The War Policies of Canada, 1939–1945* (Ottawa: Queen's Printer for Canada, 1970), 141.
7. Quoted in Stacey, *Arms, Men and Governments*, 142.
8. As readers will note in Chapter 5, the TIAA was signed during John Diefenbaker's premiership. But the crucial preparatory work had been completed while Louis St. Laurent was prime minister and Pearson the secretary of state for External Affairs.
9. Minister in United States to First Secretary, March 21, 1944, *DCER*, vol. 11, doc. 870, p. 1407.
10. On "strategical direction," see Chairman, Canadian Section, Permanent Joint Board on Defence [hereafter PJBD], to Chairman, American Section, April 29, 1942, *DCER*, vol. 8, doc. 128, p. 201; and Vice-Chief of the General Staff to Chief of the General Staff, May 14, 1941, *DCER*, vol. 8, doc. 131, p. 206. See also Stacey, *Arms, Men and Governments*, 349–54.
11. Stacey, *Arms, Men and Governments*, 160.
12. Chief of the General Staff to Acting USSEA, March 28, 1941, *DCER*, vol. 8, doc. 121, p. 188.
13. Memorandum from Chiefs of Staff to Minister of National Defence, April 15, 1941, *DCER*, vol. 8, doc. 124, p. 191.
14. Memorandum from Counsellor [Pearson] to Acting USSEA, May 23, 1941, *DCER*, vol. 8, doc. 135, p. 212.
15. Chairman, American Section, PBJD, to Chairman, Canadian Section," May 2, 1941, *DCER*, vol. 8, doc. 129, p. 204-05.
16. Chairman, Canadian Section, PBJD, to Chairman, American Section," May 3, 1941, *DCER*, vol. 8, doc. 130, p. 205. For interesting commentary on American "neo-

Imperialism," see Memorandum by Assistant USSEA, April 14, 1942, *DCER,* vol. 9, doc. 952, p. 1136.
17 Stacey, *Arms, Men and Governments,* 363.
18 Stacey, *Arms, Men and Governments,* 163.
19 Stacey, *Arms, Men and Governments,* 165.
20 C. P. Stacey, *Canada and the Age of Conflict: A History of Canadian External Policies* (Toronto: Macmillan of Canada, 1977), 337.
21 Stanley W. Dziuban, *Military Relations Between the United States and Canada, 1939-1945* (Washington, DC: Center of Military History, United States Army, 1990), 108.
22 Memorandum from Assistant USSEA to USSEA," December 10, 1941, *DCER,* vol. 9, doc. 966, pp. 1163–64.
23 Dziuban, *Military Relations,* 199.
24 Memorandum from First Secretary to USSEA, February 29, 1944, *DCER,* vol. 11, doc. 869, p. 1400.
25 "Memorandum by Director of Plans, Department of National Defence for Air, and by Secretary, Interdepartmental Panel on Joint Defence Projects," December 1, 1943, *DCER,* vol. 9, doc. 1016, p. 1228.

NOTES TO CHAPTER 1

1 On the Post-Hostilities Planning Committee [hereafter PHP], see Don Munton and Don Page, "Planning in the East Block: The Post-Hostilities Problems Committees in Canada 1943-5," *International Journal* 32, no. 4 (1977): 687–726, https://doi.org/10.2307/40201593; Monique Dolak, "Preparing for Peace in Time of War: Canada and the Post-Hostilities Planning Committees, 1943-1945" 15, no. 3 (2014): 124–37, https://jmss.org/article/view/58115/43732.
2 "Canadian Defence Relationships with the United States," PHP Working Committee Paper, Draft 2, May 26, 1944, LAC, RG 25, 52-C(s).
3 Field Marshall Lord Alanbrooke, *War Diaries, 1939-1945,* eds. Alex Danchev and Daniel Todman (London: Weidenfeld & Nicholson, 2001), 575.
4 Michael S. Goodman, *The Official History of the Joint Intelligence Committee: Volume 1: From the Approach of the Second World War to the Suez Crisis* (London: Routledge, 2014), 248–55. Quote at 255.
5 Larry A. Valero, "The American Joint Intelligence Committee and Estimates of the Soviet Union, 1945-1947" *Studies in Intelligence* 44, no. 3 (Summer 2000): 4, https://www.cia.gov/resources/csi/static/american-joint-intel-committee.pdf.
6 See Denis Smith, *Diplomacy of Fear: Canada and the Cold War, 1941-1948* (Toronto: University of Toronto Press, 1988) and chapter 3 in Robert Bothwell, *Alliance and Illusion: Canada and the World, 1945-1984* (Vancouver: UBC Press, 2007), 55–72.
7 Kuibyshev no. 80 to Ottawa, July 3, 1943, LAC, RG 25, 2-AE(s), part 1, CDTT00002; Moscow no. 107 to Ottawa, August 23, 1943, LAC, RG 25, 2-AE(s), part 1, CDTT00004; Moscow no. 200 to Ottawa, November 18, 1943, LAC, RG 25, 2-AE(s), part 1, CDTT00007.
8 "Canadian Defence Relationships with the United States," May 26, 1944.

9   Canadian Defence Relationships with the United States," May 26, 1944.

10 "For the Under-Secretary," from J.A.G. [James George], April 12, 1944, LAC, RG 25, 52-C(s).

11 "Canada's Post-war Defence Relationship with the United States," April 11, 1944, revised June 29, 1944, LAC, RG 25, 52-C(s).

12 "For the Under-Secretary" April 12, 1944.

13 Barnes, "A Confusion, Not a System," 464–65. See also Jensen, *Cautious Beginnings*, 117–36.

14 Barnes, "A Confusion, Not a System," 465.

15 Secretary, Chiefs of Staff Committee [hereafter CSC], to Secretary, Canadian Joint Staff [hereafter CJS] Washington, July 26, 1944, LAC, RG 25, 52-C(s).

16 CJS Washington JS 101 to Secretary, CSC, August 5, 1944, LAC, RG 25, 52-C(s).

17 Hume Wrong to Lester Pearson, January 3, 1944 [but should be 1945], LAC, RG 25, 52-C(s).

18 Memorandum to Mr. Wrong from Maurice Pope, January 4, 1945, LAC, RG 25, 52-C(s).

19 Moscow no. 368 to Ottawa, September 25, 1945, LAC, RG 25, 2-AE(s), part 1, CDTT00009, p. 3.

20 "Post War Canadian Defence Relationships with the United States: General Considerations," CWC [Cabinet War Committee], January 4, 1945, LAC, RG 25, 52-C(s). While this document is marked "Final – Second Revision," a slightly revised version was truly finalized on January 23, 1945, and is available in the same folder.

21 "Post War Canadian Defence Relationships with the United States," January 23, 1945.

22 "Post War Canadian Defence Relationships with the United States," January 23, 1945.

23 "Post War Canadian Defence Relationships with the United States," January 23, 1945.

24 "Continental Defence Value of the Canadian Northwest," by Major General Guy V. Henry, June 8, 1945, LAC, RG 25, 52-C(s); "Postwar Collaboration," by Major General Guy V. Henry, June 8, 1945, LAC, RG 25, 52-C(s).

25 Untitled memorandum from Pope to several recipients, July 28, 1945, LAC, RG 25, 52-C(s).

26 "Suggested draft of observations on General Henry's statement on (a) Continental Defence Value of Canadian Northwest and (b) Canada-United States Post-War Collaboration, to be made by Canadian section at Meeting of the PJBD to be held in Montreal, 4th September 1945," August 10, 1945, LAC, RG 25, 52-C(s).

27 "Suggested draft of observations on General Henry's statement," August 10, 1945.

28 "Suggested draft of observations on General Henry's statement," August 10, 1945.

29 "Brief of Informal Remarks by the Acting Secretary, United States Section, PJBD, New York, November 7, 1945, on the Subject of Continuing Canadian-American Military Collaboration," undated, LAC, RG 25, 52-C(s). See also Memorandum for Mr. Wrong from RMM [Ronald Macalister Macdonnell], November 16, 1945, LAC, RG 25, 52-C(s).

30 "Brief of Informal Remarks by the Acting Secretary," undated. See also Memorandum for Mr. Wrong from RMM, November 16, 1945.

31 "Brief of Informal Remarks by the Acting Secretary," undated. See also Memorandum for Mr. Wrong from RMM, November 16, 1945.
32 Memorandum of the PJBD Canada-United States, January 17, 1946, LAC, RG 25, 52-C(s).
33 For a full discussion of the replacement of ABC-22, see the excellent account in Chapter 5 of Richard Goette, *Sovereignty and Command in Canada-US Continental Air Defence, 1940–57* (Vancouver: UBC Press, 2018). Note that if the US preliminary continental defence plan focused on offence as the best defence, that was not entirely clear to the Canadians: Goette, *Sovereignty and Command*, 113.
34 Arnold Heeney to Douglas Abbott, November 19, 1945, LAC, RG 25, 52-C(s).
35 Unsent telegram, Secretary of State for External Affairs [hereafter SSEA] to Washington, January 30, 1946, LAC, RG 25, 52-C(s).
36 "Postwar defence collaboration with the United States," December 19, 1945, LAC, RG 25, 52-C(s).
37 "Progress Report No. 1," from the Joint Planning Committee, CSC, October 29, 1946, LAC, RG 24, CSC 1652:1, part 1, CDNW15194, p. 4.
38 Goodman, *The Official History*, 258.
39 Quoted in Goodman, *The Official History*, 258–62, quote at 262. See brief discussion in Jensen, *Cautious Beginnings*, 140–41.
40 "The Chargé in the Soviet Union (Kennan) to the Secretary of State," February 22, 1946, *Foreign Relations of the United States* [hereafter *FRUS*], 1946, vol. VI, Eastern Europe, The Soviet Union, doc. 475, p. 707.
41 Moscow no. 185 to Ottawa, April 24, 1946, LAC, RG 25, series 2(AE)s, part 1, CDTT00014, p. 1.
42 "Combined Canada-United States Intelligence Appreciations," Memorandum for JPC to CSC, October 29, 1946, *DCER*, vol. 12, doc. 977, p. 1660.
43 "An Appreciation of the Basic Security Requirements for Canadian-U.S. Security," No. 1, May 23, 1946, LAC, RG24, CSC 1652:1, part 1, CDNW15173, p. 3.
44 "An Appreciation of the Basic Security Requirements," No. 1, May 23, 1946, p. 2.
45 "An Appreciation of the Basic Security Requirements," No. 1, May 23, 1946, p. 5.
46 Excerpt from the 353rd Meeting of the CSC, June 7, 1946, LAC, CSC 1652:1, part 1, CDNW15176, p. 1.
47 Excerpt from the 356th Meeting of the CSC, June 25, 1946, LAC, CSC 1652:1, part 1, CDNW15184.
48 "Canadian-United States Joint Appreciation and Basic Security Plan; comments thereon by the Chief of Staff," Memorandum for the CDC, July 15, 1946, LAC, CSC 1652:1, part 1, CDNW15192, p. 1.
49 "Canadian-United States Joint Appreciation and Basic Security Plan; comments thereon by the Chief of Staff," July 15, 1946, p. 1.
50 Woodrow J. Kuhns, ed., *Assessing the Soviet Threat: The Early Cold War Years* (Washington: Centre for the Study of Intelligence, Central Intelligence Agency, 1997), 6, https://www.cia.gov/resources/csi/static/Assessing-the-Soviet-Threat-The-Early-Cold-

War-Years.pdf. The declassified document is also available online at the CIA FOIA RR, https://www.cia.gov/readingroom/docs/DOC_0000256601.pdf.

51 Kuhns, *Assessing the Soviet Threat*, 10.

52 Valero, "The American Joint Intelligence Committee"; Donald P. Steury, "Origins of CIA's Analysis of the Soviet Union" in *Watching the Bear: Essays on CIA's Analysis of the Soviet Union*, eds. Gerald K. Haines and Robert E. Leggett (Langley: Center for the Study of Intelligence, Central Intelligence Agency, 2003).

53 Raymond L. Garthoff, "Estimating Soviet Military Intentions and Capabilities" in *Watching the Bear: Essays on CIA's Analysis of the Soviet Union*, eds. Gerald K. Haines and Robert E. Leggett (Langley: Center for the Study of Intelligence, Central Intelligence Agency, 2003). ORE-1, along with JCS 1696, were prepared to support the Clifford-Elsey Report to Harry S. Truman, but had much less significance than Kennan's long telegram.

54 "The Possibility of War with the Soviet Union," Memorandum by Associate USSEA, June 28, 1946, *DCER* 12, doc. 961, p. 1632.

55 Excerpt from the 354th Meeting of the CSC, June 11, 1946, LAC, CSC 1652:1, part 1, CDNW15177; Excerpt from the 355th Meeting of the CSC, June 20, 1946, LAC, CSC 1652:1, part 1, CDNW15182.

56 Secretary, JIC, to JIC Members, August 15, 1946, LAC, RG 25, 50028-B-40, part 1, CDIM00630. The appreciation itself is "Strategic Appreciation of the Capabilities of the U.S.S.R. to Attack the North American Continent," undated, LAC, RG 25, 50028-B-40, part 1, CDIM00629.

57 "Strategic Appreciation," undated, p. 2.

58 Memorandum for Mr. Riddell from Crean, August 23, 1946, LAC, RG 25, 50028-B-40, part 1, CDIM00632, p. 2.

59 Memorandum for Mr. Riddell from Crean, August 23, 1946, p. 1.

60 The Ambassador in Canada (Atherton) to the Secretary of State, August 28, 1946, *FRUS*, 1946, vol. V, The British Commonwealth, Western and Central Europe, doc. 33, pp. 53–55.

61 Special Study No. 3, "Current Soviet Intentions," August 24, 1946, in Kuhns, *Assessing the Soviet Threat*, 9. Special Study No. 3 is available online in the CIA FOIA Reading Room: https://www.cia.gov/readingroom/docs/CIA-RDP84-00022R000200040021-6.pdf. On Turkey, see Melvyn P. Leffler, "National Security and US Foreign Policy," in *Origins of the Cold War: An International History*, eds. Melvyn P. Leffler and David S. Painter (London: Routledge, 1994), 15–52.

62 Special Study No. 3, "Current Soviet Intentions," August 24, 1946, p. 2.

63 Memorandum from Senior United States Army Member, PJBD, to PJBD, September 9, 1946, *DCER*, vol. 12, doc. 967, p. 1642.

64 Memorandum from Senior United States Army Member, September 9, 1946, p. 1643.

65 Memorandum from JPC to CSC, October 29, 1946, *DCER*, vol. 12, doc. 977, p. 1660. Emphasis in original.

66 Ambassador in United States to USSEA, June 21, 1946, *DCER*, vol. 12, doc. 960, p. 1632.

67 Ambassador in United States to USSEA, November 14, 1946, *DCER*, vol. 12, doc. 987, p. 1683. For American understanding of the Canadian need to be aware of the strategic concept, see Memorandum by the Assistant Chief of the Division of British Commonwealth Affairs (Parsons), November 12, 1946, *FRUS*, 1946, vol. V, The British Commonwealth, Western and Central Europe, doc. 38, pp. 63–65.

68 Memorandum from USSEA to Prime Minister, November 12, 1946, *DCER*, vol. 12, doc. 983, p. 1671.

69 Memorandum from USSEA to Prime Minister, November 12, 1946, p. 1672.

70 Minutes of a Meeting of the CDC, November 13, 1946, *DCER*, vol. 12, doc. 984, p. 1674.

71 Minutes of a Meeting of the CDC, November 13, 1946, p. 1675.

72 J. W. Pickersgill and D. F. Forster, *The Mackenzie King Record Volume 3, 1945/46* (Toronto: University of Toronto Press, 1970), 366–67.

73 Pickersgill and Forster, *The Mackenzie King Record*, 369.

74 Pickersgill and Forster, *The Mackenzie King Record*, 366–67.

75 Pickersgill and Forster, *The Mackenzie King Record*, 369–70.

76 Pickersgill and Forster, *The Mackenzie King Record*, 370.

77 Statement by Minister of National Health and Warfare to Cabinet, November 15, 1946, *DCER*, vol. 12, doc. 988, p. 1684.

78 Statement by Minister of National Health and Warfare to Cabinet, November 15, 1946, p. 1685.

79 Statement by Minister of National Health and Warfare to Cabinet, November 15, 1946, p. 1685.

80 Statement by Minister of National Health and Warfare to Cabinet, November 15, 1946, p. 1685.

81 Statement by Minister of National Health and Warfare to Cabinet, November 15, 1946, p. 1686.

82 Memorandum from Minister of National Defence to Prime Minister, January 7, 1947, *DCER*, vol. 13, doc. 866, p. 1482.

83 Cabinet Conclusions, November 15, 1946, *DCER*, vol. 12, doc. 989, p. 1690.

84 Cabinet Conclusions, November 15, 1946, p. 1691. The Canadians advised the Americans, informally, that they would prepare their own appreciation of Soviet intentions, and the US officers said they would welcome a Canadian assessment: Memorandum by Head, Third Political Division, November 26, 1946, *DCER*, vol. 12, doc. 993, p. 1700.

85 Memorandum by Head, First Political Division, November 21, 1946, *DCER*, vol. 12, doc. 992, p. 1697.

86 Memorandum by Head, First Political Division, November 21, 1946, 1697.

87 Memorandum by Head, First Political Division, November 21, 1946, 1698.

88 "Political Appreciation of the Objectives of Soviet Foreign Policy," Appendix A, November 30, 1946, LAC, RG 25, 50028-B-40, part 1, CDIM00634. Also published in *DCER*, vol. 12, doc. 994, p. 1703.

89   Memorandum by Head, Third Political Division, December 10, 1946, *DCER*, vol. 12, doc. 996, p. 1711.
90   Memorandum from USSEA to Prime Minister, December 23, 1946, *DCER*, vol. 12, doc. 999, p. 1721.
91   Memorandum from USSEA to Prime Minister, December 23, 1946, p. 1722. On reference to earlier disagreements, see Pope to Robertson, September 6, 1945, LAC, RG 25, 52-C(s).
92   Minutes of a Meeting Between Representatives of Canada and the United States, December 21, 1946, *DCER*, vol. 12, doc. 998, p. 1714.
93   Minutes of a Meeting Between Representatives, December 21, 1946, p. 1714.
94   Minutes of a Meeting Between Representatives, December 21, 1946, p. 1715.
95   Memorandum from USSEA to Prime Minister, December 23, 1946, p. 1723.
96   Memorandum from USSEA to Prime Minister, December 23, 1946, p. 1723.
97   Memorandum from USSEA to Prime Minister, December 23, 1946, p. 1723.
98   Memorandum from USSEA to Prime Minister, December 23, 1946, p. 1721.
99   Jensen, *Cautious Beginnings*, 142. A Joint Intelligence Staff was created for this purpose. For an early account of this document, see Lawrence Aronsen, "Preparing for Armageddon: JIC 1 (Final) and the Soviet Attack on Canada," *Intelligence and National Security* 19, no. 3 (2004): 490–510, https://doi.org/10.1080/0268452042000316250.
100 "Joint Intelligence Committee Strategic Appreciation," March 15, 1947, LAC, RG 25, 50028-AK-40, part 1, CDIM00645, p. 2.
101 "Joint Intelligence Committee Strategic Appreciation," March 15, 1947, LAC, RG 25, 50028-AK-40, part 1, CDIM00645, p. 6.
102 Memorandum for Mr. Pearson from Reid, February 13, 1947, LAC, RG 25, 50028-B-40, part 1, CDIM00639, p. 2.
103 Memorandum for Mr. Pearson from Reid, February 13, 1947, p. 2.
104 Untitled memo drafted by Crean, March 12, 1947, LAC, RG 25, 50028-B-40, part 1, CDIM00644.
105 Excerpt from the 400th Meeting of the CSC, September 4, 1947, LAC, CSC 1652:1, part 2, CDNW15267, p. 2; "Revisions of the Appreciation and the Basic Security Plan," Memorandum by the Canada-United States Military Cooperation Committee, July 24, 1947, LAC, CSC 1652:1, part 2, CDNW15258.
106 "Canada-U.S. Defence Planning," by H. N. Lay, July 16, 1947, LAC, CSC 1652:1, part 2, CDNW15255, p. 2.
107 Lay, quoting the JPC in a memorandum to the CSC, March 12, 1947, in "Canada-U.S. Defence Planning," July 16, 1947, p. 2.
108 "Canada-U.S. Defence Planning," July 16, 1947, p. 2.
109 Excerpt from the 400th Meeting of the CSC, September 4, 1947, LAC, CSC 1652:1, part 2, CDNW15268, p. 2.
110 "Canada-U.S. Defence Planning," July 16, 1947, p. 3.
111 Excerpt from the 406th Meeting of the CSC, October 14, 1947, LAC, CSC 1652:1, part 2, CDNW15273, p. 1.

112 Excerpt from the 406th Meeting of the CSC, October 14, 1947, p. 1.
113 "The United States and the Soviet Union: A Study of the Possibility of War and Some of the Implications for Canadian Policy," Memorandum by Escott Reid, August 30, 1947, LAC, RG 25, 52-F(s).
114 Maurice Pope to Lester Pearson, September 29, 1947, LAC, RG 25, 52-F(s).
115 Pope to Pearson, September 29, 1947.
116 Memorandum for Mr. Teakles from Marcel Cadieux, October 17, 1947, LAC, RG 25, 52-F(s).
117 Dana Wilgress to Lester Pearson, November 6, 1946, LAC, RG 25, 52-F(s).
118 Wilgress to Pearson, November 6, 1946.
119 Untitled and undated drafting notes from Ford, attached to his letter to Pearson of October 10, 1947, LAC, RG 25, 52-F(s).
120 Comments on Draft Memorandum of August 30, 1947, attached to RMM to Pearson, September 25, 1947, LAC, RG 25, 52-F(s).
121 Untitled comments sent from Ritchie in Paris, November 6, 1947, LAC, RG 25, 52-F(s).
122 Untitled comments sent from Ritchie in Paris, November 6, 1947.
123 "Influences Shaping the Policy of the United States Towards the Soviet Union," Memorandum by Hume Wrong, December 4, 1947, LAC, RG 25, 52-F(s).
124 "Comment on Draft Memorandum Dated August 30th Entitled 'United States and the Soviet Union,'" December 3, 1947, LAC, RG 25, 52-F(s).
125 "Influences Shaping the Policy," December 4, 1947.
126 "Influences Shaping the Policy," December 4, 1947.
127 Memorandum for the USSEA from Reid, January 17, 1948, LAC, RG 25, 52-F(s); Memorandum for the Prime Minister from USSEA, drafted by Reid on January 17, 1947, and sent from Pearson to SSEA on January 22, 1948, LAC, RG 25, 52-F(s).
128 "Comment on Draft Memorandum," December 3, 1947.
129 "Canada-U.S. Basic Security Plan, Implementation Programme – Fiscal Year 1948–49," Memorandum to Cabinet Defence Committee, October 20, 1947, LAC, CSC 1652:1, part 2, CDNW15274, p. 1.
130 "Canada-U.S. Basic Security Plan," October 20, 1947, p. 1.

NOTES TO CHAPTER 2

1 Extracts from Minutes of Meeting of CSC and Minister of National Defence, January 22, 1948, *DCER*, vol. 14, doc. 954, p. 1567.
2 Extracts from Minutes of Meeting of CSC, January 22, 1948, p. 1568.
3 Extracts from Minutes of Meeting of CSC, January 22, 1948, p. 1568.
4 Finletter, Thomas K., *Survival in the Air Age: A Report by the President's Sir Policy Commission* (Washington: US Government Printing Office, 1948).
5 Extracts from Minutes of Meeting of CSC, January 22, 1948, p. 1568.
6 Excerpt from 414th Meeting of the CSC, February 12, 1948, LAC, CSC 1652:1, part 2, CDNW15333, p. 1.

7   Excerpt from 418th Meeting of the CSC, March 9, 1948, LAC, CSC 1652:1, part 3, CDNW15360, p. 1.
8   Excerpt from 418th Meeting of the CSC, March 9, 1948, p. 1.
9   "Review by the JIC of Appreciation of the Requirements for Canada-United States Security," Memorandum by the Canada-United States Military Cooperation Committee, March 19, 1948, LAC, RG 24, CSC 1652:1, part 3, CDNW15362, p. 1.
10 "An Appreciation of the Possible Military Threat to the Security of Canada and the United States," JIC 3/48 (Final), May 3, 1948, LAC, RG 24, CSC 1652:1, part 3, CDNW15365, p. 1.
11 "An Appreciation of the Possible Military Threat," May 3, 1948, p. 1
12 "An Appreciation of the Possible Military Threat," May 3, 1948, p. 2.
13 "An Appreciation of the Possible Military Threat," May 3, 1948, p. 3.
14 "An Appreciation of the Possible Military Threat," May 3, 1948, p. 3.
15 "An Appreciation of the Possible Military Threat," May 3, 1948, p. 6.
16 "An Appreciation of the Possible Military Threat," May 3, 1948, p. 7.
17 Extract from 422nd Meeting of CSC, May 11, 1948, LAC, RG 24, CSC 1652:1, part 3, CDNW15369. Emphasis added.
18 "Appreciation for the Requirements of Canada-U.S. Security," Secretary, JIC, to Secretary, CSC, May 6, 1948, LAC, RG 24, CSC 1652:1, part 3, CDNW15366; Extract from 422nd Meeting of CSC, May 11, 1948.
19 "An Appreciation of the Possible Military Threat," May 3, 1948, p. 3.
20 "Report on the Acceptability of the American Revisions to the Appreciation of the Requirements of Canada-United States Security dated 23rd May, 1946," JIC 5/48 (Final), June 12, 1948, LAC, RG 24, CSC 1652:1, part 3, CDNW15399, p. 2.
21 "An Appreciation of the Possible Military Threat," May 3, 1948.
22 "Report on the Acceptability of the American Revisions," June 12, 1948, p. 3.
23 Extract from Minutes of Meeting of CDC, April 15, 1948, *DCER*, vol. 14, doc. 959, p. 1580.
24 Extract from Minutes of Meeting of CDC, April 15, 1948, p. 1580.
25 "J.I.S. Paper on the U.S.S.R.," undated, attached to Excerpt from meeting of the 164th Meeting of the JIC, May 3, 1948, LAC, RG 24, 9042-34/0-1.
26 "JIC Appreciation — Soviet Aims, Strategy and Capabilities," Foulkes to USSEA, April 10, 1948, LAC, RG 25, 50028-B-40, part 1, CDIM00652, p. 1.
27 "An Outline of Soviet Capabilities and Strategic Objectives in a War Beginning before July, 1949," JIC 4/48 (Final), May 31, 1948, LAC, RG 25, 50028-B-40, part 1, CDIM00654, p. 3.
28 "An Outline of Soviet Capabilities and Strategic Objectives," May 31, 1948, p. 1.
29 "An Outline of Soviet Capabilities and Strategic Objectives," May 31, 1948, pp. 1–2.
30 "An Outline of Soviet Capabilities and Strategic Objectives," May 31, 1948, p. 2.
31 Extract from Minutes of Meeting of CDC, June 2, 1948, *DCER*, vol. 14, doc. 960, p. 1582.
32 Extract from Minutes of Meeting of CDC, June 2, 1948, p. 1581.

33 Extract from Minutes of Meeting of CDC, June 2, 1948, p. 1582.
34 "The Requirement for a Combined Canada-United States Long Term Strategic Estimate (Appreciation)," Secretary, Canadian Section, MCC, to Secretary, CSC, August 20, 1948, LAC, RG 24, CSC 1652:1, part 3, CDNW15406. The Terms of Reference are attached to this document. CSC approval of the request is "Requirements for Combined Canada-U.S. Long-Term Strategic Estimate (Appreciation)," Acting Secretary, CSC, to Secretary, Canadian Section, MCC, August 31, 1948, LAC, RG 24, CSC 1652:1, part 1, CDNW15411.
35 "Soviet Capabilities and Probable Courses of Action Against Canada, the United States, and the Areas Adjacent Thereto, 1949–1956," ACAI 5 (Final), October 21, 1948, LAC, RG 24, 1480-29.
36 "Report on the Preparation of an Agreed Canada-United States Strategic Appreciation," Memorandum JIC 1-8-11 for the Joint Intelligence Committee, undated, LAC, RG 24, 1480-29.
37 "Report on the Preparation of an Agreed Canada-United States Strategic Appreciation," undated.
38 "Report on the Preparation of an Agreed Canada-United States Strategic Appreciation," undated.
39 Memorandum for the Secretary, JIC, from Director of Naval Intelligence (hereafter DNI) Atwood, November 2, 1948, LAC, RG 24, 1480-29.
40 "Report on the Preparation of an Agreed Canada-United States Strategic Appreciation," undated.
41 G. G. Crean to W. E. Todd, November 9, 1948, LAC, RG 24, 1480-29.
42 Minutes of the 192nd Meeting of the JIC, November 5, 1948, LAC, RG 24, 1274-10, part 3.
43 "Discrepancies in A.C.A.I. 5 (Final)," Memorandum to DNI, undated, LAC, RG 24, 1480-29.
44 Minutes of the 192nd Meeting of the Joint Intelligence Committee, November 5, 1948, LAC, RG 24, 1274-10, part 3.
45 Memorandum for the JIC from Secretary, JIC, December 3, 1948, LAC, RG 24, 1480-29.
46 "Report on the Preparation of an Agreed Canada-United States Strategic Appreciation," Memorandum for the JIC, December 15, 1948, LAC, RG 24, 1480-29.
47 "American-British Agreed Intelligence," Memorandum to Chiefs from Secretary, CSC, January 26, 1949, LAC, RG 24, 1480-29. See also Minutes of the 438th Meeting of the CSC, January 4, 1949, DHH/DND 2002/17, Box 74, File 10.
48 "American-British Agreed Intelligence," January 26, 1949.
49 Todd to Crean, February 21, 1949, LAC, RG 24, 1480-29, part 2.
50 Minutes of the 197th Meeting of the JIC, March 9, 1949, LAC, RG 24, 1274-10, part 3.
51 Minutes of the 197th Meeting of the JIC, March 9, 1949.
52 Minutes of the 202nd Meeting of the JIC, May 18, 1949, LAC, RG 24, 1274-10, part 4.
53 Crean to Todd, April 7, 1949, LAC, RG 24, 1480-29, part 2; Crean to Todd, undated draft, LAC, RG 24, 1480-29, part 2.
54 Todd to Crean, May 5, 1949, LAC, RG 24, 1480-29, part 2.

55 Minutes of the 202nd Meeting of the JIC, May 18, 1949.

56 "Agreed Canada-United States Intelligence Estimate (Appreciation), Request for" Secretary, JPC, to Secretary, JIC, through Secretary, CSC, May 13, 1949, LAC, RG 24, CSC 1652:1, part 3, CDNW15423, p. 2.

57 Jensen, *Cautious Beginnings*, 150–52. Kurt Jensen mentions some of the joint intelligence efforts in this era without naming them directly.

58 "Canada-United States Basic Security Plan Progress Report No. 9," Report by the JPC to the CSC, June 7, 1949, LAC, RG 24, CSC 1652:1, part 3, CDNW15441.

59 "Status of Canada-United States Basic Security Plan," Memorandum for the members, PJBD, Canada-United States, from the Acting Chairman of the US Section, June 16, 1949, LAC, RG 24, CSC 1652:1, part 3, CDNW15461, p. 1.

60 Note from DNI Atwood, August 22, 1949, LAC, RG 24, 1480-29, part 2.

61 Minutes of the 204th Meeting of the JIC, June 29, 1949, LAC, RG 24, 1272-10, part 4.

62 "ACAI 5/2," Secretary, JIC, to Secretary, CSC, August 16, 1949, LAC, RG 24, 1480-29, part 2; JCS WAR 93017 [to Ennis], August 18, 1949, LAC, RG 24, 1480-29, part 2.

63 "Memorandum for C.S.C.," from Secretary JIC, July 12, 1949, LAC, RG 24, 1480-29, part 2.

64 "ACAI 5/2," Acting Secretary, JIC, to Secretary, CSC, September 1, 1949, LAC, RG 24, CSC 1652:1, part 3, CDNW15482. The agreed document is "Probable Soviet Courses of Action against Canada, the United States, and the Areas Adjacent Thereto, 1 Jan 1957," ACAI 5/2, June 24, 1949, LAC, RG 24, CSC 1652:1, part 3, CDNW15471.

65 Secretary, JIC, to Secretary, CSC, August 8, 1949, LAC, RG 24, CSC 5-11-2, part 1. See also Crean to Todd, June 15, 1949, LAC, RG 24, 1272-17.

66 Ministry of Defence [hereafter MOD] 622 to UKSLS, June 10, 1949, LAC, RG 24, 1272-17.

67 JIC (40) 49th Meeting, May 13, 1949, NAUK, CAB 159/5.

68 Crean to Todd, June 15, 1949.

69 Crean to Todd, June 15, 1949.

70 Crean to Todd, June 15, 1949.

71 Crean to Todd, June 15, 1949.

72 On developments in NATO before the Korean War, see Lawrence S. Kaplan, *NATO before the Korean War: April 1949–June 1950* (Kent, OH: The Kent State University Press, 2013).

73 Minutes of the 205th meeting of the JIC, July 20, 1949, LAC, RG 24, 1274-10, part 4.

74 Washington WA-1662 to External, June 17, 1949, LAC, RG 24, 1272-17.

75 Todd to Crean, July 6, 1949, LAC, RG 24, 1272-17. Ultimately, tripartite efforts did not replace the ACAI process, which continued (and was later renamed "CANUS").

76 Todd to Crean, September 1, 1949, LAC, RG 24, 1272-17.

77 In preparation of the conference, the British prepared a brief on a revision of the original document, also called "Soviet Intentions and Capabilities," JIC (49)55, June 18, 1949, available from the subscription online resource "Secret Files from World Wars to Cold War," published by Taylor and Francis.

78   Directive to the JIS, from Acting Secretary, JIC, September 9, 1949, LAC, RG 24, 1272-17.
79   Directive to the JIS, September 9, 1949.
80   ABCI 6, Minutes of the 1st Meeting between the United Kingdom and Canadian Joint Intelligence Teams and the United States Joint Intelligence Committee, September 12, 1949, LAC, RG 24, 1272-17-1, part 1.
81   "U.K.-U.S.-Canadian Intelligence Appreciation – ABCI.15," Memorandum for the JIC from G/C W. W. Bean, September 30, 1949, LAC, RG 24, 1272-17-1, part 2.
82   Crean to JIC, September 20, 1949, LAC, RG 24, 1272-17-1, part 1.
83   ABCI 6, September 12, 1949.
84   ABCI 6/1, Minutes of the 2nd Meeting between the United Kingdom and Canadian Joint Intelligence Teams and the United States JIC, September 12, 1949, LAC, RG 24, 1272-17-1, part 1. The working committees were named "Political," "Economic," "Scientific," "Army," "Navy," "Air Force," "Editorial," and "Summary."
85   ABCI 6/1, September 12, 1949.
86   ABCI 6/1, September 12, 1949.
87   ABCI 6/1, September 12, 1949.
88   ABCI 6/5, Minutes of the 6th Meeting between the United Kingdom and Canadian Joint Intelligence Teams and the United States Joint Intelligence Committee, September 20, 1949, LAC, RG 24, 1272-17-1, part 1.
89   For "pressure," see "U.K.-U.S.-Canadian Intelligence Appreciation – ABCI.15," September 30, 1949; Notes on Draft Reply Suggested by the Chairman, JIC, undated, LAC, RG 24, 1272-17-1, part 1. CSC minutes on ABCI 15 (Bean's report) are in *DCER*, vol. 15, doc. 917, p. 1564.
90   ABCI 9, Memorandum by the Scientific Committee, September 14, 1949, LAC, RG 24, 1272-17-1, part 1.
91   See opinion and dissent in "The Effect of the Soviet Possession of Atomic Bombs on the Security of the United States," ORE 32–50, Central Intelligence Agency, June 9, 1950, CIA FOIA RR https://www.cia.gov/readingroom/docs/DOC_0000258838.pdf.
92   ABCI 6/8, Minutes of the 9th Meeting between the United Kingdom and Canadian Joint Intelligence Teams and the United States Joint Intelligence Committee, September 23, 1949, LAC, RG 24, 1272-17-1, part 1; ABCI 6/10, Minutes of the 11th Meeting between the United Kingdom and Canadian Joint Intelligence Teams and the United States Joint Intelligence Committee, September 27, 1949, LAC, RG 24, 1272-17-1, part 1.
93   ABCI 15, September 27, 1949, LAC, RG 24, 1272-17-1, part 2; see also CANAWASH GI 161 to SECY JIC, September 23, 1949, LAC, RG 24, 1272-17-1, part 1; ABCI 7/1, Memorandum by the Co-Chairmen, September 16, 1949, LAC, RG 24, 1272-17-1, part 1.
94   MOD Feudal 552 to JSM Washington and UKSLS, October 28, 1949, LAC, RG 24, 1272-17-1, part 2. See also Feudal 551 in same part.
95   ABCI 15, September 27, 1949.
96   ABCI 15, September 27, 1949.
97   ABCI 7/2, Memorandum by the Co-Chairmen, September 17, 1949, LAC, RG 24, 1272-17-1, part 1. The briefing committee consisted of four UK members, four US members,

and one Canadian. See also "Agreed Action Between U.S.-U.K.-Canadian Planners," enclosure to ABCM-18, Memorandum for the U.S.-U.K.-Canadian Planners, December 9, 1949, LAC, RG 24, CSC 5:11:2, part 1.

98 Kenneth W. Condit, *History of the Joint Chiefs of Staff: The Joint Chiefs of Staff and National Policy, 1947–1949*, vol. 2 (Washington, DC: Office of Joint History, Office of the Chairman of the Joint Chiefs of Staff, 1996), 154–60; Robert A. Wampler, "Ambiguous Legacy: The United States, Great Britain and the Foundations of NATO Strategy, 1948–1957" (PhD diss., Harvard University, 1991), 2–13. The Canadians noted that it was the "differences which have developed between the US and UK in discussion of defence problems connected with the Mediterranean area" that led to no agreed plan: "HICKORY – Short Range Emergency Plan," Secretary, JPC, to Secretary, CSC, January 6, 1950, LAC, RG 24, CSC 5-11-2.

99 "'Bullmoose,' ABC 101 and ABC 105," March 16, 1949, LAC, RG 24, CSC 5-11-2. ABC 105 superseded BULLMOOSE (ABC 101) and Canadians looked for a new code word.

100 "Agreed Action Between U.S.-U.K.-Canadian Planners," December 9, 1949.

101 "Agreed Action Between U.S.-U.K.-Canadian Planners," December 9, 1949.

102 "Security Arrangements for Handling ABCI. 15," Memorandum for JIC from the Secretary, December 13, 1949, LAC, RG 24, 1272-17-1, part 2.

103 "ABC 109 and ABCI 15," Secretary of the CSC to Chairman CSC and Chairman CJS (L), December 12, 1949, LAC, RG 24, CSC 5-11-2.

104 Part I, dubbed JIC (UK)(49)80 (Final) in the UK, would be sent to the King's printers for typing on February 6, 1950: "American-British-Canadian Agreed Intelligence: Soviet Intentions and Capabilities, 1950," printed for His Majesty's Government, LAC, RG 24, 1272-17-1, part 2.

105 Lt-Col T. McCoy, A/DMI, to Secretary, JIC, October 19, 1949, LAC, RG 24, 1272-17-1, part 2.

106 Lt-Col T. McCoy, A/DMI, to Secretary, JIC, October 19, 1949.

107 "U.K.-U.S.-Canadian Intelligence Appreciation – ABCI.15," September 30, 1949.

108 "ABC Intelligence," Draft memorandum from Secretary, JIC, to Secretary, CSC, undated [November 2, 1949], LAC, RG 24, 1272-17-2. The result was "Re-examination of Future Soviet Intentions as a Basis for Long-Term Planning," undated paper sent to JIS under cover of memorandum from JIC Secretary, November 26, 1949, LAC, RG 24, 1272-17, CDIW00447.

109 Memorandum to the Chairman, JIC, from Atwood, November 1, 1949, LAC, RG 24, 1272-17.

110 Memorandum to the Chairman, JIC, from Atwood, November 1, 1949.

111 Johnson to Bean, October 13, 1949, LAC, RG 24, 1272-17.

112 "Revisions of ABC Intelligence," Draft memorandum for CSC prepared by A/DMI, November 3, 1949, LAC, RG 24, 1272-17-2.

113 "ABCI. 15 – Disposition of Parts I and II," Memorandum for the JIC from the Secretary, November 2, 1949, LAC, RG 24, 1272-17-1, part 2.

114 McCoy, A/DMI, to Secretary, JIC, November 3, 1949, LAC, RG 24, 1272-17-1, part 2.

115 Extract from Minutes of Meeting of CDC, December 23, 1949, *DCER*, vol. 15, doc. 918, pp. 1566–67.
116 Memorandum for the Under-Secretary from MacKay, December 21, 1949, LAC, RG 25, 50266-40, part 1.
117 Extract from Minutes of Meeting of CDC, December 22, 1949, *DCER*, vol. 15, doc. 919, p. 1569.
118 "Re-examination of Future Soviet Intentions," November 26, 1949.
119 "Re-examination of Future Soviet Intentions," November 26, 1949.
120 "J.I.S. Format C.S.C. 1 (50) – Soviet Intentions as a Basis for Long Term Planning," January 12, 1950, LAC, RG 25, 50028-AP-40, CDIW00448, p. 2. Underline in original.
121 "J.I.S. Format C.S.C. 1 (50)," January 12, 1950, pp. 2–3.
122 "J.I.S. Format for a paper entitled 'Soviet Intentions as a Basis for Long-Term Planning,'" Memorandum for Mr. MacKay from R. L. Rogers, January 30, 1950, LAC, RG 25, 50028-AP-40, CDIW00450.
123 "J.I.S. Format C.S.C. 1 (50)," January 12, 1950, p. 3.
124 "J.I.S. Format for a paper entitled 'Soviet Intentions as a Basis for Long-Term Planning,'" January 30, 1950.
125 Memorandum for European Division from Defence Liaison [hereafter DL] (2) (R. L. Rogers), May 30, 1950, LAC, RG 25, 50028-AP-40, CDIW00479, p. 1.
126 "Soviet Intentions as a Basis for Long-Term Planning," Col. Knight, DMI, to Secretary, JIC, January 31, 1950, LAC, RG 25, 50028-AP-40, CDIW00453, p. 1.
127 "Soviet Intentions as a Basis for Long-Term Planning," January 31, 1950, p. 1.
128 "JIS Draft Format Long-Term Paper," Memorandum for Mr. R. L. Rogers from DL Division (R. A. MacKay), February 2, 1950, LAC, RG 25, 50028-AP-40, CDIW00456, p. 1.
129 Memorandum for Mr. MacDermot from R. A. MacKay, February 4, 1950, LAC, RG 25, 50028-AP-40, CDIW00455, p. 1.
130 Memorandum for MacDermot from MacKay, February 4, 1950.
131 Memorandum for MacDermot from MacKay, February 4, 1950, p. 1.
132 "JIS Draft Format Long-Term Paper," February 2, 1950; Memorandum for DL from R. A. D. Ford, February 7, 1950, LAC, RG 25, 50028-AP-40, CDIW00458; Memorandum to the Secretary, JIC, from DL Division, February 9, 1950, LAC, RG 25, 50028-AP-40, CDIW00464.
133 Handwritten note to Langille, undated, LAC, RG 25, 50028-AP-40, CDIW00472.
134 The UK paper is JIC (50)7 (Final), "The Likelihood of War with the Soviet Union and the Date by Which the Soviet Leaders Might be Prepared to Risk It," March [date obscured], 1950, LAC, RG 25, 50028-AK-40, part 1, CDIM00003.
135 "The Likelihood of War with the Soviet Union," March [date obscured], 1950, p. 1.
136 JIC (50) 28th Meeting, May 10, 1950, NAUK, CAB 159/7.
137 Memorandum for Mr. Reid, Mr. Ritchie, and Mr. MacDermot from Glazebrook, May 8, 1950, LAC, RG 25, 50028-AK-40, part 1, CDIM00001; Ritchie to Pearson, May 13, 1950, LAC, RG 25, 50028-AK-40, part 1, CDIM00002.

138 "The Likelihood and Circumstances of War with the Soviet Union," May 20, 1950, JIS(JIB) draft, LAC, RG 25, 50028-AP-40, CDIW00474, p. 1.

139 "Political Factors in the Likelihood of the Outbreak of War with the Soviet Union," June 16, 1950, LAC, RG 25, 50028-AP-40, part 1, CDIW00481, pp. 1–2; see also discussion in "Political Factors in the Likelihood of the Outbreak of War with the Soviet Union," May 23, 1950, LAC, RG 25, 50028-AP-40, CDIW00476.

140 "Political Factors in the Likelihood of the Outbreak of War," June 16, 1950, p. 1.

141 "Political Factors in the Likelihood of the Outbreak of War with the Soviet Union," Memorandum for DL from MacDermot (drafted by Ford), June 14, 1950, LAC, RG 25, 50028-AP-40, CDIW00480, p. 2.

142 "Political Factors in the Likelihood of the Outbreak of War," June 16, 1950, p. 4

143 "Political Factors in the Likelihood of the Outbreak of War," June 16, 1950, p. 4.

144 "Political Factors in the Likelihood of the Outbreak of War," June 14, 1950, p. 2.

145 "Political Factors in the Likelihood of the Outbreak of War," June 16, 1950, p. 6.

146 Memorandum for Mr. Glazebrook from R. L. Rogers, June 19, 1950, LAC, RG 25, 50028-AP-40, CDIW00482.

NOTES TO CHAPTER 3

1 The Cabinet Conclusions from the first days of the war are fascinating. On June 26, the Cabinet asserted that Korea was of "minor strategic importance": "Korea, report on recent developments," June 26, 1950, LAC CC, RG 2, A-5-a, vol. 2645, p. 2. The next day, the Cabinet had heard more from the Americans and learned that the US view was that Moscow "had no desire to provoke a general conflict": "Korea; U.S. policy," June 27, 1950, LAC CC, RG 2, A-5-a, vol. 2645, p. 4.

2 Excerpt from Minutes of the JIC's 228th Meeting, July 5, 1950, LAC, RG 25, 50028-AK-40, part 1, CDIM00004, p. 1.

3 "Imminence of War," July 6, 1950, LAC, RG 25, 50028-AK-40, part 1, CDIM00005, p. 2. Although the paper was read at the meeting on July 5, the copy in the archives was re-typed and redistributed the next day, July 6.

4 "Imminence of War," July 6, 1950, p. 1.

5 "Imminence of War," July 6, 1950, p. 2.

6 "Imminence of War," July 6, 1950.

7 "Imminence of War," July 6, 1950, p. 3.

8 Excerpt from Minutes of the JIC's 229th Meeting, July 11, 1950, LAC, RG 25, 50028-AK-40, part 1, CDIM00008, p. 1.

9 "Defence Research - Strategic Questions," Langley (DSI) to multiple addresses, July 14, 1950, LAC, RG 24, DRBS 2-1-172-10.

10 Memorandum for Mr. R. A. MacKay from Menzies, July 14, 1950, LAC, RG 25, 50028-AK-40, part 1, CDIM00011, p. 1.

11 "The Imminence of War," CSC 20(50), July 17, 1950, LAC, RG 25, 50028-AK-40, part 1, CDIM00013; "C.S.C. Meeting 9:30 a.m., Tuesday, July 18th in the Office of the C.G.S.," Memorandum for the Under-Secretary, July 17, 1950, LAC, RG 25, 50028-AK-40, part 1, CDIM00015.

12 "The Imminence of War," CSC 20(50), July 17, 1950, p. 1.
13 "The Imminence of War," CSC 20(50), July 17, 1950, p. 2.
14 "The Imminence of War," CSC 20(50), July 17, 1950, p. 2.
15 "The Imminence of War," CSC 20(50), July 17, 1950, p. 3.
16 "The Imminence of War," CSC 20(50), July 17, 1950, p. 3.
17 Excerpt from CSC Minutes of a Special Meeting, July 18, 1950, LAC, RG 25, 50028-AK-40, part 1, CDIM00016, 1. Foulkes prepared these comments in the form of an addendum that could be inserted into the paper before it was approved and sent to the Cabinet Defence Committee the following day.
18 Excerpt from CSC Minutes of a Special Meeting, July 18, 1950, p. 2.
19 Excerpt from CSC Minutes of a Special Meeting, July 18, 1950, p. 2.
20 The size of a US army division in 1950 ranged from 10,000 to 13,000 men, meaning Foulkes was anticipating that the UN required approximately 50,000 to 75,000 men. See Roy K. Flint, "Task Force Smith and the 24th Division: Delay and Withdrawal, 5–19 July 1950" in *America's First Battles, 1776–1965*, eds. Charles E. Heller and William A. Stofft (Lawrence, KS: University Press of Kansas, 1986), 269.
21 Excerpt from CSC Minutes of a Special Meeting, July 18, 1950, p. 1.
22 Excerpt from CSC Minutes of a Special Meeting, July 18, 1950, p. 1.
23 Excerpt from CDC Minutes of the 65th Meeting held at 0930 hours, Wednesday, July 19, 1950, LAC, RG 25, 50028-AK-40, part 1, CDIM00018, p. 1.
24 Excerpt from CDC Minutes of the 65th Meeting held at 0930 hours, Wednesday, July 19, 1950, p. 2. See also "Korea; communication from the Secretary-General of the United Nations," July 19, 1950, LAC CC, RG 2, A-5-a, vol. 2645.
25 "Appreciation on the Imminence of War – Re-examination," Aide Memoire prepared by Group Captain C. L. Annis, Chief Secretary of the Joint Staff, for Secretary, JIC, August 1, 1950, LAC, RG 25, 50028-AK-40, part 1, CDIM00019, p. 1.
26 "Appreciation on the Imminence of War — Re-examination," August 1, 1950, p. 1.
27 Extract from Minutes of the 233rd Meeting of the JIC, August 1 and 2, 1950, LAC, RG 25, 50028-AK-40, part 1, CDIM00021.
28 "Imminence of War," CSC 22(50), August 2, 1950, under cover of "Appreciation on the Imminence of War," August 2, 1950, LAC, RG 25, 50028-AK-40, part 1, CDIM00022, p. 1.
29 "Imminence of War," CSC 22(50), August 2, 1950, p. 3.
30 Brief for CSC, DMI (Knight) to CGS (through BGS (Plans)), August 3, 1950, DHH/DND, 2002/17, Box 70, File 9.
31 "Imminence of War," CSC 22(50), August 2, 1950, p. 7.
32 "Imminence of War," CSC 22(50), August 2, 1950, p. 8.
33 "Imminence of War," CSC 22(50), August 2, 1950, p. 7.
34 "Imminence of War," CSC 22(50), August 2, 1950, p. 8.
35 "Imminence of War," CSC 22(50), August 2, 1950, p. 8.
36 "Imminence of War," CSC 22(50), August 2, 1950, p. 9.
37 "Imminence of War," CSC 22(50), August 2, 1950, p. 12.

38 Excerpts from Minutes of the 469th Meeting of the CSC, August 3, 1950, LAC, RG 25, 50028-AK-40, part 1, CDIM00029, p. 1.
39 Excerpts from Minutes of the 469th Meeting of the CSC, August 3, 1950, p. 1.
40 Excerpts from Minutes of the 469th Meeting of the CSC, August 3, 1950, p. 1.
41 "Memorandum for the Joint Intelligence Committee," September 19, 1950, LAC, RG 25, 50028-AK-40, part 1, CDIM00032, p. 1.
42 "Memorandum for the Joint Intelligence Committee," September 19, 1950, 1.
43 The final document is "The Imminence of War," CSC 31(50), October 24, 1950, LAC, RG 25, 50028-AK-40, part 1, CDIM00043. Other drafts and related correspondence from the LAC, RG 25, 50028-AK-40, part 1, include: Memorandum for the JIS from Secretary, JIC, October 13, 1950, CDIM00036; "The Imminence of War," JIS Draft CSC 31(50), October 13, 1950, CDIM00037; "The Imminence of War," JIS Draft CSC 31(50), October 17, 1950, CDIM00038; Excerpt from Minutes of JIC's 242nd Meeting, October 18, 1950, CDIM00039; "The Imminence of War," JIC Appreciation, October 19, 1950, CDIM00041; and Memorandum to Secretary, JIC, from Pratt (DNI), October 16, 1950, LAC, RG 24, 1480-36, part 1.
44 Memorandum for Mr. MacKay and Mr. Glazebrook from Eberts, November 13, 1950, LAC, RG 25, 50028-AK-40, part 1, CDIM00056.
45 Excerpt from Minutes of the 475th Meeting, CSC, November 21, 1950, LAC, RG 25, 50028-AK-40, part 1, CDIM00059, p. 1.
46 The historical record suggests that the first — Chinese apprehension about US moves — was correct, while the second — a coordinated plan to tie up US and UN forces — was not.
47 Excerpt from Minutes of the 475th Meeting, November 21, 1950, p. 1.
48 Minutes of the 2nd Meeting of the JISC, December 1, 1950, LAC, RG 24, 1274-10-9.
49 Minutes of the 2nd Meeting of the JISC, December 1, 1950.
50 "Message CJS(L)M305 of 12 December from General Foulkes for Mr. Claxton," December 12, 1950, LAC, RG 25, 50028-AK-40, part 1, CDIM00071, p.1.
51 "Message CJS(L)M305 of 12 December from General Foulkes for Mr. Claxton," December 12, 1950, p. 1.
52 "Estimate of Soviet Intentions and Capabilities for Military Aggression," Intelligence Memorandum 301, June 30, 1950, pp. 396–402; "The Korean Situation: Soviet Intentions and Capabilities," Weekly Summary Excerpt, July 7, 1950, pp. 406–08; "Consequences of the Korean Incident," Intelligence Memorandum 302, July 8, 1950, pp. 409–13; all in Kuhns, *Assessing the Soviet Threat*.
53 JIC (50) 103rd Meeting, September 28, 1950, NAUK, CAB 159/8; Goodman, *The Official History*, 283. British officials credited themselves with moving Americans away from the conclusion that the Soviets were prepared to precipitate major war.
54 Garthoff cites NIE-15, "Probable Soviet Moves to Exploit the Present Situation," in "Estimating Soviet Military Intentions and Capabilities," 137.
55 Canadian Ambassador in Washington despatch no. 3225 to SSEA, December 14, 1950, LAC, RG 25, 50028-AK-40, part 1, CDIM00073.

56 "The International Situation," Memorandum to Cabinet, December 28, 1950, LAC, RG 25, 50028-AK-40, part 1, CDIM00078, p. 1.
57 See, for instance, Excerpt from Minutes of the JIC's 249th Meeting, December 14, 1950, LAC, RG 25, 50028-AK-40, part 1, CDIM00075; Memorandum by Joint Intelligence Committee, December 14, 1950, LAC, RG 25, 50028-AK-40, part 1, CDIM00079.
58 Memorandum for Mr. Fournier (European Division) from Ford, January 18, 1951, LAC, RG 25, 50028-AK-40, part 1, CDIM00080, p. 1.
59 Memorandum for the Under-Secretary from European Division, February 3, 1950, LAC, RG 25, 50028-AK-40, part 1, CDIM00085, p. 1.
60 Memorandum for the Under-Secretary from European Division, February 3, 1950, p. 1.
61 Memorandum for Mr. MacKay from MacDermot (drafted by Ford), January 19, 1950, LAC, RG 25, 50028-AK-40, part 1, CDIM00120, p. 1.
62 Memorandum for the Under-Secretary from European Division, February 3, 1950, p. 1.
63 Memorandum for the Under-Secretary from European Division, February 3, 1950, p. 2.
64 "An Analysis of U.S. and U.K. Joint Intelligence Committee Estimates of Soviet Intentions and Capabilities, and Canadian comments thereon," CSC 2(51), February 19, 1951, LAC, RG 25, 50028-AK-40, part 1, CDIM00127.
65 Memorandum for Mr. LePan drafted by Carter, January 17, 1951, LAC, RG 25, 50028-AK-40, part 1, CDIM00123, p. 2.
66 Memorandum for Mr. LePan drafted by Carter, January 17, 1951, p. 3.
67 Memorandum for Mr. LePan drafted by Carter, January 17, 1951, p. 3.
68 "Department of External Affairs Memorandum on Soviet Capabilities and Intentions," January 29, 1951, LAC, RG 25, 50028-AK-40, part 1, CDIM00126, p. 2.
69 "Department of External Affairs Memorandum," January 29, 1951, p. 3. Over the course of 1951, the Canadians judged that US and UK views were coming closer together. See "Likelihood of Total War with the Soviet Union up to the End of 1954," Note by the Secretaries of the [US] JIC, JIC 531/20, April 5, 1951, LAC, RG 24, CSC 1571:1, 1(TS), CDIM01739.
70 "Department of External Affairs Memorandum," January 29, 1951, p. 2.
71 "Soviet Intentions and Capabilities," Memorandum by Secretary, JIC, February 19, 1951, LAC, RG 25, 50028-AK-40, part 1, CDIM00128, p. 2.
72 "Canada-Defence," Memorandum from the Director of the Joint Staff, April 10, 1951, LAC, RG 25, 50028-AK-40, part 1, CDIM00092, p. 1.
73 "The International Situation," April 12, 1951, LAC, RG 25, 50028-AK-40, part 1, CDIM00096, p. 2. This report set the form for future imminence of war papers going forward with a *tour d'horizon* of global hot spots.
74 Memorandum for Mr. Carter from Hadwen, April 13, 1951, LAC, RG 25, 50028-AK-40, part 1, CDIM00098, p.3.
75 Memorandum for Mr. Pearson from D. V. Le Pan, April 6, 1951, LAC, RG 25, 50028-AK-40, part 1, CDIM00090, p. 1.
76 Memorandum for Mr. Pearson from D. V. Le Pan, April 6, 1951, p. 1.

77 Memorandum for the Minister from Heeney, April 5, 1951, LAC, RG 25, 50028-AK-40, part 1, CDIM00088, p. 1.
78 Memorandum for Mr. Pearson from D. V. Le Pan, April 6, 1951, pp. 1–2.
79 Memorandum for Mr. Glazebrook from Reid, April 28, 1951, LAC, RG 25, 50028-AK-40, part 1, CDIM00107, and Memorandum for the Prime Minister from Pearson, May 17, 1951, LAC, RG 25, 50028-AK-40, part 2, CDIM00145. For the paper itself, see "The Imminence of War," Memorandum to the Cabinet, April 5, 1951, LAC, RG 25, 50028-AK-40, part 2, CDIM00136; "The Imminence of War [draft]," April 30, 1951, LAC, RG 25, 50028-AK-40, part 2, CDIM00137; and "Department of External Affairs Memorandum: The Imminence of War," May 9, 1951, LAC, RG 25, 50028-AK-40, part 1, CDIM00140.
80 Memorandum for Mr. Leger from DL(2) (Glazebrook), May 1, 1951, LAC, RG 25, 50028-AK-40, part 2, CDIM00134.
81 "Comments on Departmental Memorandum of May 9th on the Imminence of War," drafted by B. A. W[allis]., June 2, 1951, LAC, RG 25, 50028-AK-40, part 2, CDIM00158, p. 1.
82 "Comments on Departmental Memorandum of May 9th," June 2, 1951, p. 2.
83 Canadian Ambassador in Washington, letter no. 2023 to USSEA, June 7, 1951, LAC, RG 25, 50028-AK-40, part 2, CDIM00160, p. 1.
84 "Comments on Departmental Memorandum of May 9th," June 2, 1951, p. 2.
85 Canadian Liaison Mission, Tokyo, letter no. 506 to USSEA, June 5, 1951, LAC, RG 25, 50028-AK-40, part 2, CDIM00159, p. 1.
86 Canadian Liaison Mission, Tokyo, letter no. 506 to USSEA, June 5, 1951.
87 Canadian Ambassador, Brussels, letter no. 402 to USSEA, June 19, 1951, LAC, RG 25, 50028-AK-40, part 2, CDIM00166, p. 1.
88 Canadian Ambassador, Brussels, letter no. 402 to USSEA, June 19, 1951, p. 1.
89 Canadian Ambassador, Brussels, letter no. 402 to USSEA, June 19, 1951, p. 1.
90 Canadian Ambassador in Washington, letter no. 2023 to USSEA, June 7, 1951, p. 2.
91 "Comments on the Department of External Affairs Memorandum 'The Imminence of War,'" sent under cover of Canadian Embassy in Paris, letter no. 989 to USSEA, June 26, 1951, LAC, RG 25, 50028-AK-40, part 2, CDIM00169, p. 1.
92 The Canadian Embassy, Belgrade, letter no. 862 to USSEA, August 24, 1951, LAC, RG 25, 50028-AK-40, part 2, CDIM00203, p. 3.
93 The Canadian Embassy, Belgrade, letter no. 862 to USSEA, August 24, 1951, p. 3.
94 "Comments on the Department of External Affairs Memorandum 'The Imminence of War,'" June 26, 1951, p. 2.
95 Quote is from "The Imminence of War," First JIS Draft, July 19, 1951, LAC, RG 25, 50028-AK-40, part 2, CDIM00182, p. 1. The actual first draft was "The Imminence of War," DAI – External Draft, July 11, 1951, LAC, RG 25, 50028-AK-40, part 2, CDIM00176.
96 "The Imminence of War," DAI – External Draft, July 11, 1951; Memorandum for Mr. Glazebrook from Carter, July 25, 1951, LAC, RG 25, 50028-AK-40, part 2, CDIM00191.
97 "The Imminence of War," July 11, 1951, p. 1.

98 "The Imminence of War," July 11, 1951, p. 2.
99 "The Imminence of War," July 11, 1951, p. 2.
100 "The Imminence of War," July 11, 1951, p. 3.
101 "The Imminence of War," July 11, 1951, p. 5.
102 "The Imminence of War," JIC 20(51), July 20, 1951, LAC, RG 25, 50028-AK-40, part 2, CDIM00184, p. 2.
103 "The Imminence of War," July 20, 1951, p. 2.
104 "Chiefs of Staff Agenda Item No. 6 for 502nd Meeting on July 20, 1951," Memorandum for the Under-Secretary, July 23, 1951, LAC, RG 25, 50028-AK-40, part 2, CDIM00189, p. 1. The JIC, as always, refused to make a more precise statement "as to the time of greatest danger of war or the circumstances under which the Soviet Union would resort to war."
105 Extracts from Minutes of the 502nd Meeting of CSC, July 25, 1951, LAC, RG 25, 50028-AK-40, part 2, CDIM00190, p. 1.
106 Extracts from Minutes of the 502nd Meeting of CSC, July 25, 1951, p. 1.
107 Memorandum for Mr. Glazebrook from Carter, July 25, 1951, p. 3.
108 Extracts from Minutes of the 502nd Meeting of CSC, July 25, 1951, p. 1.
109 Extracts from CSC Minutes of 505th Meeting, September 6 and 7, 1951, LAC, RG 25, 50028-AK-40, part 2, CDIM00206, p. 2.
110 Memorandum for the Secretary from DL(2), August 22, 1951, LAC, RG 25, 50028-AK-40, part 2, CDIM00200, p. 1.
111 Extracts from CSC Minutes of 505th Meeting, September 6 and 7, 1951, p. 2.
112 Extracts from CSC Minutes of 505th Meeting, September 6 and 7, 1951, p. 1.
113 Memorandum for the Under-Secretary, Mr. Reid, Mr. Ritchie from DL(2) (Glazebrook), September 13, 1951, LAC, RG 25, 50028-AK-40, part 2, CDIM00210, p. 1.
114 Contrast "The Imminence of War," JIC 20(51), July 25, 1951, with "The Current Risks of War," JIC 23/2 (51), October 24, 1951, LAC, RG 25, 50028-AK-40, part 2, CDIM00231.
115 Memorandum for Mr. Wershof from R. A. J. Phillips, October 4, 1951, LAC, RG 25, 50028-AK-40, part 2, CDIM00224.
116 "The Imminence of War," Memorandum for Mr. MacKay from McCordick, May 2, 1951, LAC, RG 25, 50028-AK-40, part 2, CDIM00138, p. 1.
117 "Likelihood of Total War with the Soviet Union up to the End of 1954," JIC (51)103 (Final), November 29, 1951, LAC, RG 24, CSC 1571:1, 1(TS), CDIM01834. For Canadian reactions, see Memorandum for Mr. Carter from DL(2) (Glazebrook), December 11, 1951, LAC, RG 25, 50028-AK-40, part 2, CDIM00242.
118 "Likelihood of Total War with the Soviet Union up to the End of 1954," JIC (51)103 (Final), November 29, 1951, p. 3.
119 Excerpt from Minutes of the 302nd Meeting of the JIC, January 23, 1952, LAC, RG 25, 50028-AK-40, part 3, CDIM00273.
120 Memorandum for European Divisions from DL(2), drafted by Wilgress, February 14, 1952, LAC, RG 25, 50028-AK-40, part 3, CDIM00278.

121 "Risks of General War in the Period 1952–1954," [draft] February 11, 1952, LAC, RG 25, 50028-AK-40, part 3, CDIM00277, p. 3.
122 "Risks of General War in the Period 1952–1954," February 11, 1952, p. 3.
123 "Risks of General War in the Period 1952–1954," February 11, 1952, p. 4.
124 "Risks of General War in the Period 1952–1954," February 11, 1952, p. 4.
125 "Risks of General War in the Period 1952–1954," February 11, 1952, p. 3.
126 "The Current Risks of General War," Memorandum for the JIC from Secretary, JIC, May 14, 1952, LAC, RG 25, 50028-AK-40, part 3, CDIM00290, p. 1.
127 "The Current Risks of General War," JIC 42(52), March 29, 1952, LAC, RG 25, 50028-AK-40, part 3, CDIM00285, p. 5; "deliberately" was added in "The Current Risks of General War," JIC 42/2(52), May 9, 1952, LAC, RG 25, 50028-AK-40, part 3, CDIM00289, p. 5.
128 Memorandum for Mr. Glazebrook from Ritchie, May 30, 1952, LAC, RG 25, 50028-AK-40, part 3, CDIM00293, p. 1.
129 Memorandum for Mr. Glazebrook from Ritchie, May 30, 1952, p. 1.
130 Memorandum for the JIC from Secretary, JIC, June 19, 1952, LAC, RG 25, 50028-AK-40, part 3, CDIM00299; Memorandum for the JIC from Secretary, JIC, June 17, 1952, LAC, RG 24, CSC 1571:1, 1(TS), CDIM01859.
131 "Likelihood of Total War with the Soviet Union up to the End of 1954," [UK] COS (52)285, May 28, 1952, LAC, RG 24, CSC 1571:1, 1(TS), CDIM01862, p. 2.
132 "Likelihood of the Deliberate Initiation of Full-Scale War by the USSR against the US and Its Western Allies Prior to the End of 1952," NIE 48, Central Intelligence Agency, January 8, 1952, CIA FOIA RR, https://www.cia.gov/readingroom/docs/DOC_0000269268.pdf. See also Garthoff, "Estimating Soviet Military Intentions and Capabilities," 137.
133 "Likelihood of the Deliberate Initiation of Full-Scale War by the USSR," January 8, 1952.
134 "Likelihood of the Deliberate Initiation of Full-Scale War by the USSR," January 8, 1952.
135 Memorandum for the JIC from Secretary, JIC, June 17, 1952.
136 "A Critique of the NIE's on the USSR," Memorandum for the Consultants on National Estimates, February 15, 1952, CIA FOIA RR, https://www.cia.gov/readingroom/docs/CIA-RDP79R00971A000400060060-1.pdf.
137 "The Current Risks of General War," CSC 3(52), July 3, 1952, LAC, RG 25, 50028-AK-40, part 3, CDIM00301.
138 Memorandum for the USSEA from DL(2), June 24, 1952, LAC, RG 25, 50028-AK-40, part 3, CDIM00300, p. 1.
139 Extract from Minutes of the 526th Meeting of the CSC, July 3, 1952, LAC, RG 24, CSC 1571:1, 1(TS), CDIM01867, p. 1.
140 Extract from Minutes of the 526th Meeting of the CSC, July 3, 1952, p. 1.
141 Memorandum for the JIC from Secretary, JIC, September 18, 1952, LAC, RG 25, 50028-AK-40, part 3, CDIM00306, p. 1.

142 "Review of the Risks of War," JIC 58(52), September 19, 1952, LAC, RG 25, 50028-AK-40, part 3, CDIM00307.
143 Memorandum for the JIC, from Secretary, JIC, October 21, 1952, LAC, RG 25, 50028-AK-40, part 3, CDIM00313.
144 Memorandum for Mr. Charles Ritchie from Glazebrook, October 24, 1952, LAC, RG 25, 50028-AK-40, part 3, CDIM00315, p. 1.
145 Memorandum for the JIC, from Secretary, JIC, October 21, 1952, p. 1.
146 Memorandum for the JIC, from Secretary, JIC, October 21, 1952, p. 1.
147 SSEA no. 427 to Permanent Representative of Canada to the North Atlantic Council, Paris, October 16, 1952, LAC, RG 2, I-60, part 1952. See also Memorandum for the JIC, from Secretary, JIC, October 21, 1952, p. 1.
148 Minutes of the 327th Meeting of the JIC, October 23, 1952, LAC, RG 25, 50028-AK-40, part 3, CDIM00314, p. 1. Glazebrook was also concerned with the question of evidence: Memorandum for Mr. Charles Ritchie from Glazebrook, October 24, 1952.
149 Memorandum for DL(2) Division from Far Eastern Division, November 1, 1952, LAC, RG 25, 50028-AK-40, part 3, CDIM00317, p. 1.
150 Memorandum for DL(2) Division from Far Eastern Division, November 1, 1952, p. 2.
151 Memorandum for DL(2) Division from Far Eastern Division, November 1, 1952, p. 1.
152 "The Current Risks of General War," JIC 64/2(53), February 4, 1953, LAC, RG 24, CSC 1571:1, 2(TS), CDIM01909, p. 1.
153 "The Current Risks of General War," JIC 64/1(53), January 27, 1953, LAC, RG 25, 50028-AK-40, part 3, CDIM00327, p. 1.
154 "The Current Risks of General War," February 4, 1953, p. 2.
155 Memorandum for Mr. Glazebrook from Cameron, January 29, 1953, LAC, RG 25, 50028-AK-40, part 3, CDIM00329, p. 1.
156 Memorandum for the USSEA from DL(2), February 17, 1953, LAC, RG 25, 50028-AK-40, part 3, CDIM00338, p. 2.
157 "The Likelihood of General War," JIC 79(53), June 29, 1953, LAC, RG 25, 50028-AK-40, part 4, CDIM00373.
158 Extract from Minutes of the 359th Meeting of the JIC, October 14, 1953, LAC, RG 25, 50028-AK-40, part 4, CDIM00379.
159 Likelihood of General War with the Soviet Union up to the End of 1955," [UK] JIC 53(79) (Final), September 10, 1953, LAC, RG 24, CSC 1571:1, 2(TS), CDIM01964, p. 1.
160 "Likelihood of General War with the Soviet Union up to the End of 1955," [UK] JIC 53(79) (Final), September 10, 1953, p. 3.
161 "The Current Risks of General War," JIC 79/3(53), November 9, 1953, LAC, RG 25, 50028-AK-40, part 4, CDIM00382, p. 3.
162 "The Current Risks of General War," JIC 79/3(53), November 9, 1953, p. 3.
163 "Likelihood of General War with the Soviet Union up to the End of 1955," September 10, 1953, p. 5.
164 "Likelihood of General War with the Soviet Union up to the End of 1955," September 10, 1953, p. 5.

NOTES TO CHAPTER 4

1. Minutes of the 2nd Meeting of the JISC, December 1, 1950, LAC, RG 24, 1274-10-9. On the JIC's decision to move forward periodic "imminence papers," see Minutes of the 247th Meeting of the JIC, December 9, 1950, LAC, RG 24, 1216-J2-2, part 3.
2. This story, and its possibly apocryphal nature, is recorded in Cynthia M. Grabo, "A Handbook of Warning Intelligence," vol. 1 (Defense Intelligence Agency, July 1972), p. 1-5, CIA FOIA RR, https://www.cia.gov/readingroom/docs/CIA-RDP80B00829A000800040001-6.pdf.
3. Thomas G. Belden, ed., "The National Indications Center and the Warning Process (U)" (Institute for Defense Analyses Systems Evaluation Division, July 1969), 40, CIA FOIA RR, https://www.cia.gov/readingroom/docs/CIA-RDP81B00493R000100110006-5.pdf.
4. Goodman, *The Official History*, 260. The relationship between the "check list" and these indicator lists (i.e., how and if they travelled from the field to the central machinery) is unclear and more research is required.
5. Secretary of State's Special Assistant for Research and Intelligence (Armstrong) to Director of Central Intelligence Hillenkoetter, July 29, 1949, *FRUS*, 1945–1950, Emergence of the Intelligence Establishment, doc. 391, p. 991.
6. "Agenda for IAC Meeting 19 August," Memorandum for the Director from Prescott Childs, CIA FOIA RR, https://www.cia.gov/readingroom/docs/CIA-RDP67-00059A000200030041-1.pdf.
7. "Watch Committee," Memorandum for Participating IAC Agencies Only," September 26, 1949, CIA FOIA RR, https://www.cia.gov/readingroom/docs/CIA-RDP80R01731R003600050026-4.pdf.
8. Memorandum from Director of Central Intelligence Hillenkoetter to the Director of Intelligence of the Army General Staff (Irwin), February 15, 1950, *FRUS*, 1945–1950, Emergence of the Intelligence Establishment, doc. 414, p. 1063. Emphasis in the original.
9. NSCID No. 1 as originally adopted by the NSC on December 12, 1947, is printed in Michael Warner, ed., *CIA Cold War Records, The CIA Under Harry Truman* (Washington, DC: History Staff, Center for the Study of Intelligence, Central Intelligence Agency, 1994), 169–71, https://www.cia.gov/resources/csi/static/CIA-Under-Harry-Truman-CIA-Documents-1994-Part-II-CIA-Hillenkoetter.pdf.
10. "Proposed Watch Committee," Memorandum for the Director of Central Intelligence, January 20, 1950, CIA FOIA RR, https://www.cia.gov/readingroom/docs/CIA-RDP80R01731R003600050015-6.pdf. Note that the Army's suggestions seemed to confuse the estimative and indicative goals, and seems, at least according to the marginalia on the copy in the CIA files, to misrepresent the purpose and function of the Check List Group.
11. Draft of "Proposed Watch Committee," Memorandum for the Director of Intelligence, General Staff, United States Army, February 13, 1950, CIA FOIA RR, https://www.cia.gov/readingroom/docs/CIA-RDP80R01731R003600050025-5.pdf.
12. Letter from the Department of State Member of the Standing Committee (Trueheart) to the Chief of the Coordination, Operations, and Policy Staff of the CIA (Childs), March 29, 1950, *FRUS*, 1950–1955, The Intelligence Community, doc. 3, p. 5.

13 "Proposed Interagency Operating Procedure," March 6, 1950, CIA FOIA RR, https://www.cia.gov/readingroom/document/cia-rdp61s00750a000100020092-6.

14 "Organizational History of the Central Intelligence Agency, 1950–1953," DCI Historical Series, May 1957, Chapter VIII, p. 47. Available online at https://archive.org/details/CIAHistory195053.

15 "Watch Committee," Memorandum for Executive, November 8, 1950, CIA FOIA RR, https://www.cia.gov/readingroom/docs/CIA-RDP78-04718A000100320069-2.pdf.

16 Fact Sheet, November 8, 1951, *FRUS, 1950–1955, The Intelligence Community*, doc. 91, p. 209.

17 Intelligence Advisory Committee, "Minutes of Meeting held in Director's Conference Room, Administration Building, Central Intelligence Agency, on 30 August 1951," August 30, 1951, CIA FOIA RR, https://www.cia.gov/readingroom/docs/CIA-RDP82-00400R000100030013-9.pdf.

18 Goodman, *The Official History*, 179.

19 Goodman, *The Official History*, 179–80.

20 Extract from the Minutes of the 303rd Meeting of the JIC, January 30, 1952, LAC, RG 24, CSC 1313:1, part 1, CDIW00505, p. 1.

21 "Indications of Attack," Memorandum for the JIC, January 25, 1952, LAC, RG 24, CSC 1313:1, part 1, CDIW00511, p. 1.

22 "War Room Policy," February 3, 1955, LAC, RG 24, CSC 1313:1, part 1, CDIW00580, p. 4.

23 "Proposed Changes in Organization and Functioning of the IAC Watch Committee," author sanitized, October 28, 1952, CIA FOIA RR, https://www.cia.gov/readingroom/docs/CIA-RDP91T01172R000400060005-8.pdf.

24 "IAC Action and Discussion of the Watch Committee Problem," Memorandum for Assistant Director/Current Intelligence, October 9, 1953, CIA FOIA RR, https://www.cia.gov/readingroom/docs/CIA-RDP61S00750A000100120215-8.pdf.

25 National Security Council Report, February 10, 1953, *FRUS, 1950–1955, The Intelligence Community*, doc. 146, p. 417. Italics in original.

26 "Proposed Statement to the IAC Re the Watch Committee," Memorandum for Director of Central Intelligence from Deputy Director/Intelligence, October 5, 1953, CIA FOIA RR, https://www.cia.gov/readingroom/docs/CIA-RDP94T00754R000100060001-4.pdf; "IAC Action and Discussion of the Watch Committee Problem," October 9, 1953.

27 Belden, "The National Indications Center and the Warning Process," 49.

28 Belden, "The National Indications Center and the Warning Process," 47; "Responsibility for Warning and Evolution of a 'Warning System,'" Memorandum for Director of Central Intelligence from John J. Bird, National Intelligence Officer for Warning, December 24, 1985, CIA FOIA RR, https://www.cia.gov/readingroom/docs/CIA-RDP87M00539R002103340001-5.pdf. Note that there was considerable discussion and disagreement within the ad hoc committee about the value of mechanical systems like the "indications board." See also "IAC Action and Discussion of the Watch Committee Problem," Memorandum for Assistant Director/Current Intelligence, October 9, 1953, CIA FOIA RR, https://www.cia.gov/readingroom/docs/CIA-RDP61S00750A000100120215-8.pdf.

29 Report to the National Security Council [hereafter NSC] by the Executive Secretary (Lay) [NSC 162/2], October 30, 1953, *FRUS*, 1952–1954, vol. II, part 1, National Security Affairs, doc. 101, p. 582.

30 Minutes of a Meeting of the Intelligence Advisory Committee, May 4, 1954, *FRUS*, 1950–1955, The Intelligence Community, doc. 175, p. 492.

31 "The 'Net Estimates' Problem," Paper Prepared in the CIA, August 25, 1954, *FRUS*, 1950–1955, The Intelligence Community, doc. 189, p. 530.

32 Memorandum of Discussion at the 209th Meeting of the NSC, August 5, 1954, *FRUS*, 1950–1955, The Intelligence Community, doc. 187, p. 517.

33 "National Security Council Report," March 2, 1955, *FRUS*, 1950–1955, The Intelligence Community, doc. 209.

34 Memorandum by the Intelligence Advisory Committee, November 23, 1954, *FRUS*, 1950–1955, The Intelligence Community, doc. 197.

35 Extract from the Minutes of the 339th Meeting of the JIC, March 11, 1953, LAC, RG 24, CSC 1313:1, part 1, CDIW00530, p. 1.

36 Extract from the Minutes of the 339th Meeting of the JIC, March 11, 1953, LAC, RG 24, CSC 1313:1, part 1, CDIW00530, p .1.

37 Extract from the Minutes of the 339th Meeting of the JIC, March 11, 1953, p. 1.

38 Extract from the Minutes of the 348th Meeting of the JIC, June 4, 1953, LAC, RG 24, CSC 1313:1, part 1, CDIW00533, p. 1.

39 Extract from the Minutes of the 348th Meeting of the JIC, June 4, 1953, p. 2.

40 Extract from the Minutes of the 348th Meeting of the JIC, June 4, 1953, p. 1.

41 Extract from the Minutes of the 362nd Meeting of the JIC, November 9, 1953, LAC, RG 24, CSC 1313:1, part 1, CDIW00545, p. 1.

42 "Indications of War," Memorandum for the JIC, October 23, 1953, LAC, RG 24, CSC 1313:1, part 1, CDIW00543, p. 1.

43 "Indications of War," December 8, 1953, LAC, RG 24, CSC 1313:1, part 1, CDIW00550, p. 1.

44 "The 'Indications' Project," JIC 89(53), December 3, 1953, LAC, RG 24, CSC 1313:1, part 1, CDIW00550, p. 1.

45 "The 'Indications' Project," December 3, 1953, p. 3.

46 "Indications of War," October 23, 1953; "Indications of War," December 8, 1953.

47 Extract from the Minutes of the 367th Meeting of the JIC, December 22, 1953, LAC, RG 24, CSC 1313:1, part 1, CDIW00552, p. 2.

48 Extract from the Minutes of the 367th Meeting of the JIC, December 22, 1953, p. 1.

49 "United States Indications Intelligence Project," Memorandum for the JIC, March 9, 1954, LAC, RG 24, CSC 1313:1, part 1, CDIW00555, p. 2.

50 "United States Indications Intelligence Project," March 9, 1954, p. 2.

51 "United States Indications Intelligence Project," March 9, 1954, p. 3.

52 Extract from the Minutes of the 374th Meeting of the JIC, March 17, 1954, LAC, RG 24, CSC 1313:1, part 1, CDIW00556, p. 1. Crean did not think a filing system to be as problematic as wall-mounted boards because the cards could be re-evaluated.

53 Extract from the Minutes of the 377th Meeting of the JIC, March 31, 1954, LAC, RG 24, CSC 1313:1, part 1, CDIW00557, p. 1.
54 "Arrangements for Weekly Intelligence Briefings," Directive for the JIS, April 29, 1954, LAC, RG 24, CSC 1313:1, part 1, CDIW00561, p. 1. Note that here the issue of "indications" and "current intelligence" are conflated; the US had sought to avoid conflation of these issues.
55 "Arrangements for Weekly Intelligence Briefings," April 29, 1954, p. 2.
56 Crean to Dulles, November 29, 1954, LAC, RG 24, CSC 1313:1, part 1, CDIW00568; "New Terms of Reference – US Watch Committee," from DMI, October 21, 1954, LAC, RG 25, 29-3-1-2, part 1, CDIW00003.
57 Crean to Dulles, November 29, 1954.
58 Dulles to Crean, undated, LAC, RG 24, CSC 1313:1, part 1, CDIW00577.
59 It is conceivable and likely that a specific incident touched off Crean's concerns, but the currently available record does not suggest any particular moment. The first Taiwan Straits crisis of August 1954 is one possible answer.
60 Crean to Dean, November 29, 1954, LAC, RG 25, 29-3-1-2, part 1, CDIW00005, p. 1.
61 Crean to Dean, November 29, 1954, pp. 1–2. Crean raised his point with specific reference to communication intelligence or COMINT "alerts." The National Security Agency [hereafter NSA] had apparently implemented a COMINT Alert System with four levels of alerts in 1953. Little is known about these alerts except that some levels direct US COMINT units to keep their targets under continuous analysis. CBNRC and GCHQ, it seems, were a part of this system and received both the alerts and intelligence information generated by the alerts through COMINT channels. See generally "The Suez Crisis: A Brief Comint History (U)," United States Cryptologic History, Special Series Crisis Collection Volume 2, Office of Archives and History, National Security Agency/Central Security Service, 1988, https://www.nsa.gov/news-features/declassified-documents/cryptologic-histories/assets/files/Suez_Crisis.pdf.
62 Crean to Dean, November 29, 1954, p. 2.
63 Crean to Dean, November 29, 1954, p. 2.
64 Dean to Crean, December 8, 1954, LAC, RG 25, 29-3-1-2, part 1, CDIW00008, p. 1.

NOTES TO CHAPTER 5

1 "Summary of M.C. 48 (Final)," attached to Memorandum from Head, DL(1) Division, to USSEA, December 2, 1954, *DCER*, vol. 20, doc. 365, p. 748.
2 "Summary of M.C. 48 (Final)," December 2, 1954, p. 748.
3 "Future NATO Defence Planning in Light of the Effect of New Weapons," SSEA no. 940 to Permanent Representative to North Atlantic Council, December 6, 1954, *DCER*, vol. 20, doc. 366, p. 751.
4 "Future NATO Defence Planning in Light of the Effect of New Weapons," SSEA no. 992 to Permanent Representative to North Atlantic Council, December 15, 1954, *DCER*, vol. 20, doc. 378, p. 770.
5 "Future NATO Defence Planning," December 6, 1954, pp. 751–752.

6   "Future NATO Defence Planning," December 6, 1954, p. 752; "Future NATO Defence Planning in Light of the Effect of New Weapons," SSEA no. 941 to the Permanent Representative to the North Atlantic Council, December 6, 1954, *DCER*, vol. 20, doc. 367, p. 753.

7   "Future Pattern of Military Strength," Memorandum by SSEA, December 16, 1954, *DCER*, vol. 20, doc. 379, p. 771; Memorandum of Conversation, by the Director of the Policy Planning Staff (Bowie), December 16, 1954, *FRUS*, 1952–1954, vol. V, part 1, Western European Security, doc. 287.

8   "Future Pattern of Military Strength," December 16, 1954, p. 771.

9   The fourth state was likely France, who the British and Americans frequently excluded from discussions involving nuclear matters because of security fears.

10 "Communiqué issued at the Conclusion of the Truman-Attlee Discussions," attached to United States Delegation Minutes of the 6th Meeting of President Truman and Prime Minister Attlee, December 8, 1950, in *FRUS*, 1950, vol. VII, Korea, doc. 1007.

11 "Memorandum of a Conversation with Sir Anthony Eden, Paris, December 19, 1954," Memorandum by SSEA, December 19, 1954, *DCER*, vol. 20, doc. 380, p. 773.

12 "'Alert' Procedures," USSEA to High Commissioner in United Kingdom, January 25, 1955, *DCER*, vol. 21, doc. 168, p. 329. A Canadian representative had been invited to attend the JIC (London) meeting, but Crean declined as there was not adequate time to brief the Canadian JIC representative in London. See Crean to Robertson, January 11, 1955, LAC, RG 25, 29-3-1-2, part 1, CDIW0014.

13 "Alerts," Memorandum for the JIC, January 19, 1955, LAC, RG 25, 29-3-1-2, part 1, CDIW00015, p. 1. This is a Canadian document that includes a lengthy excerpt from the minutes of a UK JIC meeting.

14 [UK] MOD London to UKSLS Ottawa, January 12, 1955, LAC, RG 25, 29-3-1-2, part 1, CDIW00013.

15 "Arrangements for the Evaluation of Indicators of Soviet Preparations for Early War," Annex to "U.K. Intelligence Alert Measures," [UK] JIC/256/55, January 26, 1955, LAC, RG 24, CSC 1313:1, part 1, CDIW00595, pp. 2–4.

16 "U.K. Intelligence Alert Measures," Memorandum for the JIC, March 3, 1955, LAC, RG 24, CSC 1313:1, part 1, CDIW00596, p. 1.

17 "Alerts," January 19, 1955, p. 1.

18 "Alerts," January 19, 1955, 2.

19 "Arrangements for the Evaluation of Indicators," January 26, 1955, 2.

20 "Alerts," January 19, 1955, p. 2.

21 "Arrangements for the Evaluation of Indicators," January 26, 1955, p. 2.

22 "Alerts," January 19, 1955, p. 1.

23 "U.K. Intelligence Alert Measures," January 26, 1955, p. 1.

24 "Alerts," January 19, 1955, p. 3.

25 "Arrangements for the Evaluation of Indicators," January 26, 1955, p. 4.

26 "Alerts," January 19, 1955, p. 3.

27 Timothy Andrews Sayle, "A Pattern of Constraint: Canadian-American Relations in the Early Cold War," *International Journal*, 62, no. 3 (2007): 689–705, https://doi.org/10.1177/002070200706200316. For a short chapter that places the tripartite alert agreements in this pattern, see Greg Donaghy, "Nukes and Spooks: Canada-US Intelligence Sharing and Nuclear Consultations, 1950–1958," in *Transnationalism: Canada-United States History into the 21st Century*, eds. Michael D. Behiels and Reginald C. Stuart (Montreal: McGill-Queen's University Press, 2010).
28 Crean to Robertson, January 11, 1955, p. 1.
29 Crean to Robertson, January 11, 1955, p. 2.
30 Untitled draft or partial draft of document, by Crean, January 10, 1955, LAC, RG 25, 29-3-1-2, part 1, CDIW00012, p. 2.
31 Untitled draft or partial draft of document, by Crean, January 10, 1955, p. 1.
32 Untitled draft or partial draft of document, by Crean, January 10, 1955, p. 2.
33 Untitled draft or partial draft of document, by Crean, January 10, 1955, p. 3. The Canadians learned that the British had been considering that "responsibility for coming to a decision as to the reality of an all-out attack should rest with the two Senior Intelligence Officers in Germany of the United Kingdom and the United States" who would send pre-arranged signals to their governments: USSEA to High Commissioner in United Kingdom, January 25, 1955, *DCER*, vol. 21, doc. 168, p. 330.
34 Untitled draft or partial draft of document, by Crean, January 10, 1955, p. 3.
35 Canadian typed copy of UK paper "Possible Stages of Action When Indications of Major Russian Aggression Are Received in Good Time," undated, LAC, RG 24, CSC 1313:1, part 1, CDIW00582, p. 1.
36 "Possible Stages of Action," undated, p. 1.
37 "Possible Stages of Action," undated, p. 2.
38 "[Canadian] JIC Brief on [UK paper titled] Possible Stages of Action when Indications of Major Russian Aggression are Received in Good Time," JIC 132(55), February 17, 1955, LAC, RG 24, CSC 1313:1, part 1, CDIW00585, p. 2.
39 Extract from the Minutes of the Special Meeting of the Chiefs of Staff Committee held on February 18, 1955, LAC, RG 24, CSC 1313:1, part 1, CDIW00592, p. 1.
40 "[Canadian] JIC Brief on [UK paper titled] Possible Stages of Action," February 17, 1955, p. 2. On a war with China, see "Problems which might be posed for Canada, if the United States were to become involved in hostilities over the Chinese offshore islands," External Affairs Draft for Discussion Purposes, February 17, 1955, LAC, RG 25, 50219-AE-40, part 1, CDNW00615. On Canadian concerns about war in the Pacific, see Samuel Eberlee, "Danger in the Asia-Pacific: Canadian Intelligence Analysis and the 'Imminence' of World War, 1950–1959," Master of Arts Directed Research Paper, University of Toronto, 2021.
41 SSEA no. 290 to London, February 17, 1955, LAC, RG 24, CSC 1313:1, part 1, CDIW00604, p. 1.
42 SSEA no. 290 to London, February 17, 1955, p. 2.
43 High Commission (London) [hereafter HICLON] no. 250 to SSEA, February 28, 1955, LAC, RG 24, CSC 1313:1, part 1, CDIW00602, p. 2.

44 HICLON no. 250 to SSEA, February 28, 1955, p. 1.

45 HICLON no. 251 to SSEA, February 28, 1955, LAC, RG 24, CSC 1313:1, part 1, CDIW00601.

46 HICLON no. 250 to SSEA, February 28, 1955.

47 SSEA no. 411 to London, March 10, 1955, LAC, RG 24, CSC 1313:1, part 1, CDIW00600, p. 1.

48 SSEA no. 411 to London, March 10, 1955, p. 3.

49 HICLON no. 397 to SSEA, March 25, 1955, LAC, RG 24, CSC 1313:1, part 1, CDIW00613.

50 Letter from Director of Central Intelligence Dulles to the Director of the Bureau of the Budget (Hughes), June 25, 1955, *FRUS*, 1950–1955, The Intelligence Community, doc. 228, p. 713.

51 National Security Council Report, August 31, 1955, *FRUS*, 1950–1955, The Intelligence Community, doc. 234, p. 720.

52 National Security Council Report, August 31, 1955, p. 721.

53 National Security Council Report, August 31, 1955, p. 722.

54 "War Room," Comments on Para. 9(a), undated, LAC, RG 24, 1480-36, CDIW00695, p. 1.

55 "War Room," Memorandum from DDNI to DNI, February 15, 1955, LAC, RG 24, 1480-36, CDIW00696, p. 1.

56 "National Indications Center," Defence Research Member to Direct, JIB, March 9, 1955, LAC, RG 24, CSC 1313:1, part 1, CDIW00606.

57 "National Indications Center," under cover of distribution memo, from Director, JIB, February 1, 1955, LAC, RG 25, 29-3-1-2, part 1, CDIW00020.

58 "National Indications Center," March 9, 1955.

59 "National Indications Center," March 9, 1955, p. 2.

60 "National Indications Center," March 9, 1955, pp. 2–3.

61 "National Indications Center," March 9, 1955, p. 3.

62 "National Indications Center," March 9, 1955, p. 3.

63 "National Indications Center," March 9, 1955.

64 Extract from the Minutes of the 432nd Meeting of the JIC, March 16, 1955, LAC, RG 24, CSC 1313:1, part 1, CDIW00607. The relationship between JIC 89(53) and this discussion is not yet clear.

65 "Indications Intelligence," JIC 135/1(55), March 21, 1955, LAC, RG 24, CSC 1313:1, part 1, CDIW00610.

66 "Indications Intelligence," March 21, 1955, 2.

67 "Indications Intelligence," March 21, 1955, 2.

68 "Indications Intelligence," March 21, 1955, 2.

69 Wesley Wark, "'Favourable Geography': Canada's Arctic Signals Intelligence Mission," *Intelligence and National Security* 35, no. 3 (2020): 319–30, https://doi.org/10.1080/02684527.2020.1724629.

70   Extract from the Minutes of the 436th Meeting of the JIC, April 6, 1955, LAC, RG 24, CSC 1313:1, part 1, CDIW00619.
71   Crean to Ignatieff, July 7, 1955, LAC, RG 25, 29-3-1-2, part 1, CDIW00022, p. 1. For more detailed discussions of Merchant/Dean conversation, see Dean to Crean, July 29, 1955, LAC, RG 25, 29-3-1-2, part 1, CDIW00024.
72   Canadian Embassy, Washington [hereafter EmbWA] no. WA-1278 to SSEA, July 28, 1955, LAC, RG 24, CSC 1313:1, part 1, CDIW00626.
73   Crean to Dean, July 15, 1955, LAC, RG 25, 29-3-1-2, part 1, CDIW00023.
74   Uren to Bowen, July 22, 1955, LAC, RG 25, 29-3-1-2, part 1, CDIW00025, p. 1. For the Pentagon-CIA spat, see "Alerts Procedures," Ignatieff to USSEA, October 28, 1955, LAC, RG 25, 29-3-1-2, part 1, CDIW00028.
75   Uren to Bowen, July 22, 1955, p. 2.
76   Ambassador in United States to USSEA, October 25, 1955, *DCER*, vol. 21, doc. 183, p. 345.
77   SSEA no. 1341 to Washington and London, July 27, 1955, LAC, RG 24, CSC 1313:1, part 1, CDIW00625, p. 1.
78   Since 1951, Canada and the United States held regular meetings of consultation on the threat of atomic war as one element of the American promise to consult Canada (time permitting) on the use of atomic weapons.
79   Léger to Foulkes, September 27, 1955, LAC, RG 25, 29-3-1-2, part 1, CDIW00027, p. 2.
80   "Alerts Procedures," Memorandum from Ignatieff to USSEA, October 28, 1955, LAC, RG 25, 29-3-1-2, part 1, CDIW00028, p. 1.
81   Copy of "Aide-Memoire," Department of State, November 18, 1955, attached to a draft letter to Robertson, December 20, 1955, LAC, RG 25, 29-3-1-2, part 1, CDIW00034, pp. 8–11.
82   Crean to Glazebrook, December 30, 1955, LAC, RG 25, 29-3-1-2, part 1, CDIW00039, p. 2. Indeed, there is a hint that the president himself directed a review of intelligence sharing with the British and Canadians. This is an avenue for further research.
83   Glazebrook to Crean, November 19, 1955, LAC, RG 25, 29-3-1-2, part 1, CDIW00031, p. 1.
84   "Aide-Memoire," November 18, 1955.
85   Glazebrook to Crean, November 19, 1955, p.1.
86   Extract from the Minutes of the 468th Meeting of the JIC, November 30, 1955, LAC, RG 24, CSC 1313:1, part 1, CDIW00628.
87   "Aide-Memoire," November 18, 1955, p. 3.
88   "Aide-Memoire," Department of State, November 18, 1955.
89   Glazebrook to Crean, November 19, 1955, p. 1.
90   Crean to Glazebrook, December 30, 1955, p. 1.
91   "Meeting of Consultation – December 5, 1955," Memorandum for the Minister from USSEA, November 30, 1955, LAC, RG 25, 29-3-1-2, part 1, CDIW00033, p. 3.
92   "Meeting of Consultation – December 5, 1955," November 30, 1955, p. 2.
93   "Meeting of Consultation – December 5, 1955," November 30, 1955, p. 3.

94 "Meeting of Consultation – December 5, 1955," November 30, 1955, p. 5.
95 Copy of EmbWA no. 2044 to External Ottawa [hereafter EXTOT], December 15, 1955, LAC, RG 25, 29-3-1-2, part 1, CDIW00035, p. 2.
96 Glazebrook to Crean, January 25, 1956, LAC, RG 25, 29-3-1-2, part 1, CDIW00043, p. 2.
97 Glazebrook to Crean, January 25, 1956, p. 3.
98 Glazebrook to Crean, January 25, 1956, p. 3.
99 Uren would become the first JIC Liaison Officer Washington (JICLO(W)) in 1957 but was already serving in Washington.
100 Glazebrook to Crean, January 25, 1956, p. 4.
101 Glazebrook to Crean, January 25, 1956, p. 5.
102 Copy of "Memorandum on Intelligence Procedures Related to Alerts: Discussions in Washington," February 15, 1956, attached to Memorandum for the Under-Secretary, February 23, 1956, LAC, RG 25, 29-3-1-2, part 1, CDIW00048, p. 3.
103 "Memorandum on Intelligence Procedures Related to Alerts," February 15, 1956, p. 5.
104 Memorandum for the Under-Secretary, February 23, 1956, p. 1.
105 "Memorandum for File," February 20, 1956, attached to Memorandum for the Under-Secretary, February 23, 1956, p. 8.
106 "Memorandum for File," February 20, 1956, p. 7.
107 Memorandum for the Under-Secretary, February 23, 1956, p. 1.
108 Memorandum for the Under-Secretary, February 23, 1956, p. 2.
109 "Exchange of Indications Between USA and Canada," Aide Memoire, G/C R. B. Ingalls, DAI, March 9, 1956, LAC, RG 25, 29-3-1-2, part 1, CDIW00054, p. 1.
110 "Chiefs of Staff Meeting, Monday, March 19," from DL(2) to R. M. Macdonnell, March 16, 1956, LAC, RG 25, 29-3-1-2, part 1, CDIW00059.
111 Extract from Cabinet Defence Committee Minutes, Meeting 109 – April 19, 1956 – Item I, LAC, RG 25, 29-3-1-2, part 1, CDIW00067, p. 1.
112 Memorandum for Cabinet Defence Committee, March 8, 1956, LAC, RG 25, 29-3-1-2, part 1, CDIW00056, p. 3.
113 "Alerts," Memorandum for the Minister from USSEA, March 7, 1956, LAC, RG 25, 29-3-1-2, part 1, CDIW00053.
114 "Procedures for Consultation on Alerts," Memorandum for the Minister, February 19, 1957, LAC, RG 25, 29-3-1-2, part 1, CDIW00100.
115 EmbWA no. 682 to SSEA, May 14, 1956, LAC, RG 25, 29-3-1-2, part 1, CDIW00081.
116 "Alerts," Memorandum from Crean to Ignatieff, October 16, 1956, LAC, RG 25, 29-3-1-2, part 1, CDIW00096; USSEA no. DL-[original damaged] to EmbWA, September [original damaged], 1956, LAC, RG 25, 29-3-1-2, part 1, CDIW00091.
117 USSEA no. DL-546 to EmbWA, May 14, 1956, LAC, RG 25, 29-3-1-2, part 1, CDIW00079.
118 USSEA no. 711 to EmbWA, May 18, 1956, LAC, RG 25, 29-3-1-2, part 1, CDIW00083, p. 1.
119 "Proposed Tripartite Discussions on Alerts," USSEA no. DS-1243 to HICLON, September 26, 1956, LAC, RG 25, 29-3-1-2, part 1, CDIW00094, p. 2.

120 "Alerts Procedures," Ignatieff to Bryce, August 24, 1956, LAC, RG 25, 29-3-1-2, part 1, CDIW00089, p. 1; "Proposed Tripartite Discussions on Alerts," September 26, 1956.

121 On the context of the Thor deployment, see Matthew Jones, *The Official History of the UK Strategic Nuclear Deterrent: Volume 1: From the V-Bomber to the Arrival of Polaris, 1945–1964* (London: Routledge, 2017), 96–154.

122 "Tripartite Discussions on Alerts," Macdonnell to Foulkes, February 22, 1957, LAC, RG 25, 29-3-1-2, part 1, CDIW00101, p. 2.

123 External no. DS-60 to London, March 6, 1957, LAC, RG 25, 29-3-1-2, part 1, CDIW00109, p. 1.

124 External no. DS-60 to London, March 6, 1957, p. 2.

125 External no. DS-60 to London, March 6, 1957, p. 3.

126 EXTOT no. DS-50 for HICLON, February 25, 1957, LAC, RG 25, 29-3-1-2, part 1, CDIW00103. See also EXTOT no. DS-51 for HICLON, "Draft Formula for Exchanging Intelligence Relating to Alerts in the NATO Area between the United States, United Kingdom and Canadian Governments," February 25, 1957, LAC, RG 25, 29-3-1-2, part 1, CDIW00104.

127 EXTOT no. DS-51 for HICLON, February 25, 1957, p. 1.

128 EXTOT no. DS-51 for HICLON, February 25, 1957, p. 2.

129 London no. 364 to External, February 28, 1957, LAC, RG 25, 29-3-1-2, part 1, CDIW00106, p. 1.

130 London no. 364 to External, February 28, 1957, p. 2.

131 External DS-60 to London, March 6, 1957, p. 2.

132 London no. 413 to External, March 8, 1957, LAC, RG 25, 29-3-1-2, part 1, CDIW00111, p. 1.

133 London no. 439 to External, March 12, 1957, LAC, RG 25, 29-3-1-2, part 1, CDIW00112, p. 2.

134 London no. 439 to External, March 12, 1957, p. 3.

135 London no. 439 to External, March 12, 1957, p. 3.

136 EXTOT no. DS-65 to EmbWA, March 14, 1957, LAC, RG 25, 29-3-1-2, part 1, CDIW00121, p. 1

137 EXTOT no. DS-65 to EmbWA, March 14, 1957, LAC, RG 25, 29-3-1-2, part 1, CDIW00121, p. 1; "Tripartite Discussions on Alerts," Foulkes to Macdonnell, March 13, 1957, LAC, RG 25, 29-3-1-2, part 1, CDIW00116, p. 1.

138 "Tripartite Discussions on Alerts," Foulkes to Macdonnell, March 13, 1957, LAC, RG 25, 29-3-1-2, part 1, CDIW00116, p. 1.

139 "Tripartite Discussions on Alerts," Foulkes to Macdonnell, March 15, 1957, LAC, RG 25, 29-3-1-2, part 1, CDIW00122, p. 1.

140 Bryce to Macdonnell, March 12, 1957, LAC, RG 25, 29-3-1-2, part 1, CDIW00113, p. 1.

141 London no. 523 to External, March 19, 1957, LAC, RG 25, 29-3-1-2, part 1, CDIW00124.

142 London no. 465 to External, March 14, 1957, LAC, RG 25, 29-3-1-2, part 1, CDIW00120, p. 1.

143 Glazebrook to Crean, November 19, 1955, p. 2.

144 Extracts from the Minutes of the 471st Meeting of the JIC, December 20, 1955, LAC, RG 24, CSC 1313:1, part 1, CDIW00635, p. 1.

145 Memorandum for the Under-Secretary, February 23, 1956, p. 1.

146 "Communications between J.I.C. and U.S. Intelligence Advisory Committee," Crean to Secretary, JIC, April 23, 1956, LAC, RG 25, 29-3-1-2, part 1, CDIW00070.

147 "Chiefs of Staff Meeting, May 10, Indications Intelligence," DL(2) to USSEA, May 9, 1956, LAC, RG 25, 29-3-1-2, part 1, CDIW00074, p. 1.

148 Excerpts from Minutes of the 593rd Meeting of the CSC, Thursday, May 10, 1956, LAC, RG 25, 29-3-1-2, part 1, CDIW00078.

149 "Action in event of special message from Washington," DL(1) to various DEA officials, July 1956, LAC, RG 25, 29-3-1-2, part 1, CDIW00087.

150 "Joint Weekly Indications Report," Bowen to Secretary, JIC, November 22, 1956, LAC, RG 24, CSC 1313:1, part 1, CDIW00682, p. 1.

151 "Joint Weekly Indications Report," Bowen to Secretary, JIC, November 22, 1956, p. 1.

152 "Tripartite Alerts Procedure," Norman Brook to PM, April 16, 1957, NAUK, PREM 11/2276.

153 The American contingent included Cabell, but also, intriguingly Frank Wisner, deputy director of plans, along with Huntington "Ting" Sheldon, Park Armstrong and H. E. Furnas. Dean brought Paul Jones and John Roper and Crean brought Saul Rae from the embassy.

154 On Crick, see Michael S. Goodman, "The Foundations of Anglo-American Intelligence Sharing," *Studies in Intelligence* 59, no. 2 (June 2015): 9–10, https://www.cia.gov/resources/csi/static/Foundations-of-Anglo-American.pdf.

155 "Meeting at C.I.A. on March 28 to Discuss the Exchange of Intelligence Relating to Alerts in the NATO Area," March 27, 1957, LAC, RG 25, 29-3-1-2, part 1, CDIW00129, p. 2. Included here is a draft letter to Dulles. It is essentially a re-working of the "formula" into a letter, which would be identical coming from Canadians and British.

156 "Meeting at C.I.A. on March 28 to Discuss the Exchange of Intelligence," March 27, 1957, p. 3.

157 EmbWA no. 753 to External, April 2, 1957, LAC, RG 25, 29-3-1-2, part 2, CDIW00130; Dean to Crean, April 2, 1957, LAC, RG 25, 29-3-1-2, part 2, CDIW00131.

158 "Tripartite Alerts – Intelligence," Léger to Foulkes, April 4, 1957, LAC, RG 25, 29-3-1-2, part 2, CDIW00133, p. 2.

159 "Tripartite Discussions on Alerts," Macdonnell for Foulkes, March 20, 1957, LAC, RG 25, 29-3-1-2, part 1, CDIW00126; Bryce to Léger, April 12, 1957, LAC, RG 25, 29-3-1-2, part 2, CDIW00138.

160 EXTOT no. DS-95 to EmbWA, April 16, 1957, LAC, RG 25, 29-3-1-2, part 2, CDIW00140.

161 EmbWA no. 1052 to External, May 6, 1957, LAC, RG 25, 29-3-1-2, part 2, CDIW00144, p. 1.

162 Crean to Foulkes, May 7, 1957, LAC, RG 25, 29-3-1-2, part 2, CDIW00146, p. 1.

163 Murphy to Heeney, May 8, 1957, CDIW00150; SSEA no. DS-608 to EmbWA, May 31, 1957, CDIW00155; "Tripartite Alerts – Intelligence," April 4, 1957; all in LAC, RG 25, 29-3-1-2, part 2.

164 London no. 964 to External, May 7, 1957, LAC, RG 25, 29-3-1-2, part 2, CDIW00147, p. 1.

NOTES TO CHAPTER 6

1 "Probable Intelligence Warning of Soviet Attack on the US," NIE 11-3-57, Central Intelligence Agency, June 18, 1957, CIA FOIA RR, https://www.cia.gov/readingroom/docs/DOC_0000267691.pdf.

2 "Probable Intelligence Warning of Soviet Attack on the US," NIE 11-3-57, June 18, 1957.

3 "Probable Intelligence Warning of Soviet Attack on the US (US NIE 11-3-57)," Memorandum for the JIC, November 25, 1957, LAC, RG 25, 29-3-1-2, part 2, CDIW00165, p. 1.

4 "Probable Intelligence Warning of Soviet Attack on the US (US NIE 11-3-57)," November 25, 1957, p. 1.

5 Crean to Dean, December 16, 1957, LAC, RG 25, 29-3-1-2, part 2, CDIW00169, p. 1.

6 "Exercises of Friendly Forces," July 14, 1959, LAC, RG 24, CSC 1313:1, Part 3, CDIW01472.

7 HICLON no. 3 to External, November 14, 1957, LAC, RG 25, 29-3-1-2, part 2, CDIW00160. When the CBNRC director Edward Drake and C. E. Denning were next in London, they called on Dean to discuss communications channels.

8 Dean to Crean, November 20, 1957, LAC, RG 25, 29-3-1-2, part 2, CDIW00164, p. 1. Underline in original.

9 EXTOT no. XT-12 to HICLON, November 15, 1957, LAC, RG 25, 29-3-1-2, part 2, CDIW00161, p. 2.

10 Lindsay Grant, "The Many Heads of HYDRA: Canada as Cold War Signals Intelligence Hub," *Canada Declassified*, accessed June 2023, https://declassified.library.utoronto.ca/exhibits/show/the-many-heads-of-hydra--canad/summary.

11 Crean to Colonel C. A. Peck, January 7, 1958, LAC, RG 25, 29-3-1-2, part 2, CDIW00170, p. 1.

12 Crean to Dean, February 6, 1958, LAC, RG 25, 29-3-1-2, part 2, CDIW00175, p. 1

13 Crean to Dean, February 6, 1958, p. 1.

14 Crean to Dean, February 6, 1958, pp. 2–3.

15 Crean to Dean, February 6, 1958, p. 4.

16 Crean to Dean, February 6, 1958, pp. 3–4.

17 Lt-Col P. E. Amyot to Crean, March 13, 1958, LAC, RG 25, 29-3-1-2, part 2, CDIW00190; HICLON no. 10 to EXTOT, February 12, 1958, LAC, RG 25, 29-3-1-2, part 2, CDIW00178; HICLON no. 16 to EXTOT, February 24, 1958, LAC, RG 25, 29-3-1-2, part 2, CDIW00181.

18 Dean to Crean, February 25, 1958, LAC, RG 25, 29-3-1-2, part 2, CDIW00184, p. 1.

19 Drake to Crean, March 3, 1958, LAC, RG 25, 29-3-1-2, part 2, CDIW00185.

20 Lt-Col Paul Amyot to Crean, March 13, 1958, p. 1.
21 EXTOT no. XT-34 to EmbWA for Uren, April 2, 1958, LAC, RG 25, 29-3-1-2, part 2, CDIW00200, p. 1.
22 EmbWA no. WX73 to EXTOT for Southam, April 9, 1958, LAC, RG 25, 29-3-1-2, part 2, CDIW00203, p. 2.
23 Southam to Uren, April 15, 1958, LAC, RG 25, 29-3-1-2, part 2, CDIW00209, p. 1.
24 Southam to Uren, April 15, 1958, p. 2.
25 "Transmittal of Communications Meeting Minutes," from Coffey (CIA) to Uren and Bremner, May 6, 1958, LAC, RG 25, 29-3-1-2, part 2, CDIW00222; EmbWA no. WX76 to EXTOT for Southam, April 16, 1958, LAC, RG 25, 29-3-1-2, part 2, CDIW00210.
26 Dean to Dulles, April 21, 1958, LAC, RG 25, 29-3-1-2, part 2, CDIW00212, p. 1.
27 Uren to Southam, May 12, 1958, LAC, RG 25, 29-3-1-2, part 2, CDIW00224, p. 1.
28 EmbWA no. WX317 to EXTOT for Southam, June 4, 1958, LAC, RG 25, 29-3-1-2, part 2, CDIW00240.
29 "Procedures for the Committing to the Attack of Nuclear Retaliatory Forces in the United Kingdom," Report to the President and Prime Minister, June 9, 1958, online at https://unredacted.com/wp-content/uploads/2016/10/98-245-1-3.pdf, p. 1. On the resulting Murphy-Dean Agreement, see Matthew Jones, "'A Matter of Joint Decision': The Origins of British Nuclear Retaliation Procedures and the Murphy–Dean Agreement of 1958," *The English Historical Review*, 2024: 1–41, early access, https://doi.org/10.1093/ehr/ceae161.
30 "Procedures for the Committing to the Attack of Nuclear Retaliatory Forces in the United Kingdom," June 9, 1958, p. 5.
31 Jebb to Hoyer Millar, July 23, 1959, NAUK, PREM 11/3002.
32 Southam to Dean, April 30, 1958, LAC, RG 24, CSC 1313:1, part 2, CDIW01074.
33 EmbWA no. WX243 to EXTOT for Southam, May 30, 1958, LAC, RG 25, 29-3-1-2, part 2, CDIW00232, p. 1.
34 EmbWA no. WX243 to EXTOT for Southam, May 30, 1958, p. 2.
35 EmbWA no. WX243 to EXTOT for Southam, May 30, 1958, pp. 2–3.
36 EmbWA no. WX243 to EXTOT for Southam, May 30, 1958, p. 3.
37 EmbWA no. WX318 to EXTOT for Southam, June 5, 1958, LAC, RG 25, 29-3-1-2, part 2, CDIW00244.
38 EmbWA no. WX318 to EXTOT for Southam, June 5, 1958.
39 Dean to Webb (US Embassy), July 22, 1958, LAC, RG 25, 29-3-1-2, part 2, CDIW00263, p. 1.
40 EmbWA no. WX318 to EXTOT for Southam, June 5, 1958, p. 1.
41 EmbWA no. WX318 to EXTOT for Southam, June 5, 1958. See also "Nature of Intelligence Information to be Passed on Tripartite Alert Communications Facility," Memorandum for the JIC, June 11, 1958, LAC, RG 25, 29-3-1-2, part 2, CDIW00254.
42 Extract from the Minutes of the 600th Meeting of the JIC, May 14, 1958, LAC, RG 24, CSC 1313:1, part 2, CDIW01078. See also Extract from the Minutes of the 597th

Meeting of the JIC, April [date obscured], 1958, LAC, RG 24, CSC 1313:1, part 2, CDIW01063.

43 Extract from the Minutes of the 597th Meeting, JIC, April [date obscured], 1958. Iterations include: "Indications Intelligence Communications and Watch Procedures," JIC 278(58), April 28, 1958, RG 24, CSC 1313:1, part 2, CDIW01068; JIC 278/1(58), May 22, 1958, LAC, RG 24, CSC 1313:1, part 2, CDIW01080; JIC 278/2(58), May 27, 1958, LAC, RG 24, CSC 1313:1, part 2, CDIW01082; and JIC 278/3(58), May 29, 1958, LAC, RG 24, CSC 1313:1, part 2 CDIW01155.

44 "Indications Intelligence – Procedures," April 22, 1958, LAC, RG 25, 29-3-1-2, part 2, CDIW00215, p. 3.

45 HICLON no. 51 to EXTOT, May 30, 1958, LAC, RG 25, 29-3-1-2, part 2, CDIW00231, p. 1.

46 HICLON no. 104 to EXTOT, July 29, 1958, LAC, RG 25, 29-3-1-2, part 2, CDIW00269.

47 HICLON no. 104 to EXTOT, July 29, 1958.

48 Uren to Southam, September 10, 1958, LAC, RG 25, 29-3-1-2, part 3, CDIW00305; Dean to Southam, October 31, 1958, LAC, RG 25, 29-3-1-2, part 3, CDIW00328.

49 E. P. Black to Southam, September 19, 1958, LAC, RG 25, 29-3-1-2, part 3, CDIW00310, p. 1.

50 "The Continuing Need for Indications Intelligence," Annex A, by Bowen, May 14, 1958, LAC, RG 25, 3-10-2, CDIW00425.

51 "The Continuing Need for Indications Intelligence," May 14, 1958, p. 1.

52 "The Continuing Need for Indications Intelligence," May 14, 1958, p. 1.

53 Minutes of the 607th Meeting of the JIC, June 5, 1958, LAC, RG 24, CSC 1313:1, part 2, CDIW01096, p. 2.

54 EXTOT no. XT-14 to HICLON, January 28, 1959, LAC, RG 24, CSC 1313:1, part 3, CDIW01277.

55 GCHQ to CBNRC, July 30, 1958, LAC, RG 25, 29-3-1-2, part 2, CDIW00276. On the reversion to Stages 1, 2, and 3, see Extracts from the Minutes of the 681st Meeting of the JIC, March 25, 1959, LAC, RG 24, CSC 1313:1, part 3, CDIW01346.

56 "Notes on Use of Tripartite Indications Communications System," Annex A, marked "First Draft," undated, LAC, RG 25, 29-3-1-2, part 3, CDIW00295, p. 1. This seems to be an excerpt of JIC 1103/1(58), a document still withheld by the Privy Council Office.

57 "Notes on Use of Tripartite Indications Communications System," Annex A, marked "First Draft," undated, p. 2.

58 "Notes on Use of Tripartite Indications Communications System," Annex A, marked "First Draft," undated, p. 3.

59 EmbWa WX 341 to EXTOT for Southam, August 25, 1958, LAC, RG 25, 29-3-1-2, part 3, CDIW00297, p. 1.

60 Extract from the Minutes of the 632nd Meeting, JIC, August 27, 1958, LAC, RG 24, CSC 1313:1, part 2, CDIW01175, p. 1.

61 Southam to S. F. Rae, September 12, 1958, LAC, RG 25, 29-3-1-2, part 3, CDIW00307, p. 1.

62 "Report of the Tripartite Working Group on Tripartite Alert System," Memorandum for Dulles, Dean, and Southam, October 2, 1958, LAC, RG 25, 29-3-1-2, part 3, CDIW00315, p. 6.

63 "Report of the Tripartite Working Group on Tripartite Alert System," October 2, 1958, p. 8.

64 "Report of the Tripartite Working Group on Tripartite Alert System," October 2, 1958, p. 2.

65 EmbWA no. WI-65 to USSEA, December 31, 1958, LAC, RG 25, 29-3-1-2, part 3, CDIW00345.

66 "Report of the Tripartite Working Group on Tripartite Alert System," October 2, 1958, p. 3.

67 "Tripartite Alert System," Memorandum for the JIC, November 14, 1958, LAC, RG 25, 29-3-1-2, part 3, CDIW00338.

68 EmbWA no. WI-66 to USSEA, December 31, 1958, LAC, RG 25, 29-3-1-2, part 3, CDIW00344.

69 Greg Donaghy, "When the Chips Are Down: Eisenhower, Diefenbaker, and the Lebanon Crisis, 1958," in *Reassessing the Rogue Tory: Canadian Foreign Relations in the Diefenbaker Era*, eds. Janice Cavell and Ryan M. Touhey, (Vancouver: UBC Press, 2019), 95.

70 The JIC minutes referring to this crisis remain heavily sanitized. See Minutes of the 615th Meeting of the JIC, July 15, 1958; Minutes of the 616th Meeting of the JIC, July 16, 1958; Minutes of the 617th Meeting of the JIC, July 17, 1958; Minutes of the 626th Meeting of the JIC, July 30, 1958; all from PCO A-2016-00694.

71 HICLON no. HC-26 to EXTOT, April 2, 1959, LAC, RG 24, JIBS 266-2000-1, part 2.

72 EmbWA no. EX2028 to EXTOT, March 23, 1959, LAC, RG 24, JIBS 266-2000-1, part 2.

73 "Tripartite Alert System – Report on Traffic," Memorandum for the JIC, December 5, 1958, LAC, RG24, CSC 1313:1, part 3, CDIW01238. See also "Tripartite Alert System," G. P. Hartling to Uren, November 10, 1958, CDIW01212; "Tripartite Alert System," Memorandum for the JIC, November 14, 1958, CDIW01225; "Tripartite Alert System – Interpretation and Procedures," January 12, 1959, CDIW01262; CIAWAS 05 (Director CIA Washington to JIC London, JIC Ottawa), December 22, 1958, CDIW01260; all from LAC, RG 24, CSC 1313:1, part 3.

74 "Tripartite Intelligence Alerts Agreement – Interpretation and Procedures," Memorandum for the JIC, January 9, 1959, LAC, RG 25, 29-3-1-2, part 3, CDIW00355.

75 Uren to Southam, December 19, 1958, LAC, RG 25, 29-3-1-2, part 3, CDIW00339, p. 1.

76 Uren to Southam, December 19, 1958, p. 2. Uren reported to Ottawa that the initiative had been useful for it exercised the system and resolved some minor problems.

77 HICLON no. 181 to EXTOT, December 31, 1958, LAC, RG 25, 29-3-1-2, part 3, CDIW00342, p. 1.

78 EmbWA no. WX1 to EXTOT for Southam, January 22, 1959, LAC, RG 25, 29-3-1-2, part 3, CDIW00363, p. 1.

79 USSEA no.DI-9 to EmbWA, January 26, 1959, LAC, RG 25, 29-3-1-2, part 3, CDIW00377.

80 EmbWA no. WX2011 to EXTOT, February 12, 1959, LAC, RG 25, 29-3-1-2, part 3, CDIW00385, p. 1.
81 EmbWA no. WX2011 to EXTOT, February 12, 1959, p. 2.
82 "Tripartite Alerts – Interpretation and Procedures," G. C. Cook to Starnes, February 17, 1959, LAC, RG 25, 29-3-1-2, part 3, CDIW00386, pp. 1–2.
83 EmbWA no. WX2018 to EXTOT, February 27, 1959, LAC, RG 25, 29-3-1-2, part 3, CDIW00393, p. 1.
84 EmbWA no. WX2026 to EXTOT, March 13, 1959, LAC, RG 25, 29-3-1-2, part 3, CDIW00398, p. 1.
85 EmbWA no. WX2026 to EXTOT, March 13, 1959, p. 1.
86 EXTOT no. XT-36 to EmbWA, March 20, 1959, LAC, RG 25, 29-3-1-2, part 3, CDIW00404, p. 1.
87 Dean to Starnes, April 2, 1959, LAC, RG 25, 29-3-1-2, part 3, CDIW00405, p. 1.
88 Dean to Starnes, April 2, 1959, p. 1.
89 "Tripartite Intelligence Alerts Agreement," Starnes to LePan, April 10, 1959, LAC, RG 25, 29-3-1-2, part 3, CDIW00406, p. 2.
90 Dean to Dulles, April 30, 1959, LAC, RG 25, 29-3-1-2, part 3, CDIW00407, p. 1.
91 Dean to Starnes, April 30, 1959, LAC, RG 25, 29-3-1-2, part 3, CDIW00408.
92 "Tripartite Intelligence Alerts Agreement," Bowen to Secretary, JIC, May 8, 1959, LAC, RG 24, CSC 1313:1, part 3, CDIW00413, p. 1.
93 "Tripartite Intelligence Alerts Agreement," May 8, 1959, p. 1.
94 Extract from the Minutes of the 693rd Meeting, JIC, June 3, 1959, LAC, RG 24, CSC 1313:1, part 3, CDIW01417.
95 Dulles to Starnes, June 4, 1959, LAC, RG 24, CSC 1313:1, part 3, CDIW01453, p. 1; Extracts from the Minutes of the 697th Meeting, JIC, June 30, 1959, LAC, RG 24, CSC 1313:1, part 3, CDIW01462–CDIW01464.
96 Dulles to Starnes, August 27, 1959, LAC, RG 24, CSC 1313:1, part 4, CDIW01524.
97 Starnes to Foulkes, September 14, 1959, LAC, RG 24, CSC 1313:1, part 4, CDIW01528, p. 1; Foulkes to Starnes, September 21, 1959, LAC, RG 24, CSC 1313:1, part 4, CDIW01532; EXTOT no. XT-118 to EmbWA, October 5, 1959, LAC, RG 24, CSC 1313:1, part 4, CDIW01555.
98 HICLON no. HC-26 to EXTOT, April 2, 1959.
99 HICLON no. HC-26 to EXTOT, April 2, 1959.
100 "Tripartite Alerts System – Monthly Report of Traffic," Memorandum for the JIC, March 11, 1959, LAC, RG 24, CSC 1313:1, part 3, CDIW01331.
101 Extract UK JIC (59) 19th Meeting, undated, LAC, RG 24, CSC 1313:1, part 3, CDIW01327. The author has found no evidence of the result of this operation.
102 Extract from the Minutes of the 700th Meeting held on 22 Jul 59, JIC, July 22,1959, LAC, RG24, CSC 1313:1, part 4, CDIW01490, p. 1.
103 Extract UK JIC (59) 19th Meeting, undated, p. 1.
104 Extract UK JIC (59) 19th Meeting, undated, p. 1.

105 Canadian records of these studies are still closed in LAC, RG 24, CSC 1860:1 and CSC 1860:2.
106 Starnes to Dean, July 16, 1959, LAC, RG 24, CSC 1313:1, part 4, CDIW01478, p .1.
107 Dean to Starnes, March 23, 1960, CDIW00881; "Soviet Interdiction of Allied Communications," Starnes to Secretary, JIC, April 5, 1960, CDIW00882; "Tripartite Intelligence Alerts Agreement – Soviet Interdiction of Allied Communications," Secretary, JIC, to Secretary, JTC [Joint Telecommunications Committee], April 28, 1960, CDIW00892; H. S. Stephenson (on behalf of Dean) to Starnes, August 15, 1960, CDIW00894; all in LAC, RG 24, 1480-12, part 2.
108 "Reporting on Indications Intelligence," Bowen to Secretary, JIC, February 20, 1959, LAC, RG 24, 1480-12, part 1, CDIW00810.
109 "Reporting on Indications Intelligence," February 20, 1959, p .1.
110 "Probable Enemy Activities Prior to the Outbreak of War," Draft Letter of Transmittal for JIC 312/2(59), February 5, 1959, CDIW00809; "Canadian Intelligence Alert Stages," JIC 323(59), March 9, 1959, CDIW00813; "JIS List of Critical Intelligence Indicators," JIC 321(59), March 9, 1959 (with updates as JIC 3211/1(59) on April 24, 1959, and JIC 321/2(59) on May 4, 1959), CDIW00814; all from LAC, RG 24, 1480-12, part 1.
111 "Reporting on Indications Intelligence," Starnes to Secretary, JIC, March 24, 1959, LAC, RG 24, CSC 1313:1, part 3, CDIW01352, p .1; Appendix A to [UK] JIC (58)79 (Final), undated, LAC, RG 24, CSC 1313:1, part 3, CDIW01348.
112 "Transmittal of General Indicator List (Information Bearing on a Possible Soviet Decision to Initiate Hostilities)," To All Diplomatic Missions and Berlin, Hongkong and Singapore, March 17, 1959, LAC, RG 24, CSC 1313:1, part 3, CDIW01371.
113 "Probable Enemy Activities Prior to Outbreak for War," for JIC from Secretary, JIC, April 7, 1959, LAC, RG 24, CSC 1313:1, part 3, CDIW01349, p. 1.
114 "Probable Enemy Activities Prior to Outbreak for War," April 7, 1959.
115 "FALLEX 62 – JIC POST EXERCISE REPORT," October 8, 1962, LAC, RG 24, 1216-J2-3, part 5.
116 "Intelligence Warning of Military Attack on North America," JIC 443/2(62), September 6, 1962, LAC, RG 25, 1-3-12-2, part 3.
117 "Intelligence Warning of Military Attack on North America," JIC 443/2(62), September 6, 1962.
118 "Intelligence Warning of Military Attack on North America." JIC 443/2(62). September 6, 1962.
119 Extracts of the Minutes of the 900th Meeting of the JIC, July 25, 1962, RG 24, 2433-1, part 1. This conference, which includes the five members of would come to be referred to as the "Five Eyes," was meant to build on a 1958 conference in Melbourne featuring attendees from the same five states.
120 "Cuba – Discussion with Mr. John A. McCone, Director of Central Intelligence," October 18, 1962, GAC ATIP A-2020-01164.
121 The best overview of Canada's role in the crisis remains Asa McKercher, "A 'Half-hearted Response'? Canada and the Cuban Missile Crisis, 1962," *The International History Review* 33, no. 2 (June 2011): 337, https://doi.org/10.1080/07075332.2011.555450.

122 "Interview with Mr. J. J. McCardle by John F. Hilliker for the DEA History Project," April 30, 1981, GAC ATIP A-2021-00037.

123 "Cuba," Memorandum from SSEA to Prime Minister, October 22, 1962, *DCER*, vol. 29, doc. 653, p. 1132.

124 The American memorandum of the lunch-time meeting, with the names of the Canadians excised, is also available. See Timothy Andrews Sayle, "The Moment Canada Learned about the Cuban Missile Crisis," *Canada Declassified*, October 21, 2023, https://timsayle.substack.com/p/the-moment-canada-learned-about-the.

125 Report on the Operation of the Joint Indications Room during the Cuban Crisis," Staff Officer, JIR, to Chairman, JIC, December 10, 1962, LAC, RG 24, 1480-12, part 2, CDIW00926, p. 1.

126 "Report on the Operation of the Joint Indications Room during the Cuban Crisis," December 10, 1962. Note the October 23, 1962 minutes of the 914th JIC meeting mention agreement on a state of intelligence readiness, while the JIR report on its operations suggested this alert took effect the next day, on October 24.

127 Minutes of the 914th Meeting of the JIC, October 23, 1962, LAC, RG 25, 50028-CH-40, part 2.

128 Minutes of the 914th Meeting of the JIC, October 23, 1962.

129 "Interview with Mr. J. J. McCardle by John F. Hilliker for the DEA History Project," April 30, 1981.

130 "Report on the Operation of the Joint Indications Room during the Cuban Crisis," December 10, 1962.

131 "Warning of Soviet Military Aggression," JS 3746, CCOS to SACEUR and SACLANT, October 24, 1962, LAC, RG24, CSC 1313:1, part 5, CDIW01943, p. 1.

132 "USIB Passes Its Test in the Cuban Crisis," excerpt [sanitized copy], undated, CIA FOIA RR, https://www.cia.gov/readingroom/docs/CIA-RDP79M00098A000200070001-2.pdf.

133 "Your Briefings of the NSC Executive Committee," [Retrospective] Memorandum for the Director, November 3, 1962, CIA FOIA RR, https://www.cia.gov/readingroom/docs/CIA-RDP80B01676R001800020018-4.pdf.

134 Malcolm Bow to [sanitized], March 29, 1989, GAC ATIP A-2021-00037. The author filed Access to Information requests with Library and Archives Canada (LAC A-2023-00475), the Privy Council Office (PCO A-2023-00088), and Global Affairs Canada (GAC A-2023-00243), for the records described by Bow. Based on correspondence and clarifications with each unit, the author is convinced that LAC, PCO, and GAC undertook thorough reviews. None of these departments could find the records Bow describes.

NOTES TO CONCLUSION

1 "JIR Standing Orders," Memorandum to the JIC, May 21, 1963, LAC, RG 24, 1480-12, part 1, CDIW00925.

2 "Integration of Intelligence – Department of National Defence," November 30, 1965, LAC, RG 25, 1-3-13-1, part 1.

3 "The Tripartite Intelligence Alerts Agreement," JIC 543(66), June 8, 1966, GAC ATIP A-2018-00945.

4   "A Tentative Missile Indicator List (Mark II) (Developed in NIC and checked with GMAIC)," undated, LAC, RG 24, 1480-12, part 2, CDIW00908.

5   These lists are found in LAC, RG 24, 1571:1, part 7.

6   "IAC Procedures in Crisis Situations," March 1, 1989, LAC, RG 25, 29-4-IAC, part 6. See also "Update to IAC Procedures in Crisis Situations: Additions," April 23, 1991, LAC, RG 25, 29-4-IAC, part 6.

7   On the conference, see Lindsay Grant, "28 September 1966: Provision of Tripartite Intelligence Conference Network," *Canada Declassified*, accessed June 19, 2023, https://declassified.library.utoronto.ca/exhibits/show/the-many-heads-of-hydra--canad/1966-1971--heads-and-tails--th/28-september-1966--provision-o.

8   "Tripartite Intelligence Alerts Communications Network Report February, 1972," March 4, 1972, LAC, RG 73, BAN 2016-00616, Box 19, File 7/10/A/4.

9   "Intelligence Advisory Committee Minutes of Meeting 51/80, 17 December 1980," December 18, 1980, LAC, RG 73, BAN 2016-00616, Box 10, File 7/10/A/1, part 22.

10 "Alternatives to the Tripartite Network," [presumably CIA] Memorandum, March 17, 1970, LAC, RG 73, BAN 2016-00616 Box 19 File 7/10/A/4.

11 "Alternatives to the Tripartite Network," March 17, 1970.

12 "Tripartite Intelligence Alerts Network," March 29, 1974, LAC, RG 73, BAN 2016-00616, Box 19, File 7/10/A/4.

13 "The Tripartite Intelligence Alerts Network – IAC Communications," October 3, 1973, LAC, RG 25, BAN 2017-00434-0, Box 26, File 1-3-13-1, part 1.

14 "IAC Procedures in Crisis Situations," March 1, 1989, LAC, RG 25, 29-4-IAC, part 6. See also "Update to IAC Procedures in Crisis Situations: Additions," April 23, 1991.

15 DGI [Director General Intelligence] Familiarization Guide, 2013. Available online at British Columbia Civil Liberties Association, https://bccla.org/wp-content/uploads/2023/02/AGC-0183_0225.pdf, last accessed June 30, 2023. I am grateful to Bill Robinson for drawing my attention to this document.

16 John Fraser, "The Intelligence Advisory Committee 1972-86," July 31, 1996, PCO ATIP A-2015-00214 states that Canada agreed to the "termination of this Agreement" in April 1970, but this is clearly a misreading of a document describing the Canadian agreement to terminate the communications network, not the agreement itself. See above for the discussion of network changes in the 1970s.

17 See Samuel Eberlee, "Danger in the Asia-Pacific: Canadian Intelligence Analysis and the 'Imminence' of World War, 1950–1959."

Bibliography

UNPUBLISHED PRIMARY SOURCES

Directorate of History and Heritage, Department of National Defence (DHH/DND)
    2002/17   Joint Staff Fonds

Library and Archives Canada (LAC)

Record Group 2 (Privy Council Office)
A-5-a   Cabinet Conclusions
I-60   International Situation

Record Group 24 (Department of National Defence)

1946 Army Central Registry
9042-34/0-1 Intelligence – Appreciations by Canadian Joint Intelligence Committee on Soviet capabilities and strategic objectives in a war before July 1949

Defence Research Board
DRBS 2-1-172-10 Scientific Intelligence and Defence Research, Strategic Guidance

Directorate of Military Intelligence
1216-J2-2   Intelligence – Canadian Joint Intelligence Committee – Agenda and minutes
1216-J2-3   Canadian Joint Intelligence Committee Programmes

Joint Intelligence Bureau, Registry Files
JIBS 266-2000-1 Joint Intelligence Committee – Economic and Topographic Intelligence – Exchange of Information

Joint Staff and Chiefs of Staff Committee, Central Registry

CSC 5-11-2	Hickory Indoctrination
CSC 7-18	Strategic Appreciations
CSC 1313:1	Warning of Attack – Channel of Transmission
CSC 1571:1	Imminence of War
CSC 1652:1	MCC Canada-United States Emergency Defence Plan
CSC 2433:1	Intelligence Conferences – General

Royal Canadian Navy Third Central Registry System

1272-10	Joint Planning Sub-Committee – Vice Chief of Staff Committee
1272-17	Chiefs of Staff Committee – ABC Intelligence – General
1272-17-1	Chiefs of Staff Committee – ABC Intelligence – Part 1
1272-17-2	Chiefs of Staff Committee - ABC Intelligence - ABCI 15, Part2
1274-10	Canadian Joint Intelligence Committee – Minutes
1274-10-9	Joint Intelligence Committee – Joint Intelligence Sub-Committee
1480-12	Intelligence Situation and War Measures – Indications from Intelligence Rooms
1480-29	Agreed Canada-United States Estimate Entitled "Soviet Capabilities and Probable Courses of Action Against Canada, the United States and the Areas Adjacent Thereto"
1480-36	General Intelligence – Imminence of War – Reports and Papers

Record Group 25 (Department of External Affairs)

Defence Liaison (2) Special Registry

1-3-12-2	Intelligence Policy Committee Master File Papers 1962
1-3-13-1	Intelligence Advisory Committee (IAC) [Joint Intelligence Organization (JIC)] – Organization and Terms of Reference
3-10-2	Current Intelligence, Indications & Briefing – CIIB

Foreign Intelligence Bureau Special Records Unit

29-3-1-2	Intelligence Agreements – Tripartite Intelligence Alerts Agreement (CDA/UK/USA)

Security and Intelligence Liaison – Special Registry (PSIR)

29-4-IAC	Intelligence – Conferences & Organizations Intelligence Advisory Committee

Special Registry Small S Series

2-AE(s)	Relations Between Western World and Soviet Union and Its Satellite States – (Soviet Union Foreign Policy)
52-C(s)	Canadian Post-War Defence Relationship with the United States
52-F(s)	Memoranda on United States-USSR Relations as Affecting Canadian Policy 1947–1948

Top Secret Registry, 50,000 Series

50028-AK-40	JIC - Imminence of War
50028-AP-40	JIC - Soviet Union – Long-Term Intentions
50028-B-40	JIC – Soviet Union
50028-CH-40	JIC – Cuba – General Records
50219-AE-40	Canada-USA Meeting on Consultation on Threat of Atomic War
50266-40	Emergency Defence Arrangements Hickory and Bullmoose

Record Group 73 (Ministry of the Solicitor General)

National Security Directorate Files

7/10/A/1	Minutes of Intelligence Advisory Committee Meetings
7/10/A/4	Intelligence Advisory Committee – Intelligence Alerts Communications Network

National Archives of the United Kingdom (NAUK)

Prime Minister's Office: Correspondence and Papers, 1951–1964

PREM 11/2276	Tripartite alert machinery for exchange of intelligence between United States, Canada, and UK: note of Bermuda Conference Agreement 1957
PREM 11/3002	French proposals for organisation to promote closer co-operation between UK, US, and France on defence and security matters

Records of the Cabinet Office

CAB 159/5	Joint Intelligence Sub-Committee later Committee: Minutes (JIC Series). Meetings: 1–64. [1949]
CAB 159/7	Joint Intelligence Sub-Committee later Committee: Minutes (JIC Series). Meetings: 1–68. [1950]

CAB 159/8   Joint Intelligence Sub-Committee later Committee: Minutes (JIC Series). Meetings: 69–138. [1950]

PUBLISHED PRIMARY SOURCES AND COLLECTIONS

Freedom of Information Act Reading Room (FOIA RR), Central Intelligence Agency, https://www.cia.gov/readingroom/home

Documents on Canadian External Relations (DCER)

Canada. Department of External Affairs. *Documents on Canadian External Relations*: Volume 8, 1939–1941. Ottawa: Queen's Printer for Canada.

Canada. Department of External Affairs. *Documents on Canadian External Relations*: Volume 9, 1942–1943. Ottawa: Queen's Printer for Canada.

Canada. Department of External Affairs. *Documents on Canadian External Relations*: Volume 11, 1944–1945. Ottawa: Queen's Printer for Canada.

Canada. Department of External Affairs. *Documents on Canadian External Relations*: Volume 12, 1946. Ottawa: Queen's Printer for Canada.

Canada. Department of External Affairs. *Documents on Canadian External Relations*: Volume 14, 1948. Ottawa: Queen's Printer for Canada.

Canada. Department of External Affairs. *Documents on Canadian External Relations*: Volume 15, 1949. Ottawa: Queen's Printer for Canada.

Canada. Department of External Affairs. *Documents on Canadian External Relations*: Volume 20, 1954. Ottawa: Queen's Printer for Canada.

Canada. Department of External Affairs. *Documents on Canadian External Relations*: Volume 21, 1955. Ottawa: Queen's Printer for Canada.

Canada. Department of External Affairs. *Documents on Canadian External Relations*: Volume 29, 1962–1963. Ottawa: Queen's Printer for Canada

Foreign Relations of the United States (FRUS)

Foreign Relations of the United States, 1945–1950, Emergence of the Intelligence Establishment. Washington, DC: US Government Printing Office.

Foreign Relations of the United States, 1946, Volume V, The British Commonwealth, Western and Central Europe. Washington, DC: US Government Printing Office.

Foreign Relations of the United States, 1946, Volume VI, Eastern Europe, The Soviet Union. Washington, DC: US Government Printing Office.

Foreign Relations of the United States, 1950, Volume VII, Korea. Washington, DC: US Government Printing Office.

Foreign Relations of the United States, 1950–1955, The Intelligence Community. Washington, DC: US Government Printing Office.

Foreign Relations of the United States, 1952–1954, Volume II, Part 1, National Security Affairs. Washington, DC: US Government Printing Office.

Foreign Relations of the United States, 1952–1954, Volume V, Part 1, Western European Security. Washington, DC: US Government Printing Office.

SECONDARY SOURCES

Alanbrooke, Field Marshall Lord. *War Diaries, 1939–1945*. Edited by Alex Danchev and Daniel Todman. London: Weidenfeld & Nicholson, 2001.

Aronsen, Lawrence. "Preparing for Armageddon: JIC 1 (Final) and the Soviet Attack on Canada." *Intelligence and National Security* 19, no. 3 (2004): 490–510. https://doi.org/10.1080/0268452042000316250.

Barnes, Alan. "A Confusion, Not a System: The Organizational Evolution of Strategic Intelligence Assessment in Canada, 1943 to 2003." *Intelligence and National Security* 34, no. 4 (2019): 464–79. https://doi.org/10.1080/02684527.2019.1578043.

Belden, Thomas G., ed., "The National Indications Center and the Warning Process (U)." Institute for Defense Analyses Systems Evaluation Division, July 1969. CIA FOIA RR, https://www.cia.gov/readingroom/docs/CIA-RDP81B00493R000100110006-5.pdf.

Bothwell, Robert. *Alliance and Illusion: Canada and the World, 1945–1984*. Vancouver: UBC Press, 2007.

Condit, Kenneth W. *History of the Joint Chiefs of Staff: The Joint Chiefs of Staff and National Policy, 1947-1949*, vol. 2. Washington, DC: Office of Joint History, Office of the Chairman of the Joint Chiefs of Staff, 1996.

Dolak, Monique. "Preparing for Peace in Time of War: Canada and the Post-Hostilities Planning Committees, 1943-1945." *Journal of Military and Strategic Studies* 15, no. 3 (2014): 124–37. https://jmss.org/article/view/58115/43732.

Donaghy, Greg. "Nukes and Spooks: Canada-US Intelligence Sharing and Nuclear Consultations, 1950–1958." In *Transnationalism: Canada-United*

States History into the 21st Century, edited by Michael D. Behiels and Reginald C. Stuart, 241–58. Montreal: McGill-Queen's University Press, 2010.

———. "When the Chips Are Down: Eisenhower, Diefenbaker, and the Lebanon Crisis, 1958." In *Reassessing the Rogue Tory: Canadian Foreign Relations in the Diefenbaker Era*, edited by Janice Cavell and Ryan M. Touhey, 85–102. Vancouver: UBC Press, 2019.

Dziuban, Stanley W. *Military Relations Between the United States and Canada, 1939–1945*. Washington, DC: Center for Military History, United States Army, 1990.

Eayrs, James. *In Defence of Canada Vol IV: Growing Up Allied*. Toronto: University of Toronto Press, 1985.

Eberlee, Samuel. "Danger in the Asia-Pacific: Canadian Intelligence Analysis and the 'Imminence' of World War, 1950–1959." Master of Arts Directed Research Paper, University of Toronto, 2021.

Finletter, Thomas K. *Survival in the Air Age: A Report by the President's Sir Policy Commission*. Washington: US Government Printing Office, 1948.

Flint, Roy K. "Task Force Smith and the 24th Division: Delay and Withdrawal, 5–19 July 1950." In *America's First Battles, 1776–1965*, edited by Charles E. Heller and William A. Stofft, 266–99. Lawrence, KS: University Press of Kansas, 1986.

Garthoff, Raymond L. "Estimating Soviet Military Intentions and Capabilities." In *Watching the Bear: Essays on CIA's Analysis of the Soviet Union*, edited by Gerald K. Haines and Robert E. Leggett, 135–86. Langley: Center for the Study of Intelligence, Central Intelligence Agency, 2003.

Goette, Richard. *Sovereignty and Command in Canada–US Continental Air Defence, 1940–57*. Vancouver: UBC Press, 2018.

Goodman, Michael S. "The Foundations of Anglo-American Intelligence Sharing." *Studies in Intelligence* 59, no. 2 (June 2015): 1–12, https://www.cia.gov/resources/csi/static/Foundations-of-Anglo-American.pdf.

———. *The Official History of the Joint Intelligence Committee: Volume 1: From the Approach of the Second World War to the Suez Crisis*. London: Routledge, 2014.

Grabo, Cynthia. "A Handbook of Warning Intelligence." Vol. 1. Defense Intelligence Agency, July 1972. CIA FOIA RR, https://www.cia.gov/readingroom/docs/CIA-RDP80B00829A000800040001-6.pdf.

Grant, Lindsay. "28 September 1966: Provision of Tripartite Intelligence Conference Network." *Canada Declassified*. Accessed June 19, 2023. https://declassified.library.utoronto.ca/exhibits/show/the-many-heads-of-hydra--canad/1966-1971--heads-and-tails--th/28-september-1966--provision-o.

———. "The Many Heads of HYDRA: Canada as Cold War Signals Intelligence Hub." *Canada Declassified*. Accessed June 2023. https://declassified.library.utoronto.ca/exhibits/show/the-many-heads-of-hydra--canad/summary.

Jensen, Kurt F. *Cautious Beginnings: Canadian Foreign Intelligence, 1939–51*. Vancouver: UBC Press, 2009.

Jones, Matthew. "'A Matter of Joint Decision': The Origins of British Nuclear Retaliation Procedures and the Murphy–Dean Agreement of 1958," *The English Historical Review*, 2024, early access, https://doi.org/10.1093/ehr/ceae161.

———. *The Official History of the UK Strategic Nuclear Deterrent: Volume 1: From the V-Bomber to the Arrival of Polaris, 1945–1964*. London: Routledge, 2017.

Kaplan, Lawrence S. *NATO before the Korean War: April 1949–June 1950*. Kent, OH: The Kent State University Press, 2013.

Kuhns, Woodrow J., ed. *Assessing the Soviet Threat: The Early Cold War Years*. Washington: Centre for the Study of Intelligence, 1997. https://www.cia.gov/resources/csi/static/Assessing-the-Soviet-Threat-The-Early-Cold-War-Years.pdf.

Leffler, Melvyn P. "National Security and US Foreign Policy." In *Origins of the Cold War: An International History*, eds. Melvyn P. Leffler and David S. Painter, 15–52. London: Routledge, 1994.

McKercher, Asa. "A 'Half-hearted Response'? Canada and the Cuban Missile Crisis, 1962." *The International History Review* 33, no. 2 (June 2011): 335–52. https://doi.org/10.1080/07075332.2011.555450.

———. "Neutralism, Nationalism, and Nukes, Oh My! Revisiting Peacemaker or Powder-Monkey and Canadian Strategy in the Nuclear Age." In *Nuclear North: Histories of Canada in the Atomic Age*, edited by Susan Colbourn and Timothy Andrews Sayle, 88–108. Vancouver: UBC Press, 2019.

Munton, Don, and Don Page. "Planning in the East Block: The Post-Hostilities Problems Committees in Canada 1943–5." *International Journal* 32, no. 4 (1977): 687–726. https://doi.org/10.2307/40201593.

Pickersgill, J. W., and D. F. Forster. *The Mackenzie King Record Volume 3, 1945/46*. Toronto: University of Toronto Press, 1970.

Sayle, Timothy Andrews. "Indications of War: American, British and Canadian Intelligence Diplomacy and the 1957 Tripartite Intelligence Alerts Agreement." *Intelligence & National Security* 38, no. 3 (2023): 427–46. https://doi.org/10.1080/02684527.2022.2123936.

———. "The Moment Canada Learned about the Cuban Missile Crisis." *Canada Declassified*, October 21, 2023. https://timsayle.substack.com/p/the-moment-canada-learned-about-the.

———. "A Pattern of Constraint: Canadian-American Relations in the Early Cold War." *International Journal*, 62, no. 3 (2007): 689–705. https://doi.org/10.1177/002070200706200316.

Smith, Denis. *Diplomacy of Fear: Canada and the Cold War, 1941–1948*. Toronto: University of Toronto Press, 1988.

Stacey, C. P. *Arms, Men and Governments: The War Policies of Canada, 1939–1945*. Ottawa: Queen's Printer for Canada, 1970.

———. *Canada and the Age of Conflict: A History of Canadian External Policies*. Toronto: Macmillan of Canada, 1977.

Steury, Donald P. "Origins of CIA's Analysis of the Soviet Union." In *Watching the Bear: Essays on CIA's Analysis of the Soviet Union*, edited by Gerald K. Haines and Robert E. Leggett, 1–16. Langley: Center for the Study of Intelligence, Central Intelligence Agency, 2003.

Valero, Larry A. "The American Joint Intelligence Committee and Estimates of the Soviet Union, 1945–1947." *Studies in Intelligence* 44, no. 3 (Summer 2000): 4. https://www.cia.gov/resources/csi/static/american-joint-intel-committee.pdf.

Wampler, Robert A. "Ambiguous Legacy: The United States, Great Britain and the Foundations of NATO Strategy, 1948–1957." PhD diss., Harvard University, 1991.

Wark, Wesley. "'Favourable Geography': Canada's Arctic Signals Intelligence Mission." *Intelligence and National Security* 35, no. 3 (2020): 319–30. https://doi.org/10.1080/02684527.2020.1724629.

Warner, Michael, ed. *CIA Cold War Records, The CIA Under Harry Truman.* Washington, DC: History Staff, Center for the Study of Intelligence, Central Intelligence Agency, 1994. https://www.cia.gov/resources/csi/static/CIA-Under-Harry-Truman-CIA-Documents-1994-Part-II-CIA-Hillenkoetter.pdf.

Index

A

ABAI. *See* American-British Agreed Intelligence (ABAI)
Abbott, Douglas, 90
ABC. *See* American-British-Canadian (ABC) planners
ABCI. *See* American-British-Canadian Intelligence (ABCI)
ACAI. *See* American-Canadian Agreed Intelligence (ACAI)
ADC. *See* Air Defence Command (ADC, Canada); Air Defense Command (ADC, US)
aide-mémoire (US), 135–136, 138, 144
air defence, 12, 19, 22, 118–119, 136–138
Air Defence Command (ADC, Canada), 118, 126, 137
Air Defense Command (ADC, US), 116–117, 118, 126, 137
air operations, 129, 149, 174
air power, 47–48, 50–51, 58–60, 61, 71
airplane detector equipment, 12
Alanbrooke, Field Marshall Lord, 18
Alaska, defence of, 12–13
ALE messages, 154, 156, 162, 163–164, 167, 173–174
Alert, Nunavut, 173
alerts. *See also* ALE messages
  bilateral talks on, 136–140
  intelligence *vs.* operational, 125, 156
  procedures agreements, 134–136
  stages, 158–159
  treatment of, 125–126
  trilateral discussions, 140–144
Alsop, Joseph, 43
American behaviour theories
  desire for preventive war, 79, 101–102
  galvanized by Korean invasion, 84
  isolationism, 22
  overestimation of Soviet Union, 20
  oversensitivity to Soviet actions, 18
  "provocative statements," 97, 100
  in shifting balance of power, 40
  in views of diplomats and journalists, 42–44, 91
American Telegraph and Telephone cable repair, 168
American-British Agreed Intelligence (ABAI)
  ABAI 5 "Soviet Intentions and Capabilities," 58, 62, 63–64
American-British-Canadian (ABC) planners
  ABC-22 "Joint Canadian-United States Basic Defence Plan," 11, 23
  ABCI 15 "Soviet Intentions and Capabilities," 65–72
  intelligence discussions and conference, 60–65
  military planning, 48, 54–55
American-Canadian Agreed Intelligence (ACAI)
  assessments, 48
  "Soviet Capabilities and Probable Courses of Action . . . 1949–1956" (ACAI 5), 55–60
Amory, Robert
  bilateral alert talks, 138–139
  on intelligence sharing, 133, 135, 156
  on tripartite alerts system, 159–160, 165, 166
Amyot, Paul E., 153
Anderson, William, 33
Anglo-American relationships, 8, 9, 10, 11, 64–65
appreciations (assessments)
  "An Appreciation of the Possible Military Threat to the Security of Canada and the United States" (JIC 3/48), 49–52
  "Appreciation of the Requirements for Canadian-United States Security" (MCC), 25
  defined, 23
  no agreed Government view, 84
  sharing, 100
  team composition requirement, 31–32, 35
  tripartite participation, 60–63
Arctic defence measures, 34, 37

233

Argus nuclear test explosion, 168
arms race, 34
Armstrong, Park, 117, 137–138, 139, 146–147
Asia
    Communist powers, 177
    concerns about American action in, 134
Associated Press, 130
Atherton, Ray, 30, 36
atomic bombs. *See also* nuclear weapons
    in appreciations, 50–51, 57, 66
    intelligence about, 33
    program espionage, 25
    Soviet explosions, 48, 65
    in war scenarios, 27, 31, 71
Atwood, L. L., 70–71
Australia, 177–178, 179

B

Barnes, Tracey, 153
Basic National Security Policy, 112
Basic Security Plan (BSP), 25, 33, 47–48, 52, 55
Bean, W. W., 62, 63, 64–65, 70, 77
Berlin
    Blockade, 108
    Crises, 162, 167
    and Soviet Union, 103
Bermuda conference, 143–144, 145
bilateral alerts, 136–140, 146
BJSM. *See* British Joint Staff Mission (BJSM)
Black, Pat, 157, 162–163, 167
Boucher, Valentine, 62, 64
Bow, Malcolm N., 174–175
Bowen, Ivor
    on intelligence sharing, 114, 115, 117,
        149–150, 166, 169
    on interpretation of intelligence, 145
    meeting with McCone, 171
    on risks of war, 101
    "The Continuing Need for Indications Intelligence," 158
British behaviour theories
    potential war between UK and Russia, 21
British Joint Staff Mission (BJSM), 128, 155
British Red Book, 155
BROILER (war plan), 52
Brook, Sir Norman, 122, 126
Bryce, Robert, 143, 172
BSP. *See* Basic Security Plan (BSP)
budgets
    Canadian, 34, 90, 101
    intelligence spending surge, 180
    US military, 21, 25, 58

BULLMOOSE (war plan), 52
Burgess, Woodbury M., 116

C

"C" (Sir John Sinclair), 118, 119
Cabell, Charles P., 141–142, 145, 163
Cabinet Defence Committee (CDC)
    on alerts consultation, 140
    in Cuban Missile Crisis, 174
    and defence planning, 27–28, 33, 55, 72
Cabinet War Committee (CWC), 21, 22
Cadieux, Marcel, 41–42
Camp X (Ontario), 151
Campney, Ralph, 140
Canada
    alert communications procedures, 154
    budget speeches, 90
    Cabinet briefings, 33–34, 35
    geographical exposure, 17, 19–20, 21–22, 34
    intelligence spending, 180
    and Korean War, 81
    and Military Cooperation Committee paper,
        27–29
    military planning, 39–40
    overview of officials' views and actions, 4–5
    in Second World War, 9–12
    Soviet submarines in, 82–83
    US military in, 12–13, 19, 22, 23
    US overflights agreement, 136
Canadian Indications Room, 131–132, 138,
    144. *See also* Joint Indications Room (JIR
    (Canada))
Canadian Joint Staff in Washington (CJSW),
    12, 20–21
Canol pipeline, 12
Carter, Thomas L., 90
CAS. *See* Chief of the Air Staff (CAS)
Castro, Fidel, 171
CBNRC. *See* Communications Branch,
    National Research Council (CBNRC)
CDC. *See* Cabinet Defence Committee (CDC)
Central Intelligence Agency (CIA). *See also*
    Amory, Robert; Dulles, Allen
    and Canadian appreciations, 100
    communications channels, 144–145, 153
    indications intelligence coverage, 111–112
    on intelligence sharing, 133, 135, 171–172
    on Soviet intentions, 86, 99
    and tripartite alerts system, 142, 154, 163
    and Watch Committee, 108, 113
Central Intelligence Group (CIG), 28, 30–31
CGS. *See* Chief of the General Staff (CGS)

234   Index

Chair, Chiefs of Staff (CCOS), 117. *See also* Foulkes, Charles
Check List Group (US), 108–109
check lists, 107, 108. *See also* indicator lists
Chief of the Air Staff (CAS), 21, 33, 47
Chief of the General Staff (CGS), 82, 84. *See also* Foulkes, Charles
Chiefs of Staff (UK), 63
  "The Likelihood of Total War up to the End of 1954," 98–99
Chiefs of Staff Committee (CSC)
  and ACAI 5, 60
  on Canada's exclusion in bilateral talks, 11
  composition and tasks, 20
  on "imminence of war" papers, 94, 100–101
  intelligence alert system, 127
  on Joint Indications Room, 145
  and political appreciations, 39
  on security plan, 33, 40, 48
Chiefs of Staff Committee (CSC) documents
  CSC 1(50), 72–73
  CSC 31(50), 84
  "The Imminence of War" CSC 20(50), 78–81
  "The Imminence of War" CSC 22(50), 81–84
China, 79, 84–85, 130–131, 142, 160–161. *See also* Sino-Soviet Bloc actions
CIA. *See* Central Intelligence Agency (CIA)
CIG. *See* Central Intelligence Group (CIG)
cipher equipment, 151, 152–153
civilian oversight of defence, 25, 32
Claxton, Brooke, 34–35, 55, 80–81, 86, 89, 90
Cline, Ray, 172
codewords, 124, 150, 152, 159, 161–162
Colorado Springs facility, 111, 112, 116
Combined Chiefs of Staff (CCS), 11–12
COMINT (Communications Intelligence), 118
Communications Branch, National Research Council (CBNRC), 118, 137, 151, 152, 153
communications channels, 126, 132, 146, 151–154, 157, 167–169, 178–179
communism
  American fight against, 81
  clash with capitalism dogma, 97
  Czechoslovakia coup, 52
  opposition in Soviet Union, 96
  in Soviet intentions, 66, 72, 73, 74, 75, 93
consultation policy
  in agreements, 10, 134–135, 136, 137, 139–140, 144
  on alerts, 164–165
  and Canada's exclusion, 11, 63
  in indications of war procedures, 127
  in nuclear deployment decisions, 121–122

containment policy, 37, 42, 81
"The Continuing Need for Indications Intelligence" (Bowen), 158
Cook, Geoffrey, 171
crash (emergency) meetings, 119, 131, 132
Crean, G. G. "Bill"
  on appreciation papers, 29–30, 32, 57, 59
  bilateral alert talks, 138–139
  communications implementation, 150–153
  on indications intelligence, 116–117, 118–119, 123, 125–126, 127–128
  on intelligence sharing, 135
  on Soviet intentions, 92
  trilateral alert talks, 141–144, 145–146
  on trilateral intelligence discussions, 61, 62
Crerar, Harry, 11
CRITICOMM, 178
CSC. *See* Chiefs of Staff Committee (CSC)
Cuban Missile Crisis, 171–175
Current Intelligence Indications and Briefing Section (CIIB), 177
"The Current Risks of General War" (JIC 64/1(53)), 102–103, 104
"The Current Risks of War" (JIC 42/2(51)), 95–98
"The Current Risks of War" (JIC 42/3(52)), 100
CWC. *See* Cabinet War Committee (CWC)
Czechoslovakia Communist coup, 52, 108

D

DAI. *See* Director of Air Intelligence (DAI)
D-Day and M-Day, 17, 64
DEA. *See* Department of External Affairs (DEA)
Dean, Sir Patrick
  alerts discussions, 132–133, 140–141
  communications channel implementation, 150–151, 153
  on indications intelligence, 119, 123, 128–129
  on nuclear retaliation procedures, 155
  tripartite agreement, 142–143, 145–146
  tripartite alerts terms of use, 155–156, 165–166
defence planning. *See also* Basic Security Plan (BSP)
  ABC-22, 11
  Canada-US interdependence, 19, 22, 23–25, 32, 34–35
  and offence planning, 31, 47–48, 54–55
  policy, 6, 32–33, 36
  as provocation, 19, 37
  rearmament, 94, 100–101

Index   235

Defence Research Board, 47, 80
Department of External Affairs (DEA). *See also* Crean, G. G. "Bill"; Pearson, Lester; Reid, Escott
  on American action and Soviet reaction, 113
  on bilateral alert system, 135, 137
  collaborations with State Department, 31, 35, 36–38
  communications channels, 152
  on "The Current Risks of War," 95–96
  "Imminence of War" drafts, 78, 92–94, 98
  joins Joint Intelligence Committee, 20
  on likelihood of war, 84, 89, 94, 101–103
  on Military Cooperation Committee papers, 28–29
  on military thinking, 32, 87–88
  on "national development," 9
  "Political Appreciation," 36, 38–39
  "Political Factors in the Likelihood of War with the Soviet Union," 74–76
  Soviet theory debates, 73–74
  urged to participate in studies, 53
Department of Finance, 90
Department of National Defence (DND). *See also* Claxton, Brooke
  on atomic bombs, 71
  on imminence of war, 94
  Indications of War Room, 111
  intelligence alert system, 127, 140
  Intelligence Division, 177
  on Soviet intentions, 85
  spending goals, 101
  war planning, 87
Diefenbaker, John, 147, 167, 172, 174, 175
diplomatic corps
  communications channels, 152, 153
  in intelligence indications procedures, 169–170
  on Soviet intentions, 21, 26, 41–43, 91–92
Director of Air Intelligence (DAI), 77–78, 92–94, 110–111, 139, 173
Director of Military Intelligence (DMI), 73, 82, 114, 116, 117
Director of Naval Intelligence (DNI), 114, 129, 173
Director of Scientific Intelligence (DSI), 78, 114
DMI. *See* Director of Military Intelligence (DMI)
DND. *See* Department of National Defence (DND)
DNI. *See* Director of Naval Intelligence (DNI)
DOUBLEQUICK (war plan), 52

DRUMSTICK (codeword), 161–162
Drury, Charles "Bud," 94
DSI. *See* Director of Scientific Intelligence (DSI)
Duff, Anthony, 164
Dulles, Allen
  and Indications Centre, 144–145
  on intelligence sharing, 118
  tripartite alerts terms of use, 165–167
  on tripartite discussions, 141, 142, 145–146, 147
Dulles, John Foster, 122, 128, 132–133, 140, 143

E
Eayrs, James, 5
Eden, Anthony, 121–122, 123, 126
Edwards, RCAF Group Captain, 114
Eisenhower, Dwight D., 112, 141, 143, 145, 147
Elbrick, C. Burke, 133–134, 137
espionage and counterespionage, 25, 113, 129, 149, 172, 174
"Estimate of Soviet Postwar Intentions and Capabilities" (JIC (US)), 18

F
FALLEX 62 (NATO exercise), 170
Finletter Report, 47, 48
firmness policy, 42
Five Eyes intelligence community, 179
FLEETWOOD (war plan), 52
Ford, Robert, 42, 73, 87–88
Foreign Broadcast Information Service (FBIS), 130
Formosa Straits, 166
Fortress North America, 22, 24, 38
Foulkes, Charles
  on futility of Soviet intention studies, 94
  intelligence briefing room, 115
  on Korean War, 80, 81, 84
  on risk of war, 86, 101
  on tripartite alerts system, 167
  on tripartite discussions, 143
  on war planning, 40, 47, 52–53
FROLIC (war plan), 52
Furnas, H. E., 137, 147

G
G-2 (United States Army military intelligence), 117
GCHQ. *See* Government Communications Headquarters (GCHQ)

general war
 196? scenario, 1–4
 air *vs.* ground, 47
 alerts system on, 159
 American views, 37–38, 39–40
 Canadian role in, 19, 40, 58
 and Korean War, 79
 from miscalculations, 97, 102–104, 158
 in North America, 21, 27
 overview of concerns, 7, 180
Germany, 86, 167. *See also* Berlin
Glazebrook, George
 on aide-mémoire (US), 135
 on bilateral information discussions, 137–138, 140
 on Canadian Indications Centre, 144, 146
 on Indications Project, 116
 on risk of war, 95, 96
 on Soviet intentions papers, 74
Goodman, Michael, 110
Gouzenko, Igor, 25
Government Communications Headquarters (GCHQ), 132, 152
Green, Howard, 174–175

H
Hadwen, John, 89–90
HALFMOON (war plan), 52, 63–64
Hayter, William, 60
Heeney, Arnold
 on defence planning, 37
 in intelligence sharing discussions, 128–129, 140
 on "risks of war" assessments, 29, 95, 101
 on Soviet intentions, 80
Henry, Guy, 23, 37
Hickerson, John, 32
HICKORY (war plan), 69
Hillenkoetter, R. H., 109
Hitchcock, J. J., 130–131
Horsey, Outerbridge, 137
Hydra communications hub, 132, 151
hydrogen bomb, 7, 103

I
IAC. *See* Intelligence Advisory Committee (IAC)
ICBM. *See* Intercontinental Ballistic Missile (ICBM)
imminence of war
 1944 prospects, 20–22
 assessments studies, 179–180
 Canadian overview, 4–6
 DEA concerns about, 87
 factors and situations, 82–83, 175
 systematic reviews and tracking, 85–86
imminence of war, papers and documents related to
 "Imminence of War" (DAI), 77–78
 "The Imminence of War" (CSC 20(50)), 78–81
 "The Imminence of War" (CSC 22(50)), 81–84
 "The Imminence of War" (JIC 20(51)), 92–95
 "The International Situation" (JIC (Ottawa)), 89–92
indications intelligence, papers and documents related to
 "Indications Intelligence" (JIC 135/1(55)), 131–132
 "Indications Intelligence: Communications and Watch Procedures" (JIC 278(58)), 157
 "Indications of Russian Preparedness for War" (JIC (London)), 108
 "The 'Indications' Project," JIC 89(53), 115–116
 "Possible Stages of Action when Indications of Major Russian Aggression are Received in Good Time," 126–129
indications intelligence tracking systems. *See also* Joint Indications Room (JIR (Canada)); Joint Indications Room (JIR (UK))
 American implementations, 108–110, 111–114
 British implementations, 110, 123–125, 147
 Canadian implementations, 107–108, 110–111, 117, 131–132, 145
 continuing need for, 157–158
indications of war
 British scenarios, 124
 vs. friendly forces activities, 150
 overview, 7–8
indicator lists, 115, 156, 159, 160–161, 168, 169–170, 177–178
Inglis, Thomas B., 63, 64
intelligence
 analysis sharing, 36, 152
 assessment team composition, 31–32
 availability of, 25–26, 27–28, 61, 82, 129
 Canadian deficiencies, 42, 56–57
 "critical" as defined in Tripartite Alerts System, 161

intelligence (*continued*)
　gathering, 130
　records declassification, 4, 5, 179–180
　timeliness of, 113, 117, 118–119, 123–126, 170–171
Intelligence Advisory Committee (IAC), 108–109, 112, 135–136, 146, 179–180
intelligence assessments. *See* appreciations
intelligence rooms. *See* rooms
intelligence sharing
　American responses to, 132–136
　American-British-Canadian planners, 61
　flow, 118–119
　and Joint Intelligence Committee Liaison Officers, 167
　on marginal and developing situations, 164–167
　security and secrecy of, 149–150
"Intelligence Warning of Military Attack on North America" (JIC 443/2(62)), 170–171
Intercontinental Ballistic Missiles (ICBM), 158
"The International Situation" (JIC (Ottawa)), 89–92
Iran, 36
Iraq, 162
"Is War with Russia Inevitable?" (Kennan), 73

J

JCS. *See* Joint Chiefs of Staff (JCS)
JIB. *See* Joint Intelligence Bureau (JIB)
JIC. *See* Joint Intelligence Committee (JIC (London)); Joint Intelligence Committee (JIC (Ottawa)); Joint Intelligence Committee (JIC (US))
JICLO. *See* Joint Intelligence Committee Liaison Officers
JIG. *See* Joint Intelligence Group (JIG)
JIR. *See* Joint Indications Room (JIR (Canada)); Joint Indications Room (JIR (UK))
JIS. *See* Joint Intelligence Staff (JIS)
JISC. *See* Joint Intelligence Sub-Committee (JISC)
"Joint Canadian-United States Basic Defence Plan" (ABC-22), 11
Joint Chiefs of Staff (JCS), 23, 28, 63, 113, 134–135
Joint Indications Room (JIR (Canada))
　implementation, 145, 146, 153, 156–157, 162, 173, 177
　"Joint Indication Room: Standing Orders" (JIC 378/1 (60)), 170
"Joint Indication Room: Standing Orders" JIC 471(63), 177
Joint Indications Room (JIR (UK)), 146, 157, 167
Joint Intelligence Bureau (JIB), 101, 114, 130–131, 145, 149–150
Joint Intelligence Committee (JIC (London))
　on ABCI 15, 71
　intelligence alerts, 119, 123–125, 164
　intelligence reviews, 110
　invites Canadian participation, 61
　on Soviet interests and intentions, 18, 25–26, 99
　on transatlantic communications vulnerability, 168–169
Joint Intelligence Committee (JIC (London)) documents
　"Indications of Russian Preparedness for War," 108
　"Likelihood of General War with the Soviet Union up to the End of 1955" (JIC (53)79 (Final)), 103, 104
　"Likelihood of Total War with the Soviet Union up to the End of 1954" (JIC (451)103 (Final)), 96
　"The Likelihood of War with the Soviet Union . . . " (JIC (50)7), 74
　"Russia's Strategic Interests and Intentions," 25–26
　"Soviet Intentions and Capabilities, 1950–1954" (with JIC (US)), 88–89
Joint Intelligence Committee (JIC (Ottawa))
　on ABCI 15, 70, 71
　and ACAI 5, 60
　on aide-mémoire, 135–136
　Canadian Indications Room, 131–132, 144–145
　communications channels, 152
　and Cuban Missile Crisis, 173–175
　in FALLEX 62 exercise, 170
　indications intelligence reviews and tracking system, 85–86, 107, 111
　indications of war project, 114–116, 117
　intelligence alert systems, 125–130, 162, 163, 166–167
　and Korean War, 77–78, 81–82
　origin and function, 5, 20
　Soviet intentions request, 72
Joint Intelligence Committee (JIC (Ottawa)) documents
　"A Review of the Risks of War" (JIC 58(52)), 100–101

238　Index

"An Appreciation of the Possible Military Threat to the Security of Canada and the United States" (JIC 3/48), 49–52
"An Outline of Soviet Capabilities and Strategic Objectives in a War Beginning before July, 1949" (JIC 4/48), 53–54
"The Current Risks of General War" (JIC 64/1(53)), 102–103, 104
"The Current Risks of War" (JIC 42/2(51)), 95–98, 99
"The Current Risks of War" (JIC 42/3(52)), 100
"Indications Intelligence" (JIC 135/1(55)), 131–132
"Indications Intelligence: Communications and Watch Procedures" (JIC 278(58)), 157
"Intelligence Warning of Military Attack on North America" (JIC 443/2(62)), 170–171
"The International Situation," 89–92
JIC 1 (Final), 38–39
"Joint Indication Room: Standing Orders" (JIC 378/1 (60)), 170
"Joint Indication Room: Standing Orders" (JIC 471(63)), 177
"An Outline of Soviet Capabilities and Strategic Objectives in a War Beginning before July, 1949" (JIC 4/48), 53–54
"Probable Enemy Activities Prior to the Outbreak of War" (JIC 312/2(59)), 169, 170
"A Review of the Risks of War" (JIC 58(52)), 100–101
"Strategic Appreciation of the Capabilities of the U.S.S.R. to attack the North American Continent," 29–30
"The Imminence of War" (JIC 20(51)), 92–95
"The International Situation" (JIC (Ottawa)), 89–92
"Tripartite Alerts System" (JIC 1103/1(58)), 159–160, 166
"Tripartite Intelligence Alerts Agreement" (JIC 543(66) (Final)), 177
Joint Intelligence Committee (JIC (US))
  on ABCI 15, 70–71
  appreciation drafts, 51–52
  assessments of future war, 28
  "Estimate of Soviet Postwar Intentions and Capabilities," 18
  "Soviet Intentions and Capabilities, 1950–1954" (with JIC (London)), 88–89
Joint Intelligence Committee Liaison Officers (JICLO), 154, 157, 162–164, 167
Joint Intelligence Group (JIG), 55–58

Joint Intelligence Map Room (UK), 123
Joint Intelligence Staff (JIS)
  in ABCI conference, 62–65
  ACAI 5 drafting, 55–58
  "Current Risks of War" redraft, 97–98
  indications of war project, 114, 115
  "An Outline of Soviet Capabilities and Strategic Objectives in a War Beginning before July, 1949" (JIC 4/48), 53–54
  Soviet intention appreciation, 72–73
Joint Intelligence Sub-Committee (JISC), 107
Joint Planning Committee (JPC), 31, 39–40, 81–82
Joint War Plans Committee, 52
Jones, Paul, 163
Jordan, 162
JPC. *See* Joint Planning Committee (JPC)

K

Kellogg Pact, 43
Kennan, George, 26, 28, 36–37, 73
Kennedy, John F., 172, 173, 174
Khrushchev, Nikita, 171, 174
King, Mackenzie, 10, 19–20, 33–34
Knight, A. F. B., 73, 82
Korean War
  Chinese intervention, 84–85
  and general war, 7, 77–79, 80–82, 159
  Soviet intervention, 91, 103
  status, 100, 109

L

La Guardia, Fiorella, 11
Langley, A. J., 78, 114
Lay, H. N., 39–40
Lebanon, 162
Leckie, Robert, 21, 33
Léger, Jules, 134, 136–137, 146–147
Leitrim (Ottawa Wireless Station), 132, 152, 153
"Likelihood of General War with the Soviet Union up to the End of 1955" (UK JIC (53)79 (Final)), 103, 104
"Likelihood of the Deliberate Initiation of Full-Scale War by the USSR against the US and Its Western Allies Prior to the End of 1952" (NIE 48), 98, 99
"The Likelihood of Total War up to the End of 1954" (COS (52)285, UK), 98–99
"Likelihood of Total War with the Soviet Union up to the End of 1954" (JIC (451)103 (Final), London), 96

Index   239

"The Likelihood of War with the Soviet
    Union . . . " (JIC (50)7 (London)), 74
Lloyd, Selwyn, 143, 147
London Indicator Centre, 126–127
"Long Telegram" (Kennan), 26

M

Macdonnell, R. M., 42, 92
MacKay, Robert, 71–72
Macmillan, Harold, 132, 141, 143, 145
Makins, Roger, 128, 133
Marshall, George, 91
MAYHEM (codeword), 159
MC48 (NATO strategy document), 121
MCC. *See* Military Cooperation Committee (MCC)
McCardle, J. M., 171–172, 173, 174
McCone, John, 171–172
McCordick, J. A., 96
McCoy, Tim, 70
M-Day and D-Day, 17, 64
mechanization/machinery
    in UK systems, 123–124
    in US ADC system, 116–117
    and Watch Committee, 110, 111, 130, 131
Menzies, Arthur, 91
Merchant, Livingston, 133, 172
Middle East crises, 162, 163, 164
Military Cooperation Committee (MCC), 25, 26–29, 49, 51–52, 55, 59
Ministry of Defence (UK), 123, 132
miscalculations and accidents, 97, 100, 102–103, 104, 113, 150, 175
missiles, 141, 158, 171, 172, 177
missions abroad, 169–170
Murphy, Robert, 147, 155
Murray, Ralph, 123

N

National Indications Center (NIC), 113, 118, 130–131, 134, 141, 170
National Intelligence Estimate (NIE)
    "Likelihood of the Deliberate Initiation of Full-Scale War by the USSR against the US and Its Western Allies Prior to the End of 1952" (NIE 48), 98, 99
    "Probable Intelligence Warning of Soviet Attack on the US" (NIE 11-3-57), 149–150
    on Soviet intentions, 86

National Security Agency (NSA), 118, 132, 137, 152, 153
National Security Council (NSC), 112–113, 129
NATO. *See* North Atlantic Treaty Organization (NATO)
New Zealand, 177–178, 179
NIC. *See* National Indications Center (NIC)
NIE. *See* National Intelligence Estimate (NIE)
196? war scenario, 1–4
1946 draft appreciation (MCC), 26–29, 49, 51–52
North America
    American defence strategy for, 37–38
    "Intelligence Warning of Military Attack on North America" (JIC 443/2(62)), 170–171
    vulnerability assessments, 22–24, 27, 30, 33
North American Air Defence Command (NORAD), 162, 163
North Atlantic Alliance, 69
North Atlantic Treaty Organization (NATO)
    establishment, 48–49, 61–62, 63, 69–70, 71–72
    FALLEX 62 exercise, 170
    and intelligence alerts, 126–127, 128, 156
    nuclear attack strategy (MC48), 121–122
    and nuclear weapons, 7, 144
    threats to participants, 86, 159, 163–164
    and trilateral discussions, 142, 146, 147
North Atlantic Triangle, 8
Novorossisk (MV), 168–169
NSA. *See* National Security Agency (NSA)
NSC. *See* National Security Council (NSC)
nuclear retaliation procedures (UK-US), 155
nuclear war survival exercises, 170
nuclear weapons. *See also* atomic bombs
    in 196? scenario, 1–3, 7
    decision to launch process, 121–122, 134
    and risk of war, 104
    smuggled into North America, 171
    test explosions, 48, 65, 103, 168

O

Office of Reports and Estimates (ORE), 28
"ORE 1: Soviet Foreign and Military Policy" (Office of Reports and Estimates), 28
OFFTACKLE (war plan), 69
oil pipelines, 12
"An Outline of Soviet Capabilities and Strategic Objectives in a War Beginning before July, 1949" (JIC 4/48), 53–54

P

Parsons, J. Graham, 24
PCO. *See* Privy Council Office (PCO)
Pearkes, George, 167
Pearson, Lester
   on alerts systems, 122–123, 140
   on Canada's exclusion in wartime, 10, 11
   on defence planning, 32–33
   on global war plan, 47
   on imminence of war, 89, 90, 91
   joint appreciation and basic security plan development, 36, 39
   on Korean situation, 81
   on possibility of general war, 86
   reassurances to Mackenzie King, 44
Pentagon, 69, 130, 131, 133, 134–135, 143
Perkins, George, 133
Permanent Joint Board of Defence (PJBD), 10–11, 19–20, 23–24, 31
PHP. *See* Post-Hostilities Planning (PHP) Committees
PJBD. *See* Permanent Joint Board of Defence (PJBD)
"Political Appreciation" (DEA), 35–36, 38–39
"Political Factors in the Likelihood of War with the Soviet Union" (DEA), 74–76
Pope, Maurice, 12, 23–24, 40, 41, 91–92
"Possible Stages of Action when Indications of Major Russian Aggression are Received in Good Time" (UK), 126–129
Post-Hostilities Planning (PHP) Committees, 17, 18–19, 20, 21
Privy Council Office (PCO), 29, 143, 168
"Probable Enemy Activities Prior to the Outbreak of War" (JIC 312/2(59)), 169, 170
"Probable Intelligence Warning of Soviet Attack on the US" (NIE 11-3-57), 149–150
"Procedures Preceding Attack by United States Retaliatory Forces from the United Kingdom" (TIAA), 155

R

Radford, Arthur W., 134–135, 143
RAF. *See* Royal Air Force (RAF)
RCAF. *See* Royal Canadian Air Force (RCAF)
Reid, Escott
   on Canada's options, 19, 44
   on political appreciations, 39, 49
   on Soviet intentions papers, 74
   on US balance of power, 40, 41

"Report of Tripartite Working Group on Tripartite Alert System," 160
"A Review of the Risks of War" (JIC 58(52)), 100–101
Ritchie, Charles, 42–43, 95
Roberts, Frank, 26
Robertson, Norman, 29, 142, 172
Rockex cipher machine, 152–153, 154
rooms. *See also* Joint Indications Room (JIR (Canada)); Joint Indications Room (JIR (UK))
   Air Defense Command (Colorado Springs), 111, 112, 116–117, 118
   in Canadian discussions, 111, 115, 129
   Canadian Indications Room, 131–132, 138, 144
   Indications Room (USAF), 114, 130
   Joint Intelligence Map Room (UK), 123
   London Indicator Centre, 126–127
   National Indications Center (US), 113, 118, 130–131, 141
   Watch Room (CIA building), 109
Roosevelt, Franklin, 10, 19
Royal Air Force (RAF), 28, 59, 124
Royal Canadian Air Force (RCAF), 58, 114–115, 137, 173
"Russia's Strategic Interests and Intentions" (JIC (London)), 25–26

S

SAC. *See* Strategic Air Command (SAC)
SACEUR. *See* Supreme Allied Commander, Europe (SACEUR)
Samford, John, 139
Second World War
   experiences and lessons, 9–13, 22–24
   and post hostilities planning, 17, 20
Secretary of State for External Affairs (SSEA), 36
Sheldon, Huntington "Ting," 112, 117, 163, 165
Sheldon Committee, 112, 117
signals intelligence, 118, 132, 173, 179
Sinclair, Sir John ("C"), 118, 119
Sino-Soviet Bloc actions, 160–161, 166, 177
Smith, Walter Bedell, 112
SNIE. *See* Special National Intelligence Estimate (SNIE)
Solandt, Omond, 80
Southam, Hamilton, 160
sovereignty, 19, 24–25

Index   *241*

Soviet intention and behaviour theories
   avoidance of war, 44, 87, 101
   British theory, 18
   diplomatic analyses, 26, 92
   in responses to Escott Reid's memorandum, 41–42
   tie-down of American forces in Asia, 85
Soviet intention indicators, 124, 129, 170–171, 174
Soviet intentions and capabilities, papers and documents related to
   "Russia's Strategic Interests and Intentions" (JIC (London)), 25–26
   "Soviet Capabilities and Probable Courses of Action . . . 1949–1956" (ACAI 5), 55–60
   "Soviet Foreign and Military Policy" (ORE1), 28
   "Soviet Intentions and Capabilities . . ." (ABCI 15), 65–72
   "Soviet Intentions and Capabilities" (ABAI 5), 58, 62, 63–64
   "Soviet Intentions and Capabilities, 1950–1954" (US and UK), 88–89
Soviet satellite countries, 96
Soviet trawler MV Novorossisk, 168–169
Soviet Union
   containment of, 37, 41–42
   and Cuba, 171–172, 173, 175
   espionage and counterespionage, 113
   and Korean War, 97
   military capability assessments, 49–52, 58–60, 61
   post-war activities, 25, 30, 48, 65, 82–83, 103
   as threat to North America, 17–18
   in tripartite alerts system indicators, 160–161
Special National Intelligence Estimates (SNIE)
   on intention of Communist rulers (SNIE11-54), 104
   Watch system (SNIE 11-8-54), 113
SPEEDWAY (war plan), 52
SSEA. *See* Secretary of State for External Affairs (SSEA)
St. Laurent, Louis, 36
Stacey, C. P., 12
Stalin, Joseph, 25, 97, 101, 103
Standing Group (NATO), 121, 127
Starnes, John, 165–167
State Department (US)
   aide-mémoire, 135
   bilateral alert talks, 137–140
   distrust of military thinking, 32
   on indications intelligence, 108, 109
   participation in assessments, 31
   tripartite agreement, 146–147
   views on Soviet threat, 28, 91
Steele, A. J., 144
stop lines, 37, 42
Strategic Air Command (SAC), 136, 162
"Strategic Appreciation of the Capabilities of the U.S.S.R. to attack the North American Continent" (JIC (Ottawa)), 29–30
Suez Crisis, 141, 142, 159
Supreme Allied Commander, Europe (SACEUR), 121, 122

T

Taiwan Straits, 130–131, 162
third nation information, 132
TIAA. *See* Tripartite Intelligence Alerts Agreement (TIAA)
Todd, W. E., 61, 62, 63, 64, 71
transatlantic communications cables, 151, 167–169
TRIAN terminals, 178–179
Tripartite Alert(s) Communications System
   during Cuban Missile Crisis, 173
   elements and procedures, 160–162
   legacy, 178–179
   and missions abroad, 169–170
   in operation, 163, 175
   terms of use, 155–156, 159–160, 163–167
Tripartite Intelligence Alerts Agreement (TIAA)
   communications implementations, 150–154
   finalization, 145–147
   legacy, 179, 180
   nuclear retaliation procedures, 155
   overview, 6, 8, 10
   trilateral discussions, 140–145
   "Tripartite Intelligence Alerts Agreement" (JIC 543(66) (Final)), 177
Truman, Harry, 47, 58, 65, 108
trust and distrust
   in ABC-22 negotiations, 11
   towards military thinking, 32
Turkey, 30, 37

U

U-2 aircraft, 149, 172, 174
UN. *See* United Nations (UN)
Under-Secretary of State for External Affairs (USSEA), 29, 53, 80, 85, 95, 134

United Kingdom
  alert communications procedures, 154
  embassy in Ottawa, 160
  intelligence check lists, 108
  Ministry of Defence (UK), 123, 132
  and Suez Crisis, 141, 142
United Nations (UN), 79, 80, 85, 91, 159
United States
  1952 election, 101–102
  aide-mémoire, 135–136, 138, 144
  alert communications procedures, 154
  containment/firmness policy, 37, 42, 81
  Cuban Missile Crisis, 171–175
  defence spending, 21, 25, 58
  indications intelligence tracking systems, 107, 111–114, 125
  and Korean War, 78, 80, 81, 83–84
  military facilities in Canada, 12–13, 19, 22, 23
  military facilities in United Kingdom, 141
  nuclear weapons, 7
  in Second World War, 10–13
United States Air Force (USAF)
  Air Defence Command, 111, 118, 126
  Colorado Springs facility, 112, 116–117, 137
  Indications Room, 114, 130
  Wide-Band Tropospheric Forward Scatter System, 169
United States Army, 109, 117
United States Intelligence Board (USIB), 163, 166
Uren, Phillip, 133, 138, 163
USAF. *See* United States Air Force (USAF)
USIB. *See* United States Intelligence Board (USIB)
USSEA. *See* Under-Secretary of State for External Affairs (USSEA)

W

war. *See also* general war; imminence of war; Second World War
  of nerves, 21, 26, 31
  preventive, 42–44
War Office (UK), 123–124
war planning
  1947-1948 joint plans, 52
  American *vs.* Canadian vision, 22–24, 39–40
  global, 58
  imperatives for, 21
war rooms. *See* rooms

war scenarios
  196? scenario, 1–4
  in appreciation papers, 67–68, 96–98
  Mackenzie King's fears, 34
  in North America, 27
  weapons assumptions, 7, 28
Washington Times, 43
Watch Committee
  development and expansion, 108, 109–110, 111–112, 113–114, 129, 130–131
  intelligence sharing, 117–118, 137, 139, 155, 174
Watch Room, 109
Weiser, William, 58
Wershof, Max, 96
Western powers, 74, 83, 93, 101, 102
Whitely, John, 128
Wilgress, Dana, 18, 21, 26, 42, 44, 96–98
world domination aims, 72–73, 101
Wright, Hume, 43–44
Wrong, Hume, 29, 43, 91, 92

Index   *243*

www.ingramcontent.com/pod-product-compliance
Lightning Source LLC
Chambersburg PA
CBHW050925240426
43668CB00021B/2438